THE
LYRICS

VOLUME 1

Paul McCartney
THE LYRICS

1956 TO THE PRESENT

*Edited with an Introduction
by Paul Muldoon*

LIVERIGHT PUBLISHING CORPORATION
A Division of W. W. Norton & Company
Independent Publishers Since 1923

Since this page cannot legibly accommodate
all the copyright notices, pages 866–869
constitute an extension of the copyright page.

For information about permission to reproduce
selections from this book, write to Permissions,
Liveright Publishing Corporation, a division
of W. W. Norton & Company, Inc.,
500 Fifth Avenue, New York, NY 10110

For information about special discounts for bulk
purchases, please contact W. W. Norton Special Sales
at specialsales@wwnorton.com or 800-233-4830

This book is set in Rigby, a typeface created expressly for this
book by Triboro Design.

This book is printed on paper that has been harvested from
forests that are managed with an eye to sustainability and
social and environmental responsibility.

Manufacturing through Asia Pacific Offset
Book design by Triboro
Production managers: Anna Oler and Joe Lops

Library of Congress Cataloging-in-Publication Data

Names: McCartney, Paul, author. | Muldoon, Paul, editor.
Title: The lyrics : 1956 to the present / Paul McCartney ;
    edited with an Introduction by Paul Muldoon.
Description: First edition. | New York : Liveright Publishing
    Corporation, 2021.
Identifiers: LCCN 2021012488 | ISBN 9781631492563 (set) |
    ISBN 9781324091134 (epub)
Subjects: LCSH: Songs—Texts. | Rock music—Texts. |
    LCGFT: Popular music lyrics. | Rock lyrics.
Classification: LCC ML54.6.M13 L97 2021 | DDC 782.42166—
    dc23
LC record available at https://lccn.loc.gov/2021012488

Liveright Publishing Corporation
500 Fifth Avenue, New York, N.Y. 10110
www.wwnorton.com

W. W. Norton & Company Ltd.
15 Carlisle Street, London W1D 3BS

1 2 3 4 5 6 7 8 9 0

Dedicated to my wife Nancy and my mum and dad, Mary and Jim

To thine own self be true.

—WILLIAM SHAKESPEARE, *HAMLET*, ACT I, SCENE 3

Volume 1

Volume 2

Foreword
by Paul McCartney

MORE TIMES THAN I CAN COUNT, I'VE BEEN ASKED TO write an autobiography, but the time has never been right. Usually I was raising a family or I was on tour, which has never been an ideal situation for long periods of concentration. But the one thing I've always managed to do, whether at home or on the road, is write new songs. Some people, when they get to a certain age, like to refer to a diary to recall day-to-day events from the past, but I have no such notebooks. What I do have is my songs - hundreds of them - which serve much the same purpose. And these songs span my entire life, because even at the age of fourteen, when I acquired my first guitar in our little house in Liverpool, my natural instinct was to start writing songs. Since then I've never stopped.

There's a whole process to learning songwriting, but it's different for different people. For me, the first thing was to copy other people, like Buddy Holly and Little Richard - and Elvis, who, I later heard, didn't even write his own songs. It meant memorising their songs, learning the standards of early rock and roll, but in my early to mid-teens it occurred to me to try writing my own. I'd start off with the very simplest idea, and I'd see what came out.

The earliest lyrics in this book are the words to 'I Lost My Little Girl'. I wrote them just after the death of my mother. She was only forty-seven; I was fourteen. Even as early as 1956, when I wrote the song, a musical direction was emerging: you can hear that the chord sequence descends, and the melody or the vocal ascends. I'm already playing with little musical things, very simple things, which fascinated me even though I did not know quite what they were. What's astonishing is that John Lennon, at the home of his Aunt Mimi, was doing something similar. So when we first came together and showed each other what we'd written, we quickly realised that we were both fascinated by songwriting and that by working together, we could take things a lot further.

In our early attempts you can tell we were kids. We weren't really conscious then of the act of songwriting. But when we started The Beatles, we realised we suddenly had an eager audience. So at first we were writing with this audience, mainly young girls, in mind. Early songs like 'Thank You Girl' or 'From Me to You' or 'Love Me Do' were aimed at our fans, though many were based on our personal stories. We knew that these songs might become hits, and we could have continued writing songs like those forever. But as we matured, we became aware that we could take songwriting in other directions, often to another level, which meant writing songs for ourselves.

Of course, we had to maintain a delicate balance between songs that interested us personally and those that played to the fans, but the more we experimented, the more it became apparent that we could go just about anywhere, which meant a more creative direction. We could get into a surrealist world, where the stories weren't exactly linear and where the songs didn't necessarily have to make sense. I had always been a big fan of Lewis Carroll, having read him early on and in school, so Carroll was a big inspiration as I got more into wordplay, where the lyrics are evolving into something more unexpected, as in 'Lady Madonna' or 'Penny Lane'. And this came to be an amazing revelation: we could be poetic without losing touch with our fans, or you might even say that the opposite occurred - that as we became more experimental and leaned more towards stream of consciousness, we actually gained fans.

Over time I came to see each song as a new puzzle. It would illuminate something that was important in my life at that moment, though the meanings are not always obvious on the surface. Fans or readers, or even critics, who really want to learn more about my life should read my lyrics, which might reveal more than any single book about The Beatles could do. Yet until my brother-in-law, friend and advisor, John Eastman, and my publisher, Bob Weil, provided the initial encouragement to do this book in 2015, I felt that the process of going over the hundreds of lyrics, some that I wrote in my teens, felt too cumbersome if not a bit too indulgent. It was a luxury of time I could not afford. I had always directed all my creative energies into the music. I would worry about the interior meanings, if I worried at all, only later. But once Paul Muldoon and I started discussing the origins and influences of all these songs, I became aware that delving into the lyrics of my songs could be a useful and revealing exploration.

For one, I knew Paul's was a receptive ear. He was not a biographer looking for gossip or secrets, hoping to learn more about some supposed feud between me and John or Yoko. Nor was he an over-the-top fan-turned-writer, looking to transform every word uttered into some kind of sacred text. What appealed to me immediately was that Muldoon is a poet. Like me, he is into words and understands the poetics of words - how the lyrics themselves become their own form of music that can become even more magical when paired with a melody.

Our conversations took place over five years, a few in London but most in New York. I would make a point of seeing him whenever I was in town. That's a long period of time, and the more we talked, the more we realised we had a lot in common. It was easy for me to identify with Paul, not only because he was a poet but because we shared an Irish heritage, an ancestral link in our families' pasts. Not to mention that Paul actually plays rock and roll and writes his own songs.

I never thought I would want to analyse these lyrics, many from back in the 1960s and '70s. Many of them I hadn't thought about in years, and many I hadn't played in concert for decades. But with Paul as my sounding board, it became a challenge - and a very pleasant one - to revisit the songs and pick them apart, to discover patterns that I never knew were there.

The act of writing a song is a unique experience, unlike anything else I know. You have to be in the right mood and start with a clear mind. You must trust your initial feelings because at the beginning you don't really know where you're going. Conversations with Paul were much the same. The only thing we knew in advance of each meeting was which songs we would be discussing; everything else was free rein. Inevitably, long-dormant memories were stirred up, and new meanings and patterns suddenly emerged.

The best comparison I can think of is an old snapshot album that's been kept up in a dusty attic. Someone brings it down, and suddenly you're faced with page after page of memories. Some of the old photos appear distinct and familiar, but others are a good bit hazier. When confronted with the words, I found it a challenge to remember how these songs came about: how I structured them; what event - a visit to a movie set, a row with someone I thought was a friend - might have inspired them; and what my feelings were at the time.

Given the way memory works, often the oldest songs from youth were the easiest to remember. For example, I could easily conjure up a conversation with Jane Asher's mother, a woman whom I liked a great deal, that I had when I was living in Wimpole Street in my mid-twenties, whereas memories of concerts only ten or fifteen years ago were more difficult to retrieve. But what was so invaluable about talking to Paul was that one old line would lead to another until, all of a sudden, a flood of memories I never knew were there would wash over me.

It's a lot like entering a forest. At first you see only the thicket of trees, but as you proceed deeper into the woods, you start appreciating things you might not have noticed before. You begin to look to each side, and up and down, noticing all kinds of things that weren't at first apparent. And once you've explored these things, your inclination is to head out of the forest. This is a pattern developed over many years; the tendency is to take the same path time and again, but if you continue to repeat yourself, which is so easy to do, eventually you might recognise that you haven't made any progress.

A furniture maker, a genuine craftsman, might see things differently. He's been very comfortable making the same chair over and over, but what if he pushed himself to make chairs that were different? He'd have to think about what kinds of legs they'd have, how the seats would be constructed, and how much weight they'd be able to bear. His furniture would start taking on a certain style, but no two chairs he produced could be quite alike. The same thing happened with my songs.

MANY OF MY SONGS ARE BASED ON PEOPLE I KNEW IN AND around Liverpool. And readers of these commentaries may be surprised by how often I mention my parents. When I first began this project, Jim and Mary McCartney were certainly not the first people who came to mind. But as I started to think about songs written at every stage of my career, I could not help but realise that, even without my conscious knowledge, they were the original inspiration for so much that I've written.

I was very lucky because my immediate Liverpool family were just ordinary working-class people. Their attitudes weren't religious, but they were good people and they showed us a good way. In school and in church, we were given more formal religion – Jesus's version, you might say – but my own sense of goodness, of a certain kind of spirituality, had already come from home. My parents' beliefs had a big impact, so I just naturally grew up thinking that the right thing was to be tolerant, the right thing was to be good. We were never told at home that you shalt *not* do this, you shalt *not* do that. And growing up, we thought the whole world turned in much the same way, so when I matured and was able to put my own thoughts and feelings into songs, I drew from this foundation.

I was only fourteen when my mum died. Because she died so young, you might think she did not have a great influence on my songs. But the more I think back, the more I now appreciate her effect on my identity as a songwriter. And as I'm recalling her now, I realise that today, 29 September, is her birthday, so – talk about spiritual – *she is certainly here*; the mother who made sure we ate our meals and washed behind our ears never seems to leave.

As I remember her, I think of her accent. Accents in Liverpool can vary greatly, from sort of soft and gentle to quite hard and aggressive, but hers was more lilting. That's because her ancestry was Irish, and there were influences from both Ireland and Wales. And just like her accent, she was very gentle-natured – so gentle that I never heard her shout. She never needed to. My brother Mike and I just knew that she wanted the best for her kids.

Even though mum didn't play an instrument, she appreciated music. I can still recall hearing her whistling in the kitchen whilst cooking. It could have been something that was on the radio or maybe a tune she knew. And I remember thinking, 'Oh, it's beautiful that she's happy,' and this feeling is something I've carried with me right to this day.

In those years right after the war, we would see her leaving the house and coming back home dressed in her nurse's uniform. Nursing was a role that came to her easily, both in and out of the house. If anything happened to us, if we got ill or got into a scrape in the yard, she was there, as if always on call. Sometimes she would decide we needed an enema, even though we were little kids, and that was a bit too much. But overall, she was very loving and soft-spoken.

I'd like to think that I've always been very empathetic towards women, but the point was brought home to me one day when a girl stopped me and asked, 'Have you ever realised how many of your songs are about women?' I hadn't ever really thought about it. All I could respond with was, 'Yeah, well, I do love and respect women.' But I got to thinking that my feelings towards women might have all come from my mum - the fact that I always remembered her as gentle and happy. On the most basic level, and in unexplainable ways, she embodied the humanity that you might find in my songs.

While my mother always appreciated music, my dad really was the musical one. I suppose at another time he might have been a musician himself, but he worked in Liverpool as a salesman for a company that imported cotton from America, Egypt, India, South America - the whole world. As an amateur pianist, he played in a little group called Jim Mac's Jazz Band. This was the 1920s, the flapper era in Liverpool, so playing in a band must have been pretty exciting for a young man his age. I wasn't around then, of course, but when I was a kid I'd hear him playing the piano at home. He would just sit at the family piano and play his old tunes. Generally, they were American standards, songs like 'Chicago' or 'Stairway to Paradise', performed by Paul Whiteman and his orchestra. One song that was a real education for me was a little tune that I can still hum called 'Stumbling', which I was later told was an American foxtrot song from 1922. The syncopation in 'Stumbling' fascinated me. I would lie on the carpet, my head on my knuckles, just listening to Dad play. Everyone in the house heard him play his favourite standards, but for me it was an education, listening to all these examples of rhythm, melody, and harmony.

He made sure the baton would be passed on. One day he actually took my brother and me aside to show us what harmony meant. 'If you sing that note there, and he sings that note here,' he instructed, 'there's then a blend of two notes, which is called "harmony".' Sometimes when we heard a song on the radio he'd say, 'Can you hear that low noise there?' We'd say, 'Yeah,' and he'd reply, 'Well, that's the bass.'

While Dad's entire audience was usually just the four of us, there were singsongs, big bashes that took place once a year on New Year's Eve. The extended family - the kids our age, the older kids, the younger parents, and the older parents - would come together, and we'd get a very wide, lusty view of life from all these generations. The carpets would be rolled back, and Dad would get on the piano. The ladies would sit on chairs around the edge of the room and sing, sometimes dance, while the men, who always had a good line on the latest jokes, would stand around nursing pints of beer. It was really great, and I grew up thinking everybody had a loving family like this - lovely, always nurturing. As an older lad I was shocked to find that this wasn't true - that many people had disastrous childhoods - and John Lennon was one of them.

I didn't know it when we first met, but John had suffered so many personal tragedies. His father disappeared when he was three, and reappeared only much later, when John was famous and found his dad washing dishes in the local pub. John wasn't allowed to stay with his mother, so the family sent him to live with his Aunt Mimi and Uncle George, which they thought would be better for him, and it might have been, but who really knows? John lived with Mimi and George for most of his childhood, but when he was about fourteen, George died. I didn't know his uncle, but I remember John saying to me a few years later, 'I think I'm a jinx on the male line.' I would have to reassure him and respond, 'No, it's not your fault your father left you, or that Uncle George died; it's nothing to do with you.' In this way I tried to give him the kind of reassurance I had from my home.

My own father's influence extended well beyond music. He gave me a love of words that may first have been apparent when I was in school. It was hard as a kid *not* to be aware of the way he could juggle words or how much he loved crossword puzzles. It's a very Liverpool thing to say silly things, but he carried it a good step further, and it took some doing to keep up with the subtleties of his jokes and puns. He would tell us, 'The pain is exquisite,' but he was really making a joke about the pain being excruciating, because you would not expect pain to be exquisite (I think it sounded better in person!). He wasn't particularly well-read, since he'd left school early because the family had no money. When he was fourteen, he had to go to work straightaway, but that departure from school never vanquished his love of words. As a boy, I did not realise that I was absorbing my father's love of words and phrases, but this, I believe, was the start of it all for me. Musicians get only twelve notes to work with, and in a song, often you use only about half of them. But with words the options are limitless, so it dawned on me that I, just like my dad, could play with them. It was as if I could toss them up in the air and then see when they all came down how language could become magic.

IT'S EASY FOR ME TO RECALL MY DAD, BUT THERE ARE SO many other people who also helped shape the way I would write songs. I mention Alan Durband, my teacher at the Liverpool Institute High School for Boys, a few times in these commentaries. As much as anyone else, he inspired my love of reading and opened things up for me so much that I came to live for a while in a fantasy world drawn from books. First I would learn something about a writer or poet in school; then I would head to the bookshop to augment what I didn't know. I started buying paperbacks – often novels, but also poetry books, like Dylan Thomas's *Under Milk Wood*, just to see what it was and how Thomas dealt with words. I also bought plays, like *Camino Real* by Tennessee Williams and *Salome* by Oscar Wilde.

One thing led to another, and I started going to plays in Liverpool. All I could afford was the cheapest seat in the house. I generally enjoyed these plays, works like Henrik Ibsen's *Hedda Gabler*, but I also enjoyed eavesdropping on conversations during the interval, listening to the chatter in the stairwell. I was the guy who just stood there, listening unobtrusively, and it was worth it because I would pick up opinions, criticisms, turns of phrase and stuff like that. Everything I absorbed would come to inform my own writing.

This was about the same time that I met John Lennon, and it's pretty clear now that we were a huge influence on each other. Readers might detect duelling emotions in my recollections of John; that's because my relationship with him was very mixed. Sometimes it was filled with great love and admiration, but other times not, especially around the time The Beatles were breaking up. In the beginning, though, the relationship was a young Liverpool guy looking up to another guy a year and a half older.

It was hard *not* to admire John's wit and wisdom. But as I came to see him as a person and a human being, there were, of course, arguments, though never anything violent. There's even a movie out there in which John's character punches my character, but the truth is that he never punched me. As with many friendships, there were disputes and there were arguments, but not many. Sometimes, though, I certainly thought John was being a complete idiot. Even though I was younger, I would try to explain to him why he was being stupid and why something he'd done was so unlike him. I remember him saying things to me like, 'You know, Paul, I worry about how people are gonna remember me when I die.' Thoughts like that shocked me, and I'd reply, 'Hold on; just hold it right there. People are going to think you were great, and you've already done enough work to demonstrate that.' I often felt like I was his priest and would have to say, 'My son, you're great. Just don't worry about that.'

My reassurances seemed to make him feel better, but with our songwriting I'd sometimes have to be tough. When he would suggest a line, sometimes I'd have to tell him that it was from something else, like *West Side Story*. I was the guy who had to say, 'No, that's been done before.' Sometimes I would take a song he'd written and suggest that he mould it another way. To his credit, he would take my advice - just as I would when he would tell me, 'Oh no, we can't have that' - and we would change the line. And that was the great thing about our collaboration: we respected each other's opinions in all sorts of special ways.

Just as The Beatles were beginning to fragment, Linda Eastman came into my life - as not only my wife but also my muse. No one was more influential on my writing and composing at that time. Just the fact that she got it, that she understood what I was trying to do, was very comforting, so she crops up frequently in the commentaries. If I wrote a song and played it for her, she could be very encouraging, but I always knew that she'd give me a straightforward opinion. On that level she was very helpful. Her love of music meshed with mine, and we could suggest things to each other so easily that if she had an idea for a song or two, I could take it and run with it. At the time, I really needed someone like that because The Beatles had just broken up.

Linda was especially helpful in other ways that readers of *The Lyrics* will, I hope, appreciate. When The Beatles started out, we hung on to things like newspaper clippings. After things started getting crazy with the band, my dad continued to cut out articles from the papers. He was so proud of what we were doing. But it was Linda who helped me realise the importance of the things we'd saved. Until then, we'd always seen the written-out lyrics as sort of ephemeral. We jotted them down just so that we could compose and record the song. At that time, our focus seemed to be all about the music, which is something you cannot physically see. We just threw away the lyric sheets afterwards, and it's funny to think about everything that ended up in the wastebaskets of Abbey Road Studios. Linda, though, had a background as a photographer. Producing beautiful prints was her art and craft, and she was steeped in a world of physical artefacts. She started picking up the handwritten lyrics we left in the studio, and she'd paste them into a scrapbook for me. She saw them as memories and parts of my history.

I'm told that the archive now has over a million items, which just goes to show how many objects can pass in and out of a life. I sit with these things from time to time – things that I've not seen for ages, like my old schoolbooks or the original *Sgt. Pepper* suit. For me it's a trip down memory lane, but in putting together this book, I wanted to make sure we illustrated the commentaries with objects and pictures from my past so that readers could immerse themselves in the period when the songs were written. It's all to give a sense of what was happening then.

The illustrations in the book – some quite straightforward, but others quite wild – will strike readers in unpredictable ways. By analysing the lyrics, someone might think that a particular song came from my mum or my dad, or was inspired by the Maharishi, or came out of my meeting with the queen, a person I admire very much. But songwriting, as well as the way people view songs, often comes from pure serendipity, sheer accident. Who would guess that the inverted wording of 'A Hard Day's Night' came from a malapropism that Ringo once uttered? Or that 'Lovely Rita' was inspired by a real meter maid stationed across from the Chinese embassy in Portland Place? Or that it took Hurricane Bob and the collapse of all electrical power on Long Island for me to write 'Calico Skies'? Or that the inspiration for 'Do It Now' was my father ordering me and my brother to pick up horse shit around our neighbourhood in Liverpool?

LIFE HAS TAUGHT ME THAT WE AS A SOCIETY WORSHIP CELEBrity. And for sixty years now I've had to face being a celebrity, something I could never have imagined when I was starting out in Liverpool. Even now at my age, journalists and photographers still want to break a story or expose some dirt, as if I were suddenly feuding with my fellow Beatle Ringo, or fighting with Yoko, a woman now well into her eighties. It's not hard to understand why some celebrities become reclusive, like Greta Garbo or my friend Bob Dylan. I also empathise with singers who've been crushed by fame – a list far too long.

While I do wish I could take my wife Nancy out to dinner without being stopped half a dozen times or photographed repeatedly while chewing my pasta, I'm grateful to have had parents who believed in me and my brother, loved us and provided us with a foundation that has enabled me to handle all the rough moments that have come my way. Going through more than 150 of my songs over the course of five years helped me put so many things into perspective, especially the role that Jim and Mary McCartney played in teaching me that people are basically good – sound lessons that I absorbed and imparted to my children. There are a few baddies, of course, but most people have a good heart.

I can still picture my father waiting with my brother and me at a bus stop in Liverpool, along with other people in the queue. He's wearing his trilby, a kind of hat men wore in those days like a uniform. He'd make sure we raised our own school caps to women. 'Good morning,' we'd say. It was such a sweet, old-fashioned gesture, and something that has stuck with me all these years. And I can remember Dad always talking to us about tolerance. 'Toleration' and 'moderation' were two of his favourite words.

It's a mystery how all this happened. People stop me in the street, and they can get very emotional. They say, 'Your music changed my life,' and I know what they mean - that The Beatles brought something very important to their lives. But it's still a mystery, and I don't mind ending up being a mystery. With regard to this all-pervading mystery, there's one incident I'll always remember. We were driving north in a van - just the four of us Beatles and our roadie. It was freezing cold, during a big blizzard, and we couldn't see our hands in front of our faces, and we really needed to, since we were in this van. All we could do was basically follow the tail lights of the car in front of us. The snow was so bad that we couldn't make out the road. At one point, our van spun out of control and slipped sideways down an embankment. We looked up at the road, shaken but okay, and we thought, 'How the hell are we going to get up there?' It was a mystery. But one of us - I can't remember who - said, 'Something will happen.'

Some people might find this outlook - 'something will happen' - simple or banal, but I think it's a great philosophy. Recently I told this story to one of my friends, a big guy in business, and he was so taken with what I'd told him that he repeated back to me, 'Something will happen.' The idea is that no matter how desperate you are, no matter how bad everything seems, something will happen. I find that idea helpful, and I think it's a philosophy worth holding on to.

Paul McCartney
Sussex, England
Autumn 2020

Note to
the Reader

THE CONVERSATIONS BETWEEN PAUL McCARTNEY AND Paul Muldoon, which form the basis of the commentaries in *The Lyrics*, began on the afternoon of Wednesday, 5 August 2015, in New York. Between the summer of 2015 and the final session on Wednesday, 19 August 2020, the two spoke for approximately fifty hours over twenty-four sessions. The last sessions were conducted via video call after much of the world went into lockdown because of the COVID-19 pandemic.

Although Paul McCartney's production team at MPL helped launch the book project in 2015 with a batch of initial research, it was in the summer of 2019 that we began formally working on it. The tasks were numerous, among them aiding Paul Muldoon with detailed research and transcribing the conversations for what would become the 154 songs that are included here. Various members of the team also began a deep dive into MPL's archives for images and objects to illustrate the commentaries.

One of the key challenges was standardising the lyrics. When they were available, we began with printed lyrics from album sleeves. Because the formatting can sometimes differ between releases, however, we applied a few general rules: use title case for song titles, keep repetition to a minimum, use a fairly light touch with punctuation and default to UK spelling. Where previously printed versions were unavailable, we searched the MPL archives, though on many occasions we discovered working documents, not final texts. *The Lyrics* thus presents, for the first time, what we would like to think of as the definitive lyrics for these 154 songs.

As the reader might imagine, many details and names have changed between late 1956, when Paul finished writing his first song, and the present. When The Beatles, for example, launched their recording career with George Martin in 1962, it was not Studio Two at Abbey Road Studios where they worked, but its former name of Studio Two at EMI Recording Studios. With the aim of keeping the book consistent, Paul asked us to list all these sessions as Abbey Road Studios. A similar approach was taken for other studios, such as AIR and Columbia. We standardised the location of AIR Studios in London as it changed location in the early 1990s and CBS Studios is sometimes referred to as Columbia, but here we have followed the master tapes. We have listed the studios where the majority of the song's recording took place, rather than including details of all overdubs sessions.

We have likewise devised standardised metadata. For each song, its first album appearance and single release in the UK and the US have been included. They are listed chronologically. We have restricted the information accompanying the songs to these two countries. To produce a complete list of all the various releases around the world seems a truly Sisyphean endeavour. It would require a new volume and did not feel appropriate in a book that focuses on Paul's lyrics.

The overwhelming majority of photographs and memorabilia that illustrate Paul's commentaries have been sourced from within the MPL archives. As he notes in his foreword, this archive contains over a million items, all of them digitised and keyworded. When we started researching the project, Paul asked that we include the most interesting and dynamic items we could find to contextualise and bring alive the time period in which the song was written. On a few occasions when we did not have appropriate items, we licensed imagery from third parties, to whom we are grateful (credits can be found at the end of the book). One of the considerable advantages of digging so deeply in the MPL archives is that around half the items we are publishing have not been seen before by the public. The research even turned up a previously unreleased Beatles song 'Tell Me Who He Is'.

The Lyrics, then, is a collaboration of great scope. We sincerely hope you enjoy reading the book as much as we have enjoyed assembling it for publication.

The MPL Team

Introduction
by Paul Muldoon

I T WAS TOWARDS THE END OF 2016 WHEN I HAD A PHONE CALL from an unfamiliar number. The voice, though, was immediately familiar. The newly elected Donald Trump introduced himself quite matter-of-factly. He lost no time in getting to the point: Would I be willing to come to Washington to serve as his 'Poetry Supremo'?

That Sir Paul McCartney turns out to be such a brilliant mimic shouldn't have come as a surprise. Like almost all great writers, he'd apprenticed himself to the masters of the trade, including an impressive array of literary masters: Dickens, Shakespeare, Robert Louis Stevenson, Lewis Carroll - names that roll quite naturally off his tongue. All apprenticeships are characterised by caricature and impersonation.

The context in which Paul McCartney was exposed to King Lear and, no less significantly, Edward Lear, is vital to an understanding of his achievement. Born in 1942, he was among the very first UK citizens to benefit directly from the 1944 Education Act, which allowed many more possibilities for the historically underprivileged. Paul's parents had both come from immigrant families of Irish extraction and had at once an intrinsically complex relationship to the UK and a sense of belonging to Liverpool's vast Irish community. More significantly, though, they identified with the newly confident, comparatively optimistic post-war generation.

As Paul McCartney attests, his parents always wanted 'greatness' for him and his brother Mike, so the boys were encouraged to go to the best available schools. His father, a cotton salesman, was 'very good with words', and the fact that his mother was a nurse ensured that Paul was 'the only boy in school who could spell "phlegm"'.

The single greatest influence on young McCartney turned out to be his high school English teacher, Alan Durband, who had attended Downing College, Cambridge, and had been a student of F. R. Leavis, the doyen of close reading of 'the words on the page'. Paul McCartney's capacity for textual analysis, of his own work as much as others', may then be traced directly to Durband's influence. I'm certain that, in another life, Paul McCartney would have been a schoolteacher - perhaps a university don - wearing a mortarboard as lightly as a mop top.

T O HAVE HAD SUCH A SECURE GROUNDING IN THE WORLD of English literature accounts for only part of Paul McCartney's success. That he is equally steeped in the popular song tradition - not only Little Richard and Chuck Berry, but the songwriters of the Brill Building and Tin Pan Alley - has given him a remarkably wide musical vocabulary. Among his earliest heroes were Fred Astaire, Hoagy Carmichael, George and Ira Gershwin and Cole Porter. Though he would later be in conversation with such avant-garde composers as Karlheinz Stockhausen and John Cage, Paul McCartney's immediate influences were The Everly Brothers and, preeminently, Buddy Holly. He remarks that 'Elvis wasn't a writer or a lead guitarist; he was just a singer. Duane Eddy was a guitar player but not a singer. So Buddy had it all.' Here he's referring to the fact that Buddy Holly wrote his own songs, sang them *and* played guitar.

In his own songwriting buddy, John Lennon, what Paul McCartney recognised from the outset was John's equally prodigious ventriloquistic capacities. However groundbreaking their work would turn out to be, The Beatles were constantly in dialogue with their contemporaries, whether the artists associated with Motown, The Beach Boys, or Bob Dylan, or the singers and songwriters of a slightly earlier era. Even now, Paul McCartney will psych himself into a song by channelling Little Richard or Fred Astaire. He may even occasionally channel John Lennon, in whom he recognised a partner whose name might one day be paired with his as Gilbert was paired with Sullivan, and Rodgers with Hammerstein. He acknowledges that the interplay of Lennon and McCartney was 'nothing short of miraculous', describing how they 'wrote with two guitars'. 'The joy of that was that I was left-handed and he was right-handed, so I was looking in a mirror and he was looking in a mirror.'

T HE OTHER GIFT THAT PAUL McCARTNEY RECOGNISED AB initio in John Lennon was his willingness not only to improvise but to improve. Together, they were always 'on the lookout for the kind of subject that hadn't really been the stuff of popular song'. They shared the eternal schoolboy's engagement with nonsense and nursery rhyme, and they did so with a Byronic lingering over the slightly outrageous rhyme, whether 'Edison/medicine' or 'Valerie/gallery'. They were blessed to find in

George Martin a producer who could keep pace with them – sometimes, indeed, setting the pace. Martin's suggestions for string arrangements and his openness to the inventiveness of Robert Moog and his newfangled synthesizer allowed The Beatles to be chronically inventive themselves.

A persistent component in The Beatles' soundscape that is often overlooked is the impact of radio. Paul McCartney describes *Sgt. Pepper* as 'a big radio programme'. Like the rest of The Beatles, he grew up on a diet of madcap radio comedy like *The Goon Show*, which ran from 1951 until 1960 and starred Peter Sellers, Spike Milligan and Harry Secombe. Other radio stars included the Liverpudlian zany Ken Dodd, often considered the last great music hall comedian. The influence of radio underscored Paul McCartney's fascination with 'what's missing in a piece', as well as the power of a few well-chosen words to set a scene. The impact of radio drama, including Dylan Thomas's 1954 masterpiece *Under Milk Wood*, cannot be overstated. It was a radio version of Alfred Jarry's *Ubu Cocu*, broadcast in 1966, that introduced Paul McCartney to the term 'pataphysical', referring to a particular realm of nonce science. Then there's the role of stage drama, whether Sean O'Casey's *Juno and the Paycock* or Eugene O'Neill's *Long Day's Journey Into Night*. Paul McCartney may usefully be thought of as a writer of mini-plays. He has the capacity to render a fully rounded character from what might otherwise be merely a thumbnail sketch.

Two other long-standing areas of interest for Paul McCartney fall under the rubric of the visual arts. The first is painting. He is both literally a painter, having completed hundreds of works in oil, and figuratively a presenter of images. The second is cinema. He is a presenter of the moving image, insisting along the way that 'my camera is looking around and sweeping life for clues'.

To THINK OF THE SONG AS A SHOOTING SCRIPT IS AN ANGLE OF entry into the planetary atmosphere of 'Eleanor Rigby', one of Paul McCartney's best-known songs. Here I will attempt to interpret some aspects of it as Alan Durband, *pace* F. R. Leavis, might have done. Like Leavis, Durband would probably have resisted the urge to disentangle the song from its historical moment. The other great Cambridge critic, I. A. Richards, would have insisted that the poem (or song) is a self-contained artefact, but Leavis and Durband would have been more inclined to allow for contextualisation.

Take the name of the main character. The song was released in 1966, when the most famous Eleanor in the UK was Eleanor Bron. A star of the popular 1964-65 television comedy series *Not So Much a Programme, More a Way of Life*, Bron had also appeared in the 1965 Beatles film *Help!* Visualisations of Eleanor Rigby by the very first UK audiences to hear the song are likely to have been strongly tinged by the strikingly beautiful Ms Bron. 'Rigby' is essentially a Viking name meaning 'ridge farm' or 'ridge village' and would tend to locate the song somewhere in the northern half of Great Britain. Being Scottish, Father McKenzie, the other main character of the poem, also evokes a northern-UK setting.

Part of the impact of 'Eleanor Rigby' is its filmic structure, where the two main characters are introduced in the first and second verses and are then brought together in the third. It's a version of the technique that Alfred Hitchcock used for the shower scene in his 1960 film, *Psycho*, in which he establishes the image of bloody water flowing down a drain, cuts away from it and then returns to a shot of the same drain with clear water swirling into the vortex. The shower scene in *Psycho* is also relevant because the frenzied playing of the double string quartet orchestrated by George Martin is reminiscent of Bernard Herrmann's 'stabbing' film score, so for those who first heard 'Eleanor Rigby', superimposed on the image of Eleanor Bron was the image of the mummified mother from *Psycho*. Part of the impact of 'Eleanor Rigby' is this all-but-invisible subtext of isolation and death.

THE DEATH OF HIS OWN MOTHER WHEN HE WAS FOURTEEN – something he's 'never gotten over' – is what hurt Paul McCartney into song. From 'I Lost My Little Girl' to such pieces as 'Despite Repeated Warnings', Paul McCartney has taken as his subject matter an astonishing array of topics – everything from his relationships with Jane Asher, Linda Eastman and Nancy Shevell, through climate change and racial injustice, to the family dog and the family car. Readers of *The Lyrics* will come away with a sense that they are in the presence of a poet for whom 'the London bookshops were almost as good as the guitar shops'. When Paul McCartney reminds us that 'what made The Beatles such a great band was that no two tracks are the same', we do well to remember that, throughout his long career with Wings and as a solo artist, he has had an unfailing 'aversion to being bored'. For sixty years he has embodied the restlessness we associate with the artist of the first rank. Beyond that, Paul McCartney is remarkable in that he is one of the very few who is not only influenced by his time but whose work has substantially defined that time. He is living proof of his fellow lyricist William Wordsworth's brilliant dictum that 'every great and original writer, in proportion as he is great and original, must himself create the taste by which he is to be relished'.

A WORD OR TWO ABOUT THE METHODOLOGY OF THE PRESENT tome. It's based on twenty-four separate meetings over a five-year period between August 2015 and August 2020. I'd been introduced to Paul McCartney by Robert Weil and John Eastman in early 2015. Most of these meetings took place in New York, and each involved two or three hours of intensive conversation. The process was a little reminiscent of the two-or-three-hour writing sessions that were a feature of the Lennon-McCartney partnership, though the tea was green rather than Brooke Bond or PG Tips. For snacks there were bagels with hummus, cheese and pickles, occasionally Marmite. Our times together were universally upbeat, sometimes uproariously so. Part of the reason we got on so well was our shared culture and range of reference, given that we were born a mere eleven years apart. Our birthdays are also separated by just two calendar days, and we were both named Paul for the same reason: the fact that the Feast of Saints Peter and Paul falls on the twenty-ninth of June.

However good he may be at putting people at ease, and however comfortable in his own skin he may be, there's no getting around the fact that Paul McCartney will always be a twentieth-century icon. For that reason, if no other, I did occasionally have to allow myself a starstruck moment. Successive starstruck moments occur whenever Paul McCartney takes the stage. His live shows continue to be of such high voltage that one half expects him to burst into flames. During our collaboration, then, it was a particular delight to have him quite often pick up a guitar to demonstrate a chord sequence and play a few bars of one of his songs to an audience of one.

Despite all this to-ing and fro-ing, we did somehow manage to discuss six to eight songs each time we met. Our conversations were recorded simultaneously on two devices and professionally transcribed. The commentaries on the lyrics included here I then edited into a semi-seamless narrative that eschewed my own questions and comments and was sometimes re-sequenced for sense. That text was then line-edited by the redoubtable Robert Weil and occasionally augmented with factual information by the equally redoubtable Issy Bingham and Steve Ithell, both of MPL.

T HE DEPTH AND DURABILITY THAT ARE THE HALLMARKS OF PAUL McCartney's lyrics derive from the combination of two seemingly irreconcilable forces that I characterise as the 'physics' and the 'chemistry' of the song. The physics has to do with the song's engineering, with its concomitant apprenticeship to craft that I referred to earlier. One estimate has The Beatles playing nearly 300 times in Germany between 1960 and 1962. That sheer exposure to the business of how songs are constructed lies at the root of the word 'poet', a version of the Greek term for a 'maker'. It's no accident that one Scottish term for a poet or bard is *makar*.

The chemistry component is reflected in another term for a poet: 'troubadour'. The word 'troubadour' is related to the French word *trouver*, 'to find'. Paul McCartney often uses some version of the phrase 'I came across the chords' to describe how a song begins its mysterious life. It's the magical combination of two elements – whether musical notes or the components of a simile – that causes a chemical reaction.

Paul McCartney often refers to a version of inspiration before which he is all but inert. The element of ventriloquism is one which he continues to valourise, as when he says that 'with the Little Richard thing you just have to give yourself over to it'. He remembers his father being 'into crossword puzzles' and acknowledges that he has 'inherited a love of words and crossword puzzles'. The word he uses of his attitude to the puzzle of a song – the answer to the question only it has raised – is 'fascination'. It brings to mind W. B. Yeats's insistence that 'The *fascination* of what's difficult / Has dried the sap out of my veins'. Like Yeats, Paul McCartney is committed to the serviceability of the idea of the mask, or persona, reminding us that 'starting with myself, the characters who appear in my songs are imagined' and it's 'all about making it up'.

Paul McCartney also has at least a partial regard for what the French philosopher Roland Barthes described as the 'death of the author', the idea by which the act of reading necessarily involves a degree of writing, or even rewriting, the text. In Paul McCartney's case, this idea is represented by his trust in the notion that each of his millions of fans around the world will round out their own version of the song he has offered them. The song becomes what it might most truly be only when it is heard and heralded. The single quality that makes Paul McCartney great, though, is his well-attested humility. He would be on exactly the same page as the perennially wise novelist and short story writer Donald Barthelme, who, in an essay titled 'Not-Knowing', categorised the writer as 'one who, embarking on a task, does not know what to do'. The emotional range and intellectual robustness of *The Lyrics* are testimony to Paul McCartney's profound selflessness – the implicit acknowledgment that he represents no more or less than what Barthelme calls 'the work's way of getting itself written'.

Paul Muldoon
Sharon Springs, New York
October 2020

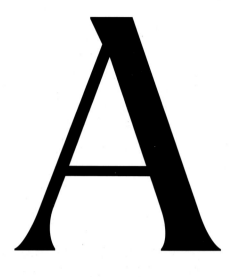

All My Loving

WRITERS   Paul McCartney and John Lennon
ARTIST   The Beatles
RECORDED   Abbey Road Studios, London
RELEASED   *With The Beatles*, 1963
Meet The Beatles! 1964

Close your eyes and I'll kiss you
Tomorrow I'll miss you
Remember I'll always be true
And then while I'm away
I'll write home every day
And I'll send all my loving to you

I'll pretend that I'm kissing
The lips I am missing
And hope that my dreams will come true
And then while I'm away
I'll write home every day
And I'll send all my loving to you

All my loving, I will send to you
All my loving, darling, I'll be true

Close your eyes and I'll kiss you
Tomorrow I'll miss you
Remember I'll always be true
And then while I'm away
I'll write home every day
And I'll send all my loving to you

All my loving, I will send to you
All my loving, darling, I'll be true
All my loving, all my loving
All my loving, I will send to you

W E WERE ON A PACKAGE TOUR, WITH PROBABLY FIVE or six other bands, because one act was not enough to sell tickets. Even in New York, a show would have Buddy Holly, Jerry Lee Lewis, Little Richard, Fats Domino, The Everly Brothers – all on the same bill!

So I was on a tour bus somewhere in the UK, with nothing to do, and I started to think of these words: 'Close your eyes . . .' Although we'd met at this point, I don't know that I was thinking specifically of Jane Asher when I wrote this, though we were courting. It's probably more of a reflection on what our lives were like then – leaving behind family and friends to go on tour and experience all these new adventures. It's one of the few songs I've written where the words came first. That almost never happens, I usually have an instrument with me. So, I'd started work on the lyrics on the bus, and back then we were playing what was known as the Moss Empires circuit. The Moss Empires company owned a number of venues across the country, which would be some of the stops on the tour. They were these large, gorgeous turn-of-the-century music halls, but nowadays most of them are bingo halls. These places had really nice, big, empty backstage areas, and I remember we were on a package tour with Roy Orbison, and we arrived at the venue, and with all the hustle and bustle around me – all the various bands and tour crews and stagehands running about – I made my way to a piano and then somehow found the chords. At that point, it was a straight country-and-western love song.

With songwriting, you conceive of it in one genre (because you can't conceive of things in thousands of genres), and you have one way of hearing it. If you get it right, however, you realise it has a certain elasticity; songs can be flexible. And when other members of The Beatles would get into the studio, often that's when that elasticity would kick in.

The thing that strikes me about the 'All My Loving' recording is John's guitar part; he's playing the chords as triplets. That was a last-minute idea, and it transforms the whole thing, giving it momentum. The song is obviously about someone leaving to go on a trip, and that driving rhythm of John's echoes the feeling of travel and motion. It sounds like a car's wheels on the motorway, which, if you can believe it, had only really become a thing in the UK at the end of the fifties. But, it was often like that when we were recording. One of us would come up with that little magic thing. It allowed the song to become what it needed to be.

It's a letter song, of course, in the same vein as the epistolary song 'P.S. I Love You', which was the B-side of 'Love Me Do'. It's part of a tradition of letter songs like Fats Waller's 'I'm Gonna Sit Right Down and Write Myself a Letter' or Pat Boone's 1956 hit 'I'll Be Home'. So, 'All My Loving' is a song that has a lineage.

'All My Loving' has somewhat of a lineage within the story of The Beatles too. It was recorded in the summer of 1963 and ended up on our second album, *With The Beatles*, released later that same year. At least, it was on *With The Beatles* in the UK. In the US the song came out on *Meet The Beatles!* in early 1964. At the beginning of our career, up until around the time of *Help!*, the US albums were different to the ones in the UK. Capitol used to take a few songs from here, a few from there, and add in a single or two, and that would be the US album. But what's great about *With The Beatles* and *Meet The Beatles!* is that they both have the same photo by Robert Freeman on the cover

Bob had worked with some really cool jazz musicians, like John Coltrane and Dizzy Gillespie, and we'd shown him some of our favourite photos taken of the band by our friend Astrid Kirchherr back in the Hamburg days. We asked Bob to keep that kind of style, and if you look at Astrid's photos of us you can definitely see the influence. I get asked about that cover a fair bit, and people are often surprised to hear how quickly it was done. It looks like it was taken in a studio with professional lighting to achieve those shadows, but the photo was actually taken in a hotel corridor in Weston-super-Mare, an old seaside town on the west coast of England. We were over there to play a string of shows at the Odeon Cinema, and Bob came to our hotel and was given an hour to get the cover. He set up a row of chairs and tried a few different arrangements - some with John at the front, some with me or George. But it was all done very quickly and with natural light. That photograph has become pretty iconic now, so we were pleased it was on the cover of both releases.

These albums came out at a time when Beatlemania was in full swing. A young lady in Washington, DC, had contacted her local radio station, asking them to play 'I Want to Hold Your Hand'. I think they had to ship a copy in from England at that point, but they put it on, and I think they even had her introduce the record on their station. That kick-started everything, and the song went to number one a few weeks later. We'd always said that we didn't want to go to America until we had a number one record, and here it was. So all that led to our first trip there.

There were crazy scenes at London Airport when we took off with a thousand-odd fans and the press waving us off and wishing us well. Cynthia, John's wife, mistook the screams for the sound of a plane. The scenes were even crazier on our arrival at JFK. At the time I don't think it necessarily occurred to us, but the airport had only recently been renamed after Kennedy. Our trip was only a few months after his assassination - which happened on the same day as the release of *With The Beatles* in the UK - and, though it's not for me to say, people have written that the country, especially teenagers, had been looking for something new and positive and fun to latch onto after mourning his death. It's one possible explanation for why Beatlemania took off so quickly in the US.

Capitol Records, our US label, had gone on a publicity drive to make sure people knew we were coming, and did they ever. We were met in New York by five thousand screaming fans and a hundred police officers trying to cordon them off. There's a film of a press conference we gave right after stepping off the plane, and you can see just how out of control it all was.

A couple of weeks after the release of *Meet The Beatles!*, we played the *Ed Sullivan Show*. Ed Sullivan was a real gentleman to us, and he always wore these finely tailored suits. There were only three major channels in the US

5

at the time, and his show defined what people talked about. You hadn't made it in America until you'd been on it. We'd heard that some of our heroes, like Buddy Holly and The Crickets, had performed on the show, and there was that story about how they'd let Elvis Presley back on after performing 'Hound Dog', but he had to be shown from the waist up.

Our first appearance has now become sort of mythical in the story of The Beatles. Just before it aired, we received a telegram from Elvis Presley, wishing us well. I'd nearly done well at school; then Elvis came along, and school was all but forgotten, and here he was saying good luck to us. Then there was the sound of the audience, which is still ringing in my ears. The show had received something like fifty thousand applications for the seven hundred studio tickets. When the show aired, seventy-three million people watched us, and it became a cultural marker. So many people have come up to me through the years to tell me they watched it. People like Bruce Springsteen, Tom Petty, Chrissie Hynde, Billy Joel - they'd all seen it. It's probably not true, but the story goes that the crime rate went down too; even the robbers were tuning in. It was such a great way for us to be introduced to the US. During our second song, 'Till There Was You', they cut to shots of each of us and put our names up on the screen. When they got to John, they added, 'Sorry girls, he's married' - which had been a badly kept secret up until that point.

Some of the press the next day were a bit mean, though. The *New York Herald Tribune* - who, I might add, are no longer with us - wrote that The Beatles were '75 percent publicity, 20 percent haircut, and 5 percent lilting lament'. But then the 'mop top' became a whole new trend in the way that teenage boys started to wear their hair. At that point, the fringe - or bangs, as they're called in the US - wasn't supposed to go anywhere near the eyebrows. That all changed. You could even buy Beatles wigs.

The *Ed Sullivan Show* brings us back to 'All My Loving'. The song had always done well live, so after he'd introduced us as 'these youngsters from Liverpool', it became the first song that America saw The Beatles play live on TV. A month or so afterwards we had the top five songs in the Billboard charts.

So to illustrate how quickly things were moving for us in those days, 'All My Loving' helped us go from the Moss Empires circuit to conquering America in a little over six months. And a few months later I turned twenty-two.

Our first appearance has now become sort of mythical in the story of The Beatles. Just before it aired, we received a telegram from Elvis Presley, wishing us well. I'd nearly done well at school; then Elvis came along, and school was all but forgotten, and here he was saying good luck to us.

Left: Robert Freeman's photograph as used on the covers of *With The Beatles*, 1963, and *Meet The Beatles!* 1964

Right: The Beatles' engagement list for the summer of 1963 as issued by Brian Epstein's management company, NEMS Enterprises Ltd. The name 'NEMS' comes from the Epstein family business (North End Music Stores) in Liverpool where Paul's dad Jim bought his piano.

Below: Robert Freeman, photographed by Paul. Miami, February 1964

NEMS ENTERPRISES LTD

DIRECTORS: B. AND C. J. EPSTEIN

PRESS OFFICE : 13, MONMOUTH STREET, LONDON W.C.2.   TELEPHONE COVent Gdn 2332

ENGAGEMENT LIST FOR THE BEATLES : MONDAY 10 JUNE to SUNDAY 1 SEPTEMBER 1963

Monday 10 June	: Pavilion, BATH
Wednesday 12 June	: Grafton Ballroom, LIVERPOOL (Charity function in aid of N. S. P. C. C.)
Thursday 13 June	: Offerton Palace Club and Southern Sporting Club, MANCHESTER
Friday 14 June	: Tower Ballroom, NEW BRIGHTON
Saturday 15 June	: City Hall, SALISBURY
Sunday 16 June	: Odeon, ROMFORD
Wednesday 19 June	: Recording 'EASY BEAT' (BBC, LONDON) for broadcast Sunday 23 June.
Friday 21 June	: Odeon, GUILDFORD
Saturday 22 June	: Town Hall, ABERGAVENNY
Sunday 23 June	: Filming 'THANK YOUR LUCKY STARS' (ABC TV, BIRMINGHAM) for screening on Saturday 29 June (special all-Merseyside edition)
Monday 24 June	: Recording 'SATURDAY CLUB' (BBC, LONDON) for broadcast Saturday 29 June.
Tuesday 25 June	: Astoria, MIDDLESBROUGH
Wednesday 26 June	: Majestic, NEWCASTLE
Friday 28 June	: Queens Hall, LEEDS
Sunday 30 June	: Regal, YARMOUTH
Wednesday 3 July	: 'THE BEAT SHOW' (BBC, MANCHESTER)
Saturday 6 July	: Memorial Hall, NORTHWICH
Sunday 7 July	: ABC BLACKPOOL
Monday 8 July to Saturday 13 July	: Week at Winter Gardens, MARGATE
Sunday 14 July	: Princess, TORQUAY
Friday 19 July	: Ritz Ballroom, RHYL
Saturday 20 July	: Ritz Ballroom, RHYL
Sunday 21 July	: Queens, BLACKPOOL
Monday 22 July to Saturday 27 July	: Week at Odeon, WESTON-SUPER-MARE
Sunday 28 July	: Regal, YARMOUTH
Wednesday 31 July	: Imperial Ballroom, NELSON
Friday 2 August	: Grafton Ballroom, LIVERPOOL
Saturday 3 August	: Cavern Club, LIVERPOOL
Sunday 4 August	: Queens, BLACKPOOL
Monday 5 August	: Urmston Show, URMSTON
Tuesday 6 August	: Springfield Hall, JERSEY
Wednesday 7 August	: Springfield Hall, JERSEY
Thursday 8 August	: Springfield Hall, JERSEY
Friday 9 August	: Springfield Hall, JERSEY
Saturday 10 August	: Springfield Hall, JERSEY
Sunday 11 August	: Queens, BLACKPOOL
Monday 12 August to Saturday 17 August	: Week at Odeon, LLANDUDNO
Sunday 18 August	: Filming 'BIG NIGHT OUT' (ABC TV, MANCHESTER) for for screening on Saturday 24 August
Monday 19 August to Saturday 24 August	: Week at Gaumont, BOURNEMOUTH
Sunday 25 August	: Queens, BLACKPOOL
Monday 26 August to Saturday 31 August	: Week at Odeon, SOUTHPORT
Sunday 1 September	: Regal, YARMOUTH

With Compliments from

Tony Barrow

Press & Public Relations Officer

Nems Enterprises Ltd.
Service House (1st Floor),
13 Monmouth Street,
LONDON, W.C.2.

Telephone: COVent Garden 2332

And I Love Her

WRITERS   Paul McCartney and John Lennon
ARTIST   The Beatles
RECORDED   Abbey Road Studios, London
RELEASED   *A Hard Day's Night*, 1964

I give her all my love
That's all I do
And if you saw my love
You'd love her too
I love her

She gives me everything
And tenderly
The kiss my lover brings
She brings to me
And I love her

A love like ours
Could never die
As long as I
Have you near me

Bright are the stars that shine
Dark is the sky
I know this love of mine
Will never die
And I love her

NEVER MIND THE BARRETTS OF WIMPOLE STREET; WHAT ABOUT the Ashers of Wimpole Street? Number 57 to be precise. The area is what many people might think of when they think of London. It's in Marylebone and a little like something out of *Mary Poppins* - Edwardian townhouses with quite a literary background: Elizabeth Barrett met Robert Browning there; Virginia Woolf wrote that it was 'the most august of London streets'; Henry Higgins supposedly lived there in *Pygmalion*. And it was in the house belonging to my girlfriend Jane Asher's family that I wrote this song.

When things really started to pick up for The Beatles, around 1963, we moved from Liverpool down to London. That happened partly because it's where the music 'business' was, but it was also a new world of adventures. The city was still pitted with bomb sites from the war, and it was undergoing a huge redevelopment: while I was staying in Wimpole Street, the Post Office Tower was built about a ten-minute walk from the Ashers' house. For a while, that was the tallest building in the city, and I could see it going up from my attic bedroom window. There was a real sense of renewal and anything goes in London; it was an exciting place to be.

I was staying with Jane partly because I didn't like where Brian Epstein had arranged for us to stay in Mayfair. He was a suave man with sophisticated taste, but the place had no soul, and even though I'd come from a poor background - especially compared to Mayfair - our house had soul, and all my uncles' and aunties' houses had soul. This was a plain, unfurnished flat. I was only twenty-one and never thought to buy some pictures and put them up. I just got annoyed that there was nothing on the wall.

Jane and I first met in the spring of 1963, when she came to the Royal Albert Hall to interview The Beatles for the *Radio Times*. I remember we were all surprised by her red hair, because we'd only ever seen her in black and white before. She and I started dating shortly afterwards, and towards the end of the year the Ashers must have heard me grumbling about Mayfair and said, 'Well, do you want to stay here?' This gesture was in the long tradition of giving a garret room to a starving artist. So, I had a little room up at the top, next to Jane's brother Peter's room. Jane would have been around

Above: Jane Asher at her family home. Wimpole Street, London, 1963

Below: The view from Wimpole Street, captured by Paul, of the BT Tower (formerly the Post Office Tower). London, 1964

seventeen or eighteen, and Peter was a little older, around nineteen or twenty at this time. And even though I was technically a lodger, I would often get to eat with the family, and I remember that it all worked out great.

It was a big eye-opener living there, because I'd never seen this class of people, except maybe on telly. I didn't know anybody like that. Brian Epstein was kind of classy but not this kind of classy; this was sort of a showbiz family in a way. Jane's mother Margaret had taken her to auditions, and Jane had been in little commercials and things. ('Don't Put Your Daughter on the Stage, Mrs. Worthington' - an old Nöel Coward song.) And because of Jane's success - she'd been acting and making films since the 1950s - I think Peter and younger sister Clare might have gone for auditions too.

So, the family knew all about art and culture and society, whereas I'd never known anyone who knew about going for auditions, or had an agent. It was really nice staying in that house. Lots of books to read, art on the walls, interesting conversations; and Margaret was a music teacher. It was at least a home, and I'd sorely missed that since I'd come down from Liverpool and since my mum had died six or seven years before.

As far as the gossip columns were concerned, Jane and I were what they would call an 'item'. So much so that we were in a theatre one night - I liked literature and theatre, and of course she, as an actress, did too, which might have explained a good deal why I was drawn to her in the first place - and we were sitting there, and the lights went up for the interval. We had decided not to go to the bar, so we were just going to sit it out. Despite some of those huge early concerts, I really was not used to the personal burdens imposed by fame, so we were just talking in our seats, and suddenly ten paparazzi came scampering in with those cameras going *flash*, *flash*, *flash*, like *La Dolce Vita*, and then, just as quickly, they all just scampered out again. They were like the Keystone Cops. But, oh my God, we were *shocked*. The theatre had probably tipped them off, to get a bit of publicity for the play.

But precisely because Jane was my girlfriend, I wanted to tell her *there* that I loved her, so that's what initially inspired this song; that's what it was. Listening to it so many years later, I do think it's a nice melody. It starts with F-sharp minor, not with the root chord of E major, and you gradually work your way back. When I'd finished it, I felt, almost immediately, proud of it. I thought, 'This is a good 'un.'

It really reached me, so I thought it might reach other people too. I brought it to the recording session where The Beatles' producer George Martin listened to it. We were about to record it, and he said, 'I think it would be good with an introduction.' And I swear, right there and then, George Harrison went, 'Well how about this?' and he played the opening riff, which is such a hook; the song is nothing without it. We were working very fast and spontaneously coming up with ideas.

Another thing worth recalling is that George Martin was inspired to add a chord modulation in the solo of the song, a key change that he knew would be musically very satisfying; we shifted the chord progression to start with G minor instead of F-sharp minor - so, up a semitone. I think George Mar-

Above: The jacket worn in *A Hard Day's Night*, 1964

Right: At the theatre with Jane Asher

tin's classical training told him that that would be a really interesting change. And it is. And this sort of help is what started to make The Beatles' stuff better than that of other songwriters. In the case of this song, the two Georges – George Harrison with the intro and then George Martin on the key change into the solo – gave it a bit more musical strength. We were saying to people, 'We're a little bit more musical than the average bear.' And then, of course, the song – which is now in F major, or arguably D minor – eventually finishes on that bright D major chord, a lovely, pleasing resolution. So, I was very proud of that. It was very satisfying to make that record and to have written that song for Jane.

Many years later, long after we had lived together in St John's Wood, I ran into her when I was going to a doctor on Wimpole Street. I'd been walking down the street from Marylebone, and I passed the house and thought, 'Wow, great memories there.' Then I went further down the street to where my doctor was, and I was just pressing the bell when I sensed someone behind me. I turned around, and it was Jane. I said, 'Oh my God, I was just thinking about you and the house.'

That was the last time I saw her, but the memories don't fade.

Another Day

WRITERS	Paul McCartney and Linda McCartney
ARTIST	Paul McCartney
RECORDED	CBS Studios, New York
RELEASED	Single, 1971

Every day she takes a morning bath she
    wets her hair
Wraps a towel around her as she's
    heading for the bedroom chair
It's just another day

Slipping into stockings, stepping into shoes
Dipping in the pocket of her raincoat
It's just another day

At the office where the papers grow she
    takes a break
Drinks another coffee and she finds it
    hard to stay awake
It's just another day

It's just another day
It's just another day

So sad, so sad
Sometimes she feels so sad
Alone in apartment she'd dwell
Till the man of her dreams comes
    to break the spell
Ah stay, don't stand her up
And he comes and he stays but he
    leaves the next day
So sad
Sometimes she feels so sad

As she posts another letter to The Sound of Five
People gather round her and she finds it
    hard to stay alive
It's just another day

It's just another day
It's just another day

So sad, so sad
Sometimes she feels so sad
Alone in apartment she'd dwell
Till the man of her dreams comes
    to break the spell
Ah stay, don't stand her up
And he comes and he stays but he
    leaves the next day
So sad
Sometimes she feels so sad

Every day she takes a morning bath she
    wets her hair
Wraps a towel around her as she's
    heading for the bedroom chair
It's just another day

Slipping into stockings, stepping into shoes
Dipping in the pocket of her raincoat
It's just another day

It's just another day
It's just another day

THINK 'ELEANOR RIGBY' MEETS HITCHCOCK'S *REAR WINDOW*. FOR, much as I hate to admit it, there is indeed a voyeuristic aspect to this song. Like many writers, I really am a bit of a voyeur; if there's a lit window and there's someone in it, I will watch them. Hands up, guilty. It's a very, very natural thing.

In a strange way, I may be interested in this subject matter because I get stared at quite a lot myself. It's because I have a recognisable face. It happens in the underground, on the subway, which I take when I can. You don't think people are looking at you until a little bit later, and you realise they were. Of course, I'm also looking back at them too. So I get to experience this from both sides.

There's a decorum, an unwritten rule that you don't say anything. But you do recognise distinct personality types. Some people will come right up to you with, 'Hey, how you doing, man?' You get the fist bumps and everything. Then there are some people who don't talk at all. The people I talk to are the ones who don't say anything. For example, I'm on the mat in the gym, and there's loads of people around. There's a guy who's doing stuff with a pole and I'm fascinated by what he's doing. I say, 'Oh, that's pretty amazing,' and then we get talking and he says, 'I remember you've got horses.' And he starts talking about horses. But it can really be anything that we'll talk about - even dipping into the contents of their raincoat. It's always interesting to hear these stories, which, in a roundabout way, can sometimes make their way into a lyric.

So, people do notice me and I am kind of aware of it, but that unwritten rule means you don't talk to each other about any of that obvious stuff. And you certainly don't take photos or ask for autographs. If they do, I often tell them I'm enjoying a private moment, and pretty much everyone gets that.

I mentioned 'Eleanor Rigby'. But while both that song and this one focus on the same idea - trying to capture the everyday of this character's life - the language here is more formal, less impressionistic. Eleanor Rigby 'lives in a dream', and that's reflected in lines like 'Wearing the face that she keeps in a jar by the door'. The protagonist here works in an office, though, and the lyrics are almost like a list, like her itinerary for the day. The person I'm gazing at here just happens to be a version of Linda living alone in New York before I met her, although *The Sound of Five* was a British radio show that people would write to about their problems. So, there's a transatlantic quality to it too. But I like to think I'm the 'man of her dreams', who shows up. So, it's rather appropriate that I recorded this in New York with Phil Ramone. Phil was a great producer who had made a lot of records I admired. He'd worked with Paul Simon and Billy Joel.

This was just after The Beatles broke up, and I was trying to establish myself as a solo artist with a new repertoire. If it was going to work like the Beatles repertoire had worked, I had to have a hit. One in two songs had to be a hit. So, this was a conscious effort to write a hit, and Phil was very helpful. We knew that if we had a hit, it would cement our relationship and we would keep working together, which we did with the *RAM* album. It would prove that we were both good - he as a producer and I as a singer-songwriter.

Releasing my first solo song after the breakup felt like a big moment. Thrilling, though tinged with sadness. It also felt like I had something to prove, and that kind of challenge is always exciting. The song went to number two in the UK singles chart and number five in the US Billboard Hot 100, so it did pretty well.

Of course, this was still a time when there was a bit of tension between John and me, and this sometimes filtered into our songwriting. John made fun of this song in one of his own, 'How Do You Sleep?'

> *The only thing you done was yesterday*
> *And since you've gone you're just another day*

One of his little piss takes.

1970   **May**
Sunday   **17**
137–228
Whit Sunday   Ember Week

1970   **May**
Monday   **18**
138–227   week 21   PAYE week 7

Another Day :
(1st) verse
Everyday she takes her morning bath.
another day (——) break

(2nd) At the office
Another day (— break)
— so sad x so sad
sometimes she feels so sad
Alone in apartment
break the spell (~~~~)

Above: McCartney family
scrapbook. Early 1970s

Left: Regent's Park,
London, 1968

There's a decorum, an unwritten rule that you don't say anything. But you do recognise distinct personality types. Some people will come right up to you with, 'Hey, how you doing, man?' You get the fist bumps and everything. Then there are some people who don't talk at all. The people I talk to are the ones who don't say anything.

Arrow Through Me

WRITER   Paul McCartney
ARTIST   Wings
RECORDED   Abbey Road Studios, London; and Spirit of Ranachan Studio, Scotland
RELEASED   *Back to the Egg*, 1979
              US single, 1979

Ooh baby, you couldn't have done
A worse thing to me
If you'd have taken an arrow
And run it right through me

Ooh baby, a bird in the hand
Is worth two flying
But when it came to love
I knew you'd be lying

It could have been a finer fling
Would have been a major attraction
With no other thing
Offering a note of distraction
Come on, get up
Get under way
And bring your love

Ooh baby, you wouldn't have found
A more down hero
If you'd have started at nothing
And counted to zero

Ooh baby, you couldn't have done
A worse thing to me
If you'd have taken an arrow
And run it right through me

It could have been a finer fling
Flying in a righter direction
With no other thing
Featuring but love and affection
Come on, get up
Get under way
And bring your love

Ooh baby, you wouldn't have found
A more down hero
If you'd have started at nothing
And counted to zero

WINGS, WHICH WE BEGAN IN 1971, WAS IN MANY WAYS an experiment to see whether there was life after The Beatles, to see whether that success could be followed. It was the result of asking myself, 'Am I going to stop now?' The Beatles were so wonderful and all-encompassing, so successful. Now, should I stop and look for something else to do? But I thought, 'No. I like music too much, so whatever the something else is, it will be music.' I actually saw Johnny Cash one night on television and he had a band, and he'd never had a band to my knowledge. I thought, 'That looks like fun,' and Johnny looked like he was having fun. I was with Linda; we'd been together for around three years at this point, and our daughter Mary would have been a little over one, so we were a relatively new family. I said to her, 'You fancy starting a band?' It felt like it would be a fun new adventure for us. And she said, 'Yeah.'

The band name, Wings, came from the time of the birth of Stella, another daughter. It had been a difficult delivery, and she'd had to go into intensive care in an incubator. I stayed on at the hospital, sleeping on a camp bed in the room next to Linda's while they were recovering. After situations like that, your mind goes into overdrive. I was thinking angelic thoughts because we'd just been through this family emergency, and the vision of an angel with big wings came to me. Wings really stuck with me. But it wouldn't be *The* Wings, like The Beatles. Just Wings.

My problem after The Beatles was, who's going to be as good as them? I thought, 'We can't be as good as The Beatles, but we can be something else.' I knew that if I were to go ahead with this project I'd have to tough it out, but I had reserves of courage from being part of The Beatles when pennies were thrown at us at the village hall in Stroud, when we were still starting out.

I had to put up with the equivalent once again. The hardest thing had to do with Linda, who was a complete amateur, but I thought, 'Well, so was George when he joined the group; so was I; so was John; so was Ringo.' I

Above: Early design for the Wings logo. First used on the band's 1972 *Wings Over Europe* tour

showed her a few things on keyboard, and then she taught herself and she had a couple of lessons, and it turned out her strength wasn't necessarily the keyboard, although she handled the job. It was more as a spirit. She was a great cheerleader, and she would get crowds going, get them clapping their hands and singing along.

In those days there weren't many women in groups, so she was sort of a pioneer in that respect, and listening back to the records, you can hear that she was a damn good singer, especially on harmonies. She would do the hand-clapping thing and singing backing vocals at the same time, and that's not easy to do – which is why people employed tapes and backing tracks. Starting off a new band is always a lot of fun, but it's a lot of hard work too; you have to establish yourself. Following The Beatles was one of the most difficult things for me, just trying to live up to those expectations. It was even more difficult for her.

I started to write songs for Wings from 1971 onwards, when we got started, and I tried to keep them away from The Beatles' style. There were avenues I could go down that I wouldn't have gone down with The Beatles, like bringing in the influence of reggae, which Linda and I got into in Jamaica. I fancied doing something crazy, and Wings allowed me a little bit more freedom. So, this is a love song in which Cupid's arrow is referenced, but it's a malevolent arrow. It's possible I'd seen an illustration of Cupid and thought, 'Cupid fires a bow, but I'll switch it. It won't be love; it will be the opposite.'

The character in the song has been wounded. He's been cheated on. And it could've been a great relationship, could've been fantastic. As things stand, you couldn't 'have found a more down hero', because there was nobody more down than me at that moment. So, get it together and bring your love.

I have always had a soft spot for this song. There's a nice horn riff in it, and it's funky. Sometimes you write to get a sort of feeling rather than a perfectly 'correct' lyric. Sometimes the lyric can be secondary to the feeling. This one has as much, or more, to do with the feel of the song, the groove.

Right: *Wings Over Europe* tour. August, 1972

In those days there weren't many women in groups, so [Linda] was sort of a pioneer in that respect, and listening back to the records, you can hear that she was a damn good singer, especially on harmonies.

22

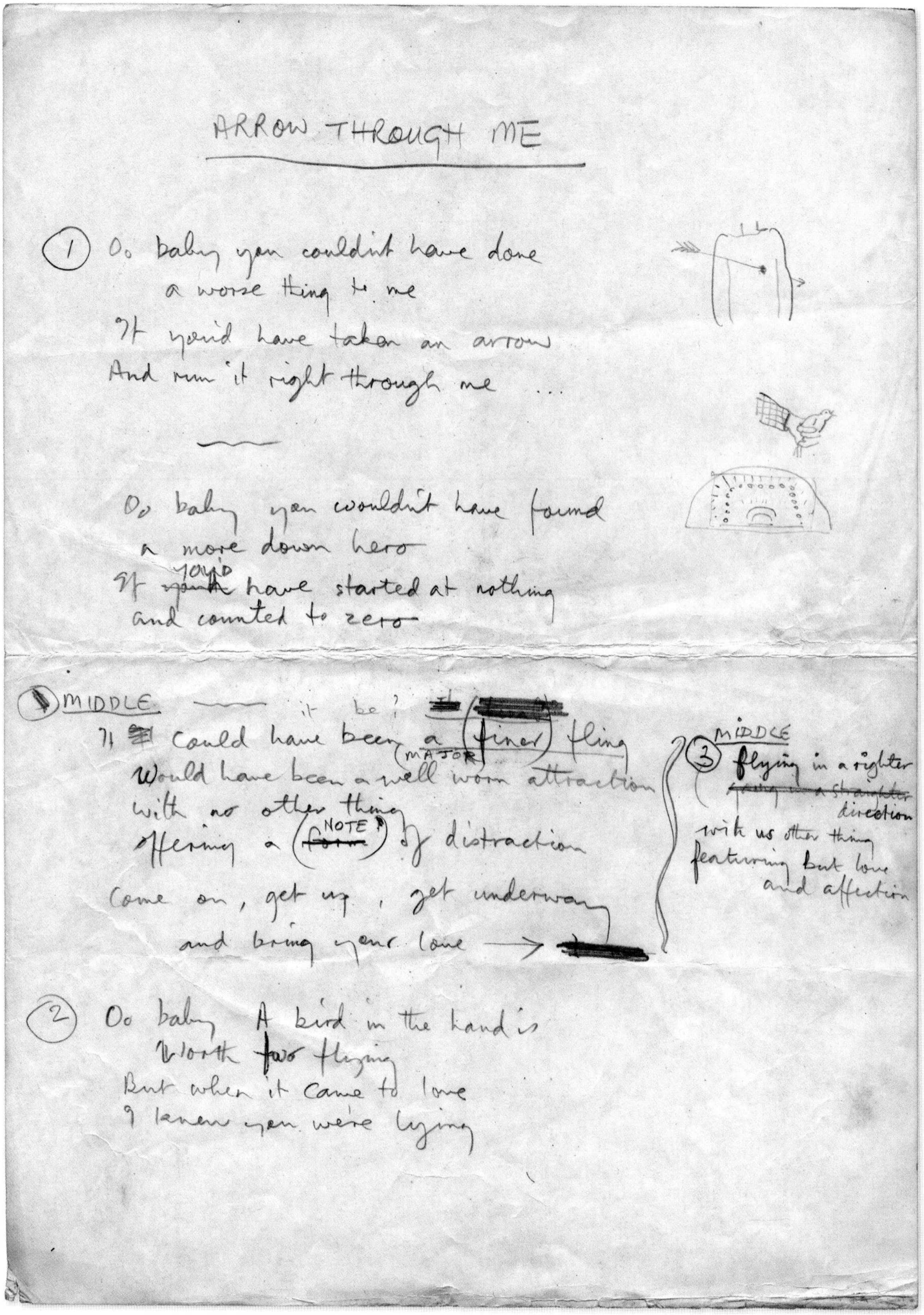

ARROW THROUGH ME

① Oo baby you couldn't have done
    a worse thing to me
  If you'd have taken an arrow
  And run it right through me ...

  ────

    Oo baby you wouldn't have found
    a more down hero
  If ~~you'd~~ you'd have started at nothing
  and counted to zero

① MIDDLE ──── it be?
    If ~~it~~ could have been a (~~finer~~) MAJOR fling
    Would have been a well worn attraction
    with no other thing
    offering a (~~form~~ NOTE) of distraction

    Come on, get up, get underway
      and bring your love ──→ ▬▬

③ MIDDLE
  flying in a righter
  ~~getting a straighter~~
              direction
  with us other thing
  featuring but love
      and affection

② Oo baby A bird in the hand is
    Worth ~~two~~ flying
  But when it came to love
  I knew you were lying

24

With Mary, Stella and
Linda on the top deck of
the *Wings Over Europe*
tour bus. Sweden, 1972

Average Person

WRITER   Paul McCartney
ARTIST   Paul McCartney
RECORDED   AIR Montserrat; and AIR Studios, London
RELEASED   *Pipes of Peace*, 1983

Look at the Average Person
Speak to the man in the street
Can you imagine the first one you'd meet?

Well I'm talking to a former engine driver
Trying to find out what he used to do
Tells me that he always kept his engine
Spit and polished up as good as new
But he said his only great ambition
Was to work with lions in a zoo
Oh to work with lions in a zoo

Yes dear, you heard right
Told me his ambition was to work with
    lions every night

Look at the Average Person
Speak to the man on the beat
Can you imagine the first one you'd meet?

Well I met a woman working as a waitress
I asked exactly what it was she did
Said she worked the summer crowd at seasides
Wintertime she ran away and hid
Once she had a Hollywood audition
But the part was given to a kid
Yes the part was given to a kid

Yes sir, you heard right
Hollywood ambition made a starlet
    grow up overnight

Well I bumped into a man who'd been a boxer
Asked him what had been his greatest night
He looked into the corners of his memory
Searching for a picture of the fight
But he said he always had a feeling
That he lacked a little extra height
Could have used a little extra height

Yes mate, you heard right
He always had a feeling that he might have
    lacked a little height

Look at the Average Person
Speak to the man in the queue
Can you imagine the first one is you?

Look at the Average Person

W*HAT'S MY LINE* WAS A GAME SHOW IN WHICH A FOUR-PERSON
panel would have to figure out the occupations of mystery guests
by asking them yes-or-no questions. It was great fun and tremendously popular. The UK version began in the early 1950s, and we often had it on in our house, so it was very much at the back of my mind and, I'd say, part of the hinterland of this song.

You're walking down the street and all the people look sort of ordinary, but one of them might be a vicar and another one might be a criminal or a plumber or a bread maker. I'm interested in the idea that people have these hidden sides and ambitions. I think writers are drawn to people like that. If you've got someone who's just purely glorious, it's not quite as interesting as if they're glorious but they've got a little Achilles' heel somewhere. All of these people are tarnished in some way. All of these people want to be something else.

I think my interest in these stories comes partly from growing up in such a tight-knit working-class community. We'd always be there for our family and our neighbours, helping out. Dad used to make me and my brother Mike go round door-to-door, canvassing for new members for the Speke Horticultural Society, where he was secretary. Knock, knock. 'Would you like to join the gardening club?' 'Piss off.' So we really got to know whose door to knock on and whose to avoid. But you'd get to hear about their lives, their troubles; this was post-war, remember, and we'd been bombed and gone through rationing. And that makes you realise we all have our stories, our own worries. It gets a little poignant, and it's about being empathetic.

It makes the story more interesting too. I know he wouldn't be counted as an 'average person', but would we be interested in Hamlet if his father had died of natural causes and he'd just ascended to the throne? Probably not. It's because he suspects that his father was murdered and thus is thrust into an agonising situation that the drama is so rich. It's his inner life and struggles that make him such a compelling character.

Another inspiration for this song was an old music hall routine having to do with the identity of a window washer that I saw on telly as a kid. My dad came from that music hall era, and the family were kind of steeped in that; we listened to it and sang all those songs at the piano. My Auntie Milly and Auntie Jin used to sing an old music hall song called 'Bread and Butterflies'. Later he worked in the cotton exchange, of course, but back in the 1920s my dad was a limelight operator - working those old stage lights - at a place in Liverpool called the Royal Hippodrome. So, I think that's how a lot of it crept into us, because every night he would be hearing 1920s and '30s music hall songs, and all those artists came through on tour. They'd do the Hippodrome in Liverpool, and then they'd go on to the Manchester Hippodrome, and so on. Dad told a story about how he trimmed the lime on the limelight - the music hall equivalent of how spotlights are used today.

So, because of my dad, these old music hall references sometimes make their way into my writing. I knew of Noël Coward's music because of my dad, and Noël was obviously hugely famous. His songs appealed to my song-writing ear. Once, he was in Rome at the same time as The Beatles, and our manager Brian Epstein, being gay and quite gregarious in his own way, knew some of the crowd that was around Noël. We were in the same hotel, but we were kind of rock and roll kids. So, we were asked whether we wanted to go meet him, and the others were a little bit more ambivalent. But I said, 'I'd better go.' I was often that guy who thought, 'Oh no, we can't not.' Now it was, 'We can't snub him; he's Noël Coward.'

So I went down with Brian and just met him in his hotel room, and he said, 'Hello, dear boy.' He was so very Noël Coward. His poise, his mannerisms - exactly as you'd imagined him to be.

But we were sometimes a little weird about meeting people like that. We were likewise very weird with Marlene Dietrich, who was a colossal star. We were on the same bill together at the Prince of Wales Theatre - the 1963 Royal Variety Performance, where John made a joke about the posh people rattling their jewellery. I think she would have sung 'Lilli Marlene' and 'Where Have All the Flowers Gone?' This was at the time when Beatlemania was getting really crazy, and someone came up from her dressing room and said, 'Would you like to meet Miss Dietrich?' and invited us to say hello. So we replied, 'Oh yeah!' They said she was very proud of her legs. Now, by this time she was getting old, maybe in her sixties, and we were all in our early twenties, so it would be like looking at your auntie's legs or your grandma's legs. I wasn't sure we wanted to do that. But as soon as we got there, one of us said, 'Oh bloody hell, what great legs you've got!' Somebody had to say it, I suppose, but it was all a bit embarrassing.

With a song like Dietrich's 'Lilli Marlene', you have the struggles of a couple in love being torn apart by war. The longing and the heartache are what make it such a poignant song. And, I think, it's this sort of pathos that I'm drawn to and that people relate to in characters like Eleanor Rigby or Father McKenzie. So that's also why, in 'Average Person', we meet the former engine driver whose ambition was to work with lions in a zoo; the waitress who had the Hollywood audition; and the boxer who always felt he lacked that little extra height. Ordinary people with ordinary problems.

THE AVERAGE PERSON

Look at the average person
Speak to the man in the (street) on the site
(beat)
Can you imagine the first one

you'd meet —

① ENGINE DRIVER

Talking to a former engine driver
Trying to find out what he used to do ...
Tells me that he always kept his engine
Spit and polished (up as) good as new (spanking)
But he said his only great ambition
was to work with (pythons) in a zoo (LIONS)
oh to work with pythons in a zoo LIONS

yes dear — you heard right
He told me his ambition was to
work with pythons in a zoo every night
once a night.

Look at the average person
Speak to the man in the street
You can imagine the first one you'd meet—

29

② WAITRESS.

Met a woman working as a waitress
Asked ~~her just~~ exactly what it was she did
Said she (worked)(served) the summer crowd at seasides
Wintertime she ran away and hid
~~S~~ Once she had a Hollywood (ambition) audition
But the part was given to a kid,
Yeah the part was given to a kid.

Yes sir, you heard right
Hollywood ambition made a starlet
grow up overnight

③ CHORUS
_____

BOXER.

Bumped into a man who'd been a boxer
Asked him what ~~(had been his greatest night)~~ ~~greatest moment was~~

(he) looked into the corners of his memory
Searching ~~for an old~~ BATFIRE OF ~~these~~ ~~(long forgotten)~~ .TITE - (fight')
~~Bath had a little known ambition~~
~~he always had a small ambition~~
~~Just to gain a little extra height~~
~~Yes Sir you heard right~~
THEN ~~But~~ he says he always had a feeling
that he ~~might~~ (MIGHT) have lacked a little height
(.could have used a little extra height)

Yes mate, you heard right

(Always had a feeling that he
might have lacked a little height –)
Yes – sir – – –
Told me his ambition

Was to never have another fight.

31

B

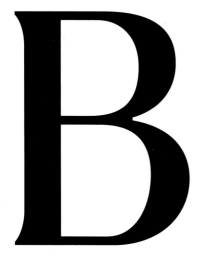

Back in the U.S.S.R.

WRITERS   Paul McCartney and John Lennon
ARTIST   The Beatles
RECORDED   Abbey Road Studios, London
RELEASED   *The Beatles*, 1968

Flew in from Miami Beach BOAC
Didn't get to bed last night
On the way the paper bag was on my knee
Man I had a dreadful flight

I'm back in the U.S.S.R.
You don't know how lucky you are, boy
Back in the U.S.S.R.

Been away so long I hardly knew the place
Gee it's good to be back home
Leave it till tomorrow to unpack my case
Honey disconnect the phone

I'm back in the U.S.S.R.
You don't know how lucky you are, boy
Back in the U.S.
Back in the U.S.
Back in the U.S.S.R.

Well the Ukraine girls really knock me out
They leave the West behind
And Moscow girls make me sing and shout
That Georgia's always on my mind

Oh show me round your snow-peaked
    mountains way down south
Take me to your daddy's farm
Let me hear your balalaikas ringing out
Come and keep your comrade warm

I'm back in the U.S.S.R.
You don't know how lucky you are, boy
Back in the U.S.S.R.

WHEN THE BEACH BOYS RELEASED *PET SOUNDS* IN 1966, we could see once and for all that they were presenting us with some serious competition. Until then, they'd seemed like a pretty good surf band. They'd already produced some great stuff, some innovative work that had itself come out of the doo-wop tradition, and we'd already nicked a few of those little things. The harmonies would be a case in point. Of course, they were nicking from us. Everybody was nicking from everybody else. There was a circularity to the whole enterprise.

One way or another, the Russian 'protagonist' of this song has certainly been influenced by The Beach Boys, and Chuck Berry's 'Back in the U.S.A.' is in there too. And it's perfectly in order for him to have been influenced by The Beach Boys. He's on a plane from Miami, after all, where he's been listening to 'California Girls' in particular, which is why our bridge section refers to how the 'Ukraine girls really knock me out'. There's a pretty blatant parody of a Beach Boys chorus in the background.

Then we've got the humorous reference to 'Georgia on My Mind', as sung by Ray Charles, but referring to Georgia in the Soviet Union rather than the US state. That this character somehow prefers the USSR to the USA is what makes this song funny. And once we start running through the USSR territories, we could go on for hours. It's almost as if the song is writing itself at this stage. The line 'show me round your snow-peaked mountains way down south' has a bit of a naughty schoolboy tinge, not to mention 'Come and keep your comrade warm'.

At a couple of points, the idea that a Russian guy is saying you don't know how lucky you are to live in the USSR is a bit undercut. I'm thinking of the reference to disconnecting the phone. Phone tapping was probably part of the back-of-the-mind view of the USSR. The reference to 'your daddy's farm' is a bit complex too, when you consider that collectivisation had been the order of the day in the USSR. So 'daddy' might be Stalin or Brezhnev, who was in power at the time.

The Beatles were banned in the USSR, needless to say, which had the usual effect of making us very popular there. When I did eventually sing 'Back in the U.S.S.R.' in Red Square, in 2003, it was a moment to savour.

Above: The Beach Boys photographed by Linda. Plaza Hotel, New York, 1968

Above: *Back in the World*
tour. Red Square, Moscow,
24 May 2003

Left: Paul's balalaika, as
featured in the lyrics

Flew in from Miami Beach B O A C
Didn't get to bed last night
On the way the paper bag was on my knee
Man I had a dreadful flight
I'm back in the U S S R
You don't know how lucky you are boy
Back in the U S S R .

Been away so long I hardly knew the place
Gee it's good to be back home.
Leave it till tomorrow to unpack my case
Honey disconnect the phone
I'm back in the U S S R ......
Well the Ukraine girls really knock me out
They leave the west behind
& Moscow girls make me sing & shout
that Georgia's always on my .... mind.
Show me round ~~the~~ your snow peaked mountains
                              way down South
Take me to your daddy's farm
Let me hear see your balalaika working out

Band on the Run

WRITERS	Paul McCartney and Linda McCartney
ARTIST	Paul McCartney and Wings
RECORDED	EMI Studios, Lagos; and AIR Studios, London
RELEASED	*Band on the Run*, 1973
	Single, 1974

Stuck inside these four walls
Sent inside forever
Never seeing no one nice again
Like you, mama, you, mama, you

If I ever get out of here
Thought of giving it all away
To a registered charity
All I need is a pint a day
If I ever get out of here
If we ever get out of here

Well the rain exploded with a mighty crash
As we fell into the sun
And the first one said to the second one there
I hope you're having fun

Band on the run
Band on the run
And the jailer man and Sailor Sam
Were searching everyone
For the band on the run
Band on the run
For the band on the run
Band on the run

Well the undertaker drew a heavy sigh
Seeing no one else had come
And a bell was ringing in the village square
For the rabbits on the run

Band on the run
Band on the run
And the jailer man and Sailor Sam
Were searching everyone
For the band on the run
Band on the run

The band on the run
The band on the run
The band on the run
The band on the run

Well the night was falling as the desert world
Began to settle down
In the town they're searching for us everywhere
But we never will be found

Band on the run
Band on the run
And the county judge who held a grudge
Will search for evermore
For the band on the run
The band on the run
Band on the run
The band on the run

THE WORD 'BAND' IN THE TITLE OF THIS SONG REFERS mostly to the idea of a group of people who've escaped prison. A band of desperadoes. Certain aspects of it remind me of *Butch Cassidy and the Sundance Kid*. The undertaker is ringing a bell because he's upset he has so few customers. Sailor Sam's a character out of *Rupert Bear*, the comic strip by Mary Tourtel. But he fitted in somehow.

As it happens, the song was recorded in Lagos, Nigeria, in an EMI studio. Lagos sounded good, exotic. It wasn't quite what I'd imagined. I hadn't imagined cholera or the mugging or the half-ready studios or my children being told they weren't allowed in the hotel swimming pool because they were naked. You block out all the worst stuff and you remember all the cool stuff.

Chief Abiola, 'Hey, hello Mac.' (He called me Mac.) 'Mac, why you no have four wives?'

'One's enough trouble, Chief.'

The main thing is it's a story song. A song about freedom. A lot of us at that time felt free from the strictures of civilisation. That's one of the great things about rock and roll: it does allow you to break rules. One rule often broken is that a piece of music has to be highly complex to be any good.

I've mentioned it time and time again, but it's worth remembering that, when The Beatles started, we had very few musicians' skills. We knew only a few chords. But we developed – to the point that when we broke up, we had become quite a sophisticated machine. With Wings, we would show up at student unions and say, 'Can we do a gig?' because we knew they had a hall and they had people. We'd charge 50p at the door. We had only eleven songs, so we had to repeat some of them. Some of the gigs must have been quite bad because we didn't really know what we were doing.

BAND ON THE RUN.

Stuck inside these four walls
Sent inside forever
Never seeing no-one, nice again,
like you, mama
You, mama ..... you...

If I ever get out of here
Thought of giving it all away,
to a registered charity
All I need is a pint a day
(If I ever get out of here
(If we ever .. ..)
        — LINK —

① Well the rain exploded with a mighty crash
As we fell into the sun
And the first one said to the second one there
I hope you're having fun
CHORUS Band on the run;)band on the run
And the jailer man, and sailor sam,
    were searching everyone
For the Band on)the run
        ,, ,, ,, ,,
        ,, ,, ,, ,,
        ,, ,, ,, ,,

Well, the undertaker drew a heavy sigh
Seeing noone else had come
And a bell was ringing in the village square
For the rabbits on the run,
CHORUS   Band on the run

and the "jailer" man etc....

(3)   Well the night was falling
As the desert world began to settle down
In the town they're searching for us everywhere
But we never will be found
CHORUS Band on the run
    "   "   "   "

And the county judge, who held a grudge
Will search forever more,
    FOR the   BAND ON THE RUN

Birthday

WRITERS	Paul McCartney and John Lennon
ARTIST	The Beatles
RECORDED	Abbey Road Studios, London
RELEASED	*The Beatles*, 1968

You say it's your birthday
It's my birthday too, yeah
They say it's your birthday
We're gonna have a good time
I'm glad it's your birthday
Happy birthday to you

Yes we're goin' to a party, party
Yes we're goin' to a party, party
Yes we're goin' to a party, party

I would like you to dance
(Birthday) Take a cha-cha-cha-chance
(Birthday) I would like you to dance
(Birthday) Dance

You say it's your birthday
It's my birthday too, yeah
They say it's your birthday
We're gonna have a good time
I'm glad it's your birthday
Happy birthday to you

'MACH SCHAU! MACH SCHAU!' WHEN THE BEATLES were first in Hamburg, in 1960, and were living on cornflakes and milk and trying to build an audience, we were told to shout, *'Mach schau!'* Putting on a show was always an important element of what The Beatles did, and what I continue to do. We were trying to pull people into the Indra Club in Hamburg, and we simply had to learn certain skills to do that. We used to do a song called 'Dance in the Street', for example, to lure people in. John stood up without his guitar and clapped as he 'danced in the street'. A little bit of spectacle, and indeed it pulled people in.

'Birthday' is one of those songs that was written to be played in a live show – with a view to being performed. There are songs like 'Sgt. Pepper', with its 'We'd like to take you home with us', which work really well at the end of a concert. 'Birthday' still works well for an audience because there's always someone who's got a birthday. Some of my songs have functions above and beyond merely getting themselves into the world.

This one came into the world one night in Abbey Road. We more or less lived in Studio Two, and a few of our friends were around. I remember Pattie Boyd, George Harrison's wife, was there. I'm pretty sure Eric Clapton was around. Normally, there weren't visitors in the studio, but this was some sort of occasion. It might even have been someone's birthday.

We decided to make something up on the spot. We often started a session with a riff, and for us the riff of riffs was Little Richard's 'Lucille'. It's the riff Roy Orbison adapted for 'Pretty Woman'. So we did the same thing for 'Birthday'. All very basic stuff.

Two of the lines I'd focus on are 'I would like you to dance / Take a cha-cha-cha-chance'. I'm reminded that another band that was very much to the fore then was The Who. They had a very memorable moment in 'My Generation', which involved what we used to call a stammer or a stutter on the phrase 'fade away'. But when you go 'f-f-f f-' on live British television, that gets people's attention. I remember that moment quite vividly. And that 'impediment', let's call it, informed the 'cha-cha-cha' in 'Birthday', just as 'Birthday' informed the 'cha-cha-cha-cha' in David Bowie's 'Changes'. Being a songwriter is about picking up the baton and holding it for a while and then passing it on.

RIFF

THEY SAY ITS YOUR BIRTHDAY
WELL ITS MY BIRTHDAY TOO YEAH
THEY SAY ITS YOUR BIRTHDAY
WE'RE GOING TO HAVE A GOOD TIME
IM GLAD ITS YOUR BIRTHDAY
    HAPPY BIRTHDAY TO YOU

DRUMS

E   ⑧ _ _ _ _ _ _

I WOULD LIKE YOU TO DANCE
TAKE A CHA CHA CHA CHANCE
I WOULD LIKE YOU TO DANCE

SOLO

STAGGERS

THEY SAY ITS YOUR BIRTHDAY
WELL ITS MY BIRTHDAY TOO YEAH
THEY SAY ITS YOUR BIRTHDAY
WE'RE GOING TO HAVE A GOOD TIME
IM GLAD ITS YOUR BIRTHDAY
    HAPPY BIRTHDAY TO YOU.

Above: Onstage with
Stuart Sutcliffe, John
Lennon and George
Harrison. Top Ten Club,
Hamburg, 1961

Right: The Beatles.
Hamburg, early 1960s

Blackbird

WRITERS   Paul McCartney and John Lennon
ARTIST   The Beatles
RECORDED   Abbey Road Studios, London
RELEASED   *The Beatles*, 1968

Blackbird singing in the dead of night
Take these broken wings and learn to fly
All your life, you were only waiting
For this moment to arise

Blackbird singing in the dead of night
Take these sunken eyes and learn to see
All your life, you were only waiting
For this moment to be free

Blackbird fly
Blackbird fly
Into the light
Of a dark black night

Blackbird singing in the dead of night
Take these broken wings and learn to fly
All your life, you were only waiting
For this moment to arise
You were only waiting
For this moment to arise
You were only waiting
For this moment to arise

THE POET ADRIAN MITCHELL WAS A GOOD FRIEND OF MINE, and I wrote a little book of poetry, called *Blackbird Singing*, that Adrian helped me with. It was edited by Bob Weil, who is working with me on this book too. I was doing some readings to promote the book, and I asked Adrian, 'What do you do at a reading? Do you just read your poems?' He said, 'Well, if you can think of any interesting anecdote about the poem, that's always a good lead-in. Then you read the poem.'

'Blackbird' was one of the pieces I was planning to read and I remembered two stories about it. One had to do with the music, the little guitar part which is so much a part of it, where the lyric goes 'Blackbird singing in the dead of night'. It was something that George Harrison and I would play as a party piece when we were kids, a lute piece by Johann Sebastian Bach. The fingerpicking style was something we admired in Chet Atkins, particularly in a piece called 'Trambone', though it was also played by Colin Manley, from a group called The Remo Four. They'd started out in Liverpool around the same time as The Beatles.

The other story has to do with 'blackbird' being slang for a Black girl. I am very conscious that Liverpool was a slave port, and also that it had the first Caribbean community in England. So we met a lot of Black guys, particularly in the music world. I'm thinking in particular of Lord Woodbine, a calypso singer and promoter who ran a couple of joints in Liverpool, including the New Cabaret Artists' Club, where he hosted The Silver Beetles. Then there was Derry of Derry and The Seniors, a band that had paved the way for us in Hamburg.

At the time in 1968 when I was writing 'Blackbird', I was very conscious of the terrible racial tensions in the US. The year before, 1967, had been a

Above: *The Beatles* recording sessions. Abbey Road Studios, London, 1968

particularly bad year, but 1968 was even worse. The song was written only a few weeks after the assassination of Martin Luther King Jr. That imagery of the broken wings and the sunken eyes and the general longing for freedom is very much of its moment.

The upshot of Adrian Mitchell's advice about the importance of the introduction in the poetry reading was that I started to do a lot more in the way of contextualising the songs in my regular concerts by telling some of the stories behind them. I think audiences really appreciate finding an angle into the planetary atmosphere of the song, by getting to see the far side of the moon.

Black bird singing
in the dead of night
Take these broken wings
and learn to fly
All your life
you were only waiting for
this moment to arise
Black bird singing
in the dead of night
Take these sunken eyes
and learn to see
All your life

Paul McCartney

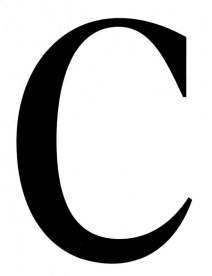

C

Café on the Left Bank

WRITER	Paul McCartney
ARTIST	Wings
RECORDED	*Fair Carol*, Virgin Islands
RELEASED	*London Town*, 1978

Café on the Left Bank
Ordinary wine
Touching all the girls with your eyes

Tiny crowd of Frenchmen
Round a TV shop
Watching Charles de Gaulle make a speech

Dancing after midnight
Sprawling to the car
Continental breakfast in the bar

English-speaking people
Drinking German beer
Talking far too loud for their ears

Café on the Left Bank
Ordinary wine
Touching all the girls with your eyes

Dancing after midnight
Crawling to the car
Cocktail waitress waiting in the bar

English-speaking people
Drinking German beer
Talking way too loud for their ears

Café on the Left Bank

VIN ORDINAIRE WAS THE ONLY KIND OF *VIN* WE KNEW about in those days. I couldn't understand why people liked wine; anytime I tasted it, it was terrible. When John and I hitchhiked to Paris in 1961, we went to a café on the Left Bank, and the waitress was older than us – easy, since John was turning twenty-one and I was nearly twenty. She poured us two glasses of *vin ordinaire*, and we noticed she had hair under her arms, which was shocking: 'Oh my God, look at that; she's got hair under her arms!' The French would do that, but no British – or, as we would later learn, American – girl would be seen dead with hair under her arms. You had to be a real beatnik. It's such a clear memory for me, so it was in my head when I was setting this scene.

I'm actually quite a fan of 'ordinary'. I hope in many ways it defines me, and so also many of the songs I've written. Don't get me wrong; I like extraordinary people and things, but if people can be great and ordinary at the same time, that to me is kind of special. So my Liverpool family – my parents, all the aunties and uncles – they were great and ordinary, and I think the fact that this combination can be easily dismissed makes it even more special. So many people would dismiss my Liverpool family, but they're actually a lot smarter than the likes of Maggie Thatcher, say. Their attitude to life was not as uptight as many people I've encountered since. They were always up for a song around the pub piano, for example. So you can choose to be highly sophisticated but very uptight, or you can be not so sophisticated but at peace with yourself. I try and be a bit of a mixture, and I draw very strongly on that ordinariness.

I remember seeing TVs in a shop window – they were still in black and white (it's hard for younger generations to imagine television without colour)

- and people were standing around watching Charles de Gaulle in his kepi hat. That's a scene we don't see much these days. In fact, we don't see it at all these days. It was, and is, a very striking image.

I have a strong recollection of recording the song with a mobile studio on a yacht moored in the US Virgin Islands. The studio had twenty-four tracks - keep in mind that *Sgt. Pepper* had been done with four tracks - so it was the next best thing to being in Abbey Road. The classic Wings line-up was involved, with Denny Laine and Jimmy McCulloch on guitars, Joe English on drums, Linda on keyboards and vocals, and me on bass and vocals. I also produced the track. That's a bit like being in a café on the Left Bank and being guest and garçon at the same time.

Above: Recording with Denny Laine. *Fair Carol*, Virgin Islands, 1977

Right: Recording with Joe English, Denny Laine, Jimmy McCulloch and Linda. *Fair Carol*, Virgin Islands, 1977

HOTEL BAKOUA MARTINIQUE

★ ★ ★ ★

BAKOUA (MARTINIQUE)
76.33.95
: 589
97207 FORT DE FRANCE CEDEX
TELEX : BAKOUA 029 666 MR

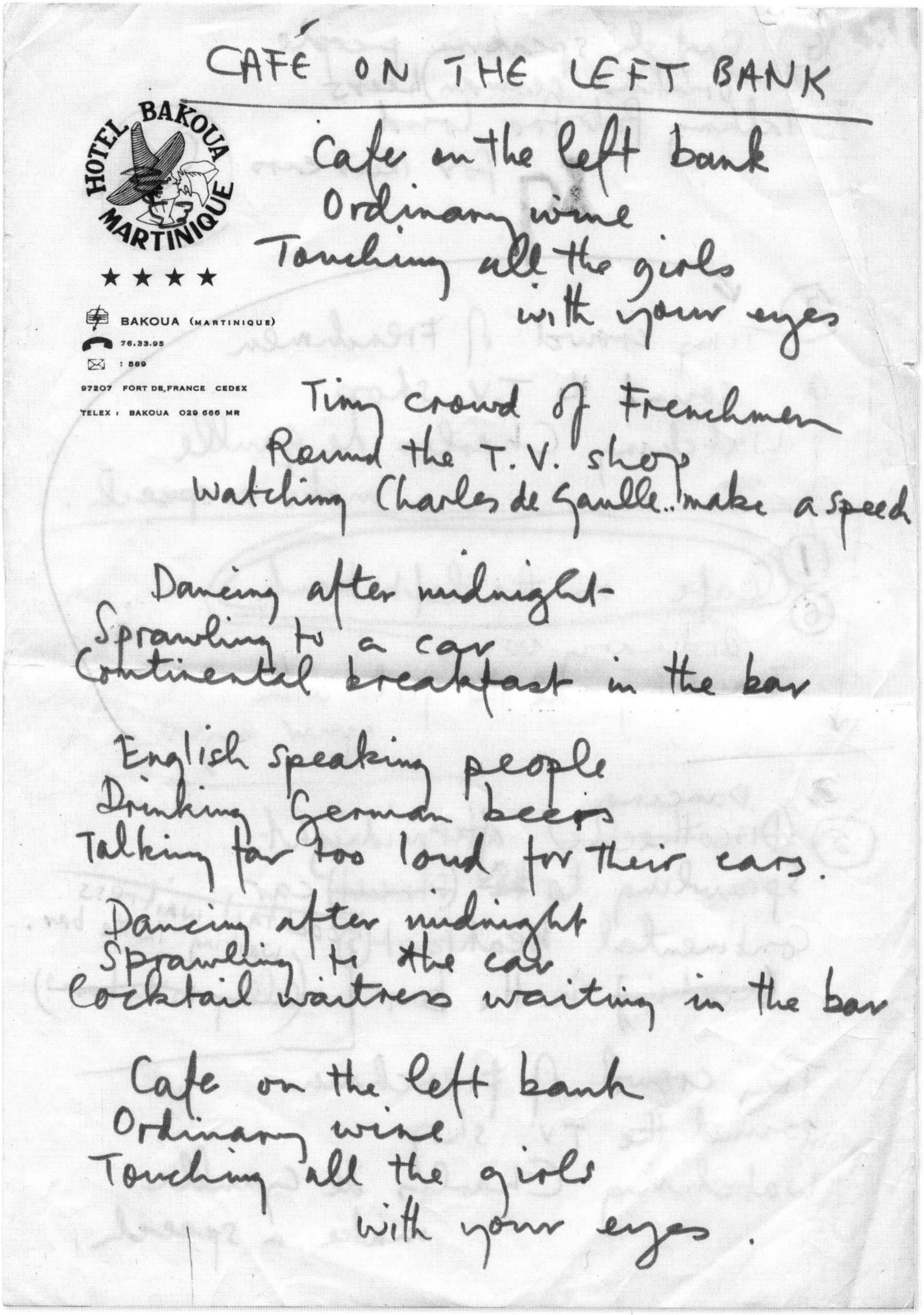

CAFÉ ON THE LEFT BANK

Cafe on the left bank
Ordinary wine
Touching all the girls
with your eyes

Tiny crowd of Frenchmen
Round the T.V. shop
Watching Charles de Gaulle.. make a speech

Dancing after midnight-
Sprawling to a car
Continental breakfast in the bar

English speaking people
Drinking German beers
Talking far too loud for their ears.

Dancing after midnight
Sprawling to the car
Cocktail waitress waiting in the bar

Cafe on the left bank
Ordinary wine
Touching all the girls
with your eyes.

④ English speaking people
Drinking (German) beers
Talking far too loud
for their ears

② Tiny crowd of Frenchmen
round the T.V. shop
Watching Charles de Gaulle
make a speech.

① Cafe on the left bank
⑥ Ordinary wine
Touching all the girls with
your eyes

③ Dancing
⑤ (Discotheque) after midnight
Sprawling to the (Street) car
Continental breakfast
(Feeding) in the bar
⑤ cocktail waitress
waiting in the bar.
(calling to the bar)

Tiny crowd of Frenchmen
round the TV shop
watching Charles de Gaulle
make a speech.

57

Calico Skies

WRITER   Paul McCartney
ARTIST   Paul McCartney
RECORDED   Hog Hill Mill, Sussex
RELEASED   *Flaming Pie*, 1997

It was written that I would love you
From the moment I opened my eyes
And the morning when I first saw you
Gave me life under calico skies
I will hold you for as long as you like
I'll hold you for the rest of my life

Always looking for ways to love you
Never failing to fight at your side
While the angels of love protect us
From the innermost secrets we hide
I'll hold you for as long as you like
I'll hold you for the rest of my life

Long live all of us crazy soldiers
Who were born under calico skies
May we never be called to handle
All the weapons of war we despise
I'll hold you for as long as you like
I'll hold you for the rest of my life
I'll hold you for as long as you like
I'll love you for the rest of my
For the rest of my life

I F LINDA WAS ASKED WHAT HER SIGN WAS, SHE USED TO SAY, 'NO Parking'. I never paid much attention to astrology, and I think that's because there was so much endless chatter about star signs in the sixties. For what it's worth, I'm a Gemini.

With Gemini you're born in the middle of the year, so there's all that bit of the year gone and there's all this bit of the year to come and you are born slap-bang in the middle. Apparently, I'm told, it affects your character. I definitely have this yin-yang thing, but I suppose everyone does: ebony and ivory; hello and goodbye; you say yes, I say no. Often I'm playing with that sense of dichotomy. I'm a true Gemini.

The opening phrase in this song – 'It was written that' – refers to the idea that one's fate is indeed 'written' in the stars. 'Calico skies'? Who knows what that might be. I might've heard the phrase somewhere, but I'm claiming it. I know calico is a kind of cotton cloth that came originally from the city I knew as Calcutta, now Kolkata, and it would be nice to think that this song increased the popularity of calico.

Today I was looking at some sleeve notes associated with the release of the album *Flaming Pie*, which this song was on, and it reminded me of how it happened. They had finally started giving boys' names to hurricanes, and a powerful one they called Bob had caused a power cut on Long Island, and everything was out. Now that's a nice opportunity, when the world shuts off, for you to create. I'm always looking for that, anyway. If I'm writing a song in a house, I will try to get as far away from the action as possible, which often means a cupboard, a closet, or a bathroom. Somewhere that I can be the hermit in the cave. So, when these power cuts happen, suddenly you don't have to secrete yourself here or there, but you can go down to the basement and just totally be at one with the song.

If you're writing a song, you're going to make it rhyme; it tends to work better than a sort of prose song. So, once I've got an idea and I know there's a good possibility I'm going to rhyme something with 'eyes', I'll just start running through potential options. I like to think my dad solved crossword puzzles in a very similar way, just shuffling through a few of the word possibilities in his head. So, in writing a song, I just look ahead and know there's going to be a rhyme and I try to make it a good one – one that advances the plot. For this song, the word 'skies' came, so I thought I'd open my eyes on a day with 'cloudy skies', 'dark blue skies', 'deep blue skies' or even 'Calico Skies'. You look for a context for that word.

'While the angels of love protect us / From the innermost secrets we hide'. Each of us has loads of stuff going on inside, but the idea of love and respect and decency protects us from innermost secrets that might not be terrific. You might not be thinking well of someone, but unless they've really angered you, you're not going to say it, and that's the angel of love protecting you. I think this goes on all the time. This can also be called your conscience. I mean I love the idea that there are two people in my head. Well, at least two.

'Long live all of us crazy soldiers'. There are certain politicians, presidents, prime ministers that we don't like, who can lie willfully, and I've fought

against them in my own way throughout my life. To me, the sort of protest that this line represents is like Pete Seeger, Bob Dylan, 'We Shall Overcome'. I put that in a romantic song, and coming as the third verse it's a bit of a wake-up call, because until this point it hasn't really been about politics or society as much as about individuals. But this puts us all into a crazy soldier brigade – we band of brothers – one that I'm very happy to belong to.

You have all these kinds of arguments and discussions as students, and in our case, The Beatles became my fellow students. We'd sit up and have a drink. Then we'd be talking about this and that, and, because of the age we were, we were discussing what we would do if a war were declared and we were actually called up. Would we fight? That is something I think a lot of people of our generation had to consider. The great thing about The Beatles was that the minute we formed the band, the UK ended the call-up, what Americans call the 'draft'.

In fact, we'd all have had to go. Ringo would've been eligible, and later I and John and George were also eligible. And none of us had that infamous lucky bone spur that some used to get out of military service. We always said that the end to the call-up was like God, in Moses fashion, opening the waters for us, and we just walked through. In truth, we were plain lucky.

So the discussion was, would we have fought? And my opinion was that I wouldn't have, unless the circumstance was something like Dunkirk or an invasion by Hitler, and then I would have felt I had to. Other than that, I was opting for peace, and that idea was very prevalent in our generation. We actually thought there might be a chance that if we could persuade these politicians, then we could indeed have peace.

In the end, it appears that you can't persuade them, but you have to keep trying. I'm glad Churchill stood up against Hitler when so many of his colleagues, including Neville Chamberlain, said, 'No, we have "peace for our time".' And Chamberlain was not alone. Loads of people thought they should give in because they – quite wrongly – considered Hitler to be mostly harmless before the war.

Rather like a certain politician's public pronouncements on COVID-19.

Above: Cloudy skies photographed by Linda

Right: East Hampton, 1991

Can't Buy Me Love

WRITERS   Paul McCartney and John Lennon
ARTIST   The Beatles
RECORDED   Pathé Marconi, Paris; and Abbey Road Studios, London
RELEASED   Single, 1964
               A Hard Day's Night, 1964

Can't buy me love, love
Can't buy me love

I'll buy you a diamond ring, my friend
If it makes you feel alright
I'll get you anything, my friend
If it makes you feel alright
'Cause I don't care too much for money
Money can't buy me love

I'll give you all I've got to give
If you say you love me too
I may not have a lot to give
But what I've got I'll give to you
I don't care too much for money
Money can't buy me love

Can't buy me love
Everybody tells me so
Can't buy me love
No, no, no, no

Say you don't need no diamond rings
And I'll be satisfied
Tell me that you want the kind of things
That money just can't buy
I don't care too much for money
Money can't buy me love

Can't buy me love
Everybody tells me so
Can't buy me love
No, no, no, no

Say you don't need no diamond rings
And I'll be satisfied
Tell me that you want the kind of things
That money just can't buy
I don't care too much for money
Money can't buy me love

Can't buy me love, love
Can't buy me love

W E THOUGHT OF OURSELVES AS LENNON AND McCARTNEY from very early on. It was because we'd heard of Gilbert and Sullivan, Rodgers and Hammerstein. Lennon and McCartney? That's good. There are two of us, and we can fall into that pattern. We put our names next to each other in our school exercise books. 'Love Me Do' came from around that period, as did 'One After 909'. That might have been as far back as 1957. About ten or fifteen years ago, I found that school exercise book. I put it in my bookcase. I've since lost it. I don't know where it is. I think it might show up somewhere. It's the first Lennon and McCartney manuscript.

In any case, one thing we always did with the records we bought, aside from checking out the title, was to check out the names in brackets underneath. Leiber and Stoller, Goffin and King. These were magic names to us – all of these, particularly these American ones – though not so much Rodgers and Hammerstein, who had been a little earlier. This was our time, and these were the writers of our time. When we moved to London, John and I started meeting professional songwriters – people like Mitch Murray and Peter Callander. They worked out of our publisher's office, and they just made hits – kind of churned them out. Mitch wrote songs like 'How Do You Do It?', which George Martin had us record, and it nearly became The Beatles' debut single. So, John and I looked at people like them and said, 'Right, we could do that. And if we get hits, we'll get money. It may not buy us love, but it'll buy us a car.'

It wasn't just the money. It was the joy of pulling a song out of a hat and then being able to play it with our band, which needed songs. So we were sort of feeding the machine. We would ask our record company, 'How many do you want, guv?' The people from Capitol Records came over, Voyle Gilmore and Alan Livingston. They were two very California gentlemen in suits, and they said, 'Well, we would like four singles and an album per year.' We thought that was very doable.

So, Brian Epstein, our soft-spoken but debonair manager, would ring us and say in his quiet but perfect upper-class accent that bore no trace of his Liverpool upbringing, 'You've got next week off, and you're to write the next album,' and we went, 'Great, okay.' We wrote a song a day. We would just meet at my house or John's. The usual two guitars, two pads, two pencils. A lot of the other stuff had been written on the road – here, there and everywhere – but to do an album you would actually allocate a week or so and just manage it.

It was always a good idea to be mid-process because it made us think, 'What if we wrote one that sounded like that?' or 'We should write one that sounds like this.' We recognised a gap that needed filling, and that was as much a part of what inspired us as anything else. And the fact that we were making records and they were successful was very helpful. It was as if you were an athlete. You were winning races, so you could sort of say, 'Oh yeah, I think I'll go in for that one as well.'

This song was written on a piano in the George V Hotel in Paris. Only a few years earlier, John and I had hitchhiked to Paris and hung around the cafés. This was a very different visit. The hotel was near the Champs-Elysées, and we had suites big enough to have a piano brought up. We were in town to play something like three weeks' worth of concerts at the Olympia Theatre. Back then, concerts were pretty short, but we'd be doing two sets every day. When I do shows now, we play about forty songs in three hours. In those days it was probably fewer than ten, so around half an hour, once you added a bit of chit-chat with the audience. We would have songs like 'From Me to You', 'She Loves You', 'This Boy', and 'I Want to Hold Your Hand' in the set. The others would be covers like 'Roll Over Beethoven' and 'Twist and Shout', finishing off with 'Long Tall Sally'. Our days in Hamburg, where we used to play all night every night, had been great training for long residencies like this.

So, as if forty-odd shows weren't enough, Brian would also arrange all these other duties, like writing and recording sessions. While we were in Paris, we ended up re-recording 'I Want to Hold Your Hand' and 'She Loves You' in German: 'Komm, gib mir deine Hand' and 'Sie liebt dich' by Die Beatles. Our producer, George Martin, came over for the recording at the Pathé Marconi studio, and at the same time we put down the basic tracks for 'Can't Buy Me Love'.

It's twelve-bar blues, with a Beatles twist on the chorus, where we bring in a couple of minor chords. Usually, minor chords are used in the verse of a song, and major chords bring a lift and lighten the mood in the chorus. We did it the other way round here. The idea is that all these material possessions are well and good, but money can't buy you what you really need. The irony here is that just before Paris, we'd been in Florida where, if not love, money certainly could buy you a lot of what you wanted. But the premise stands, I think. Money can't buy you a happy family or friends you can trust. Ella Fitzgerald recorded the song later that year too, which was a real honour.

The single did really well for us, getting to number one in the UK and US at the same time. And then, funnily enough, it was knocked off the number one spot in the UK by 'A World Without Love', a song I wrote for Jane Asher's brother Peter. He had been signed to EMI with his friend, and they put that song out as their debut under the name Peter and Gordon. I'm pretty sure it made number one in the US too. That was a song I'd written when I was sixteen at home in Liverpool. I didn't think it was strong enough for The Beatles, but it did pretty well for Peter and Gordon's career. The song starts off with the line 'Please lock me away', and when I would play it, John would respond, 'Yes, okay,' and we'd joke that that was the end of the song.

Probably quite a few people out there associate 'Can't Buy Me Love' with the film *A Hard Day's Night*. It plays in a scene where we finally manage to break out of the studio and get to have some fun, and it is sort of a proto-music video. The song was actually written especially for the soundtrack and the film, although pretty heavily scripted by Alun Owen - written in sort of short sound bites, so we wouldn't have to learn long lines - and it's sort of responsible for giving each of us public personas: John was the

HIPPY
SHIMMY
~~SHEIK~~ RED HOT
BESAME
RHYTHM + BLUES
OPEN
LOVE ME DO
POSTMAN
PICTURE
FEETS TOO BIG
SWINGIN' THING
FOOL OF SOMEBODY
DARKTOWN
BABY ITS YOU
DREAM
P.S.
MONEY
ROLL OVER BEETHOVEN
LONG TALL SALLY

smart, acerbic one; George was the quiet one; Ringo was the funny one. I was typecast as the cute one. It was strange being reduced to a couple of shorthand characteristics in the eyes of the world, and I think many people to this day still think of us in terms of how our dialogue was written in that film. That viewpoint can be pretty restrictive, but we learnt to ignore it.

One important thing hasn't changed though: my suit jacket size. I wore a velvet-trimmed tuxedo jacket to the premiere of *A Hard Day's Night* in London in 1964. In 2016, when The Beatles tour film *Eight Days a Week* premiered, again in London - and perhaps thanks to having been a vegetarian for about forty years at this point - I wore the same jacket.

Top: With John Lennon backstage at the Civic Center. Baltimore, 1964

Above: Brian Epstein photographed by Paul, 1964

Above: With Stuart Sutcliffe, George Harrison and John Lennon. Top Ten Club, Hamburg, 1961

Right: John Lennon. Paris, 1961

Below: 'A World Without Love' single. Released 1964

Right: Wearing the jacket worn to the premiere of *A Hard Day's Night* in 1964 at the premiere to *Eight Days a Week* with Ringo Starr. London, 15 September 2016

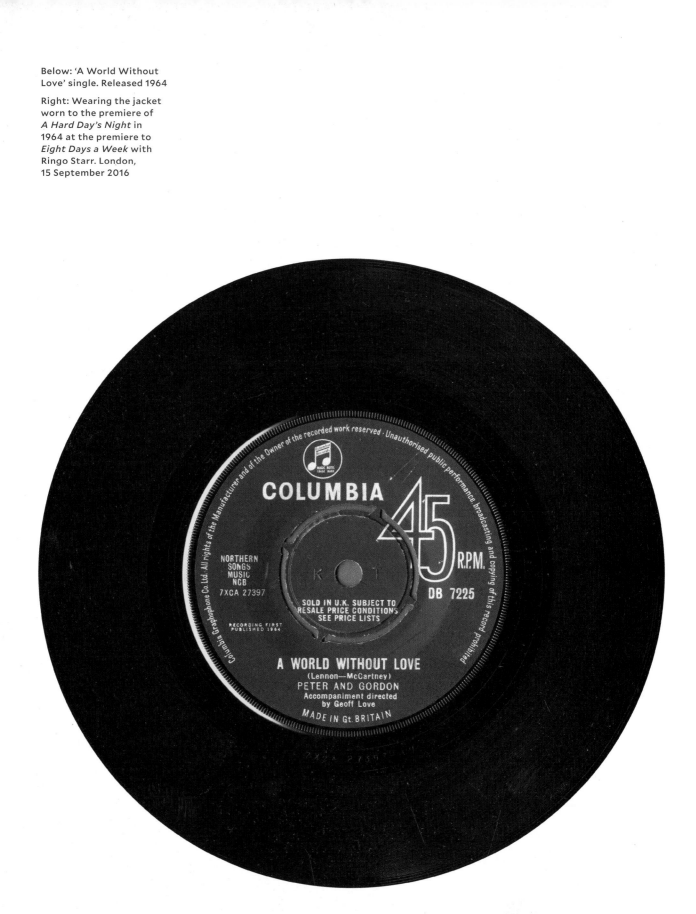

Carry That Weight

WRITERS   Paul McCartney and John Lennon

ARTIST   The Beatles

RECORDED   Abbey Road Studios, London

RELEASED   *Abbey Road*, 1969

Boy, you're gonna carry that weight
Carry that weight a long time
Boy, you're gonna carry that weight
Carry that weight a long time

I never give you my pillow
I only send you my invitations
And in the middle of the celebrations
I break down

Boy, you're gonna carry that weight
Carry that weight a long time
Boy, you're gonna carry that weight
Carry that weight a long time

WE WERE ENTERING A PERIOD IN THE MID- TO LATE SIXTIES when we were doing LSD, staying up all night, then wishing it would wear off, discovering it wouldn't. A bad trip could leave you feeling a bit heavy, instead of enjoying the normal lightness of youth. You know, we started off smoking pot, and it was just giggles. It was such fun. We loved it and it was great, and the worst that would happen was you'd fall asleep, and that was fine. Once it got into sort of more serious stuff, then you were just sort of doing it and there wasn't this light relief. It could be oppressive.

That was coupled with the business problems at Apple Records, which really were horrible. The business meetings were just soul-destroying. We'd sit around in an office, and it was a place you just didn't want to be, with people you didn't want to be with. There's a great picture that Linda took of Allen Klein, in which he's got a hammer like Maxwell's silver hammer. It's very symbolic. And that's why we have the little nod and a wink in the middle section to 'You Never Give Me Your Money', in the lines 'I never give you my pillow / I only send you my invitations'.

That whole period weighed on me to such an extent that I even began to think it was all tied in with the idea of original sin. Even though my mum had christened me as a Catholic, we weren't brought up Catholic, so I didn't buy into the concept of original sin on a day-to-day basis. It's really very depressing to think that you were born a loser.

The idea of carrying a weight may have been influenced by The Band's song 'The Weight', which had appeared on *Music From Big Pink* in July 1968. It so happens I'd already quoted that song during the fade-out section of a promotional film for 'Hey Jude'.

We'd got to know The Band mostly through Bob Dylan, whom we liked a lot. We liked the fact that he was a poet. He definitely has a way with words. We liked his vocal style too. So much so that John started singing like him; just listen to 'You've Got to Hide Your Love Away'. And, of course, it was Mr Dylan who had long since introduced us to the mysteries of pot, back in the summer of 1964 in New York City.

Above: Bob Dylan photographed by Linda. New York, 1970

Boy, you're going to carry that weight
carry that weight a long time
Boy you're gonna carry that weight
carry that weight a long time.

I never give you my pillow
I only send you my invitations
And in the middle of the celebrations
I break down,

Boy you're gonna carry that weight
carry that weight a long time.

Repeat.....

Check My Machine

WRITER	Paul McCartney
ARTIST	Paul McCartney
RECORDED	Lower Gate Farm, Sussex
RELEASED	B-side of 'Waterfalls' single, 1980

Hi George
Morning Terry
Sticks and stones may break my bones
But names will never hurt me

Check
My machine
Check
My machine
Check
My machine
Check
My machine

I want you to check
My machine

Check
My machine

THERE WAS A PERIOD WHEN I WAS WORKING IN THE STUDIO BY myself – my 'mad professor' period – around the late seventies. I would make a record, and when the time came to release it, someone at my office would realise that they needed the lyrics, so they'd just try to figure out what I'd said. I probably didn't check what they came up with. I think it's more likely that we all listened to the recording and thought, 'I'm bound to say something sensible by the end of the line.'

There's a great old tradition of scatting, and I always liked hearing it on Fats Waller or Louis Armstrong records. The greatest scatter of all was Ella Fitzgerald. The way scatters were able to find rhythms in nonsense words was so inspiring; you could tell they were having fun.

In this song I knew I'd got a lot of echo on my voice, and I knew, too, it wasn't going to matter much to anyone what the words were. I just made it up. The one idea that comes across loud and clear is 'check my machine', and that's all I want to get across.

There were a couple of kinds of machines I was thinking of. The computer was one. They said recording would be sped up massively with computers, but The Beatles would have done two songs by the time you got the computer up and running.

The promise of being much more efficient and much faster was not true. To rely on a pencil and a piece of paper and a guitar is a lot faster and a lot more efficient. Some of the best ideas have been written down on a piece of paper, or a napkin, or whatever you have to hand. But obviously, computers and technology have come a long way since then. The answering machine was also very big at this time. I can barely believe that the answering machine and the fax are now artefacts of the past.

At home. Sussex, 1980

To rely on a pencil and a piece of paper and a guitar is a lot faster and a lot more efficient. Some of the best ideas have been written down on a piece of paper, or a napkin, or whatever you have to hand.

Paul's handwritten chords for 'Check My Machine'

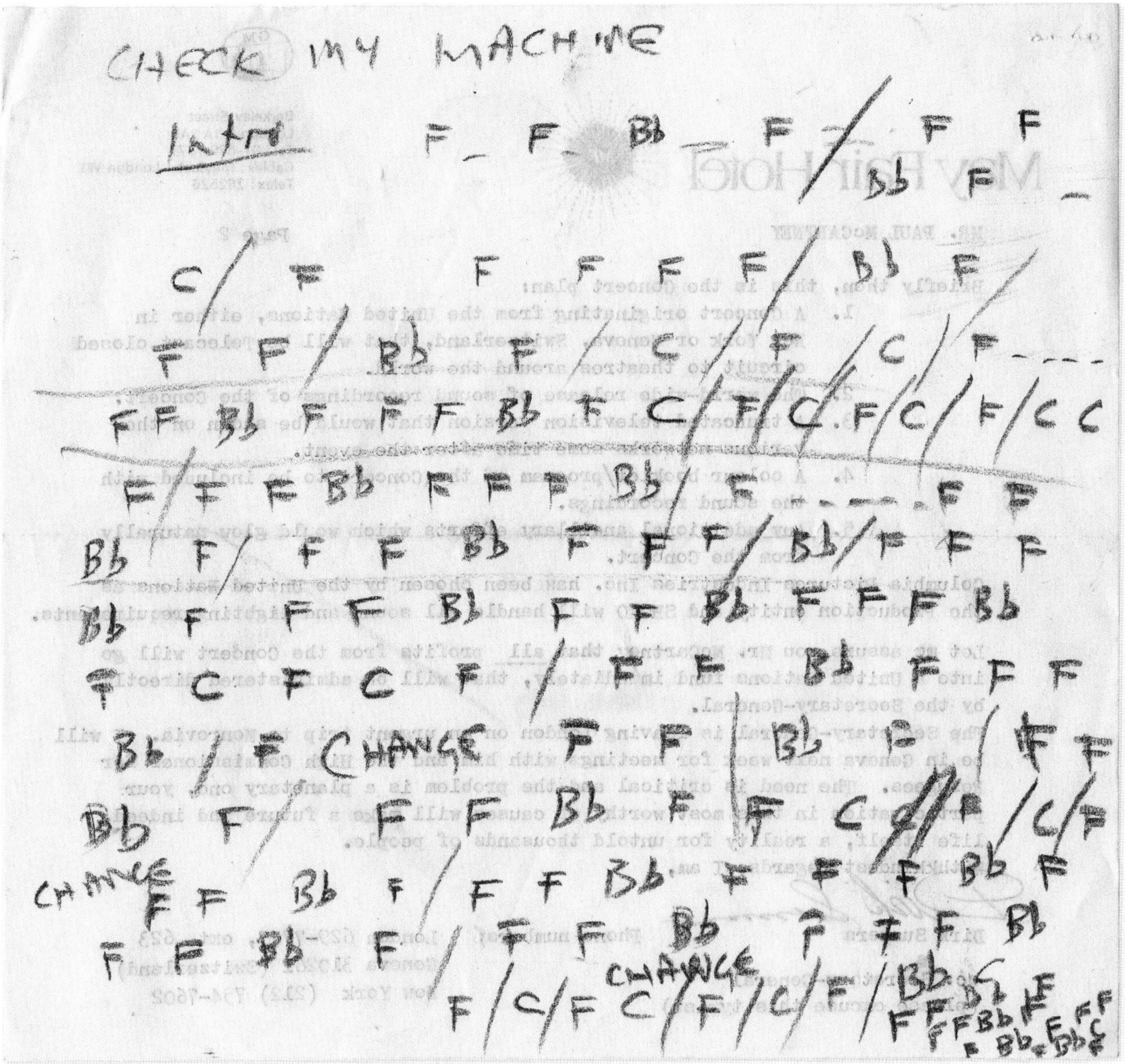

Come and Get It

WRITER	Paul McCartney
ARTIST	Badfinger
RECORDED	Abbey Road Studios, London
RELEASED	Single, 1969
	Magic Christian Music, 1970

If you want it, here it is, come and get it
Make your mind up fast
If you want it, anytime, I can give it
But you'd better hurry 'cause it may not last

Did I hear you say that there must be a catch?
Will you walk away from a fool and his money?

If you want it, here it is, come and get it
But you'd better hurry 'cause it's goin' fast

If you want it, here it is, come and get it
Make your mind up fast
If you want it, anytime, I can give it
But you'd better hurry 'cause it may not last

Did I hear you say that there must be a catch?
Will you walk away from a fool and his money,
    sonny?

If you want it, here it is, come and get it
But you'd better hurry 'cause it's goin' fast
You'd better hurry 'cause it's goin' fast
Fool and his money, sonny

If you want it, here it is, come and get it
But you'd better hurry 'cause it's goin' fast
You'd better hurry 'cause it's goin' fast
You'd better hurry 'cause it's goin' fast

TOWARDS THE END OF THE 1960S I WAS LIVING IN LONDON AND, between Beatles projects, had time to produce other artists. When we started our label, Apple Records, we took on Mary Hopkin, for example, who was already famous for winning a talent show on telly called *Opportunity Knocks*. We also signed a band called Badfinger, some English and Welsh guys whom our road manager Mal Evans had seen and suggested to us. I think, at this time, they might still have been called The Iveys, but there was confusion with another band of the same name, so they changed it to Badfinger, after 'Bad Finger Boogie', which had been the working title for 'With a Little Help From My Friends'.

I was thinking I could offer to produce them, but I wanted something to launch them with that would be a big success. I was lying in bed one night, and instead of trying to sleep I was trying to think of an idea for a song. This song started going around in my head, and then I thought, 'Oh, this is okay; this is pretty good.' So I got up quietly - Linda and I had just recently got married, and I didn't want to wake her or daughter Heather - and went downstairs where I had a little reel-to-reel tape recorder. I closed all the doors so I wouldn't make too much noise, and I wrote this. It was basically a song for Badfinger. Fairly straight-up rock and roll, very straightforward.

It's a bit like 'Love Me Do' - very similar thoughts. But again, I was trying to write a hit, so I didn't want anything too complicated. When you're writing for an audience - as Shakespeare did, or Dickens, whose serialised chapters were read to the public - there's that need to pull people in. But the interesting thing is that I knew exactly how I wanted this song to sound.

So I wrote it in the night, and then the very next day we had a session for the *Abbey Road* album, and I made a point of getting there a half hour before the session was going to start, because I knew the guys would be in on time. I said to the engineer, Phil McDonald, 'Look, I've got this thing. I'm just going to go to the drums, I'm going to go to the piano, I'm going to put a bit of bass on it and I'm going to sing it, and we can do this in a quarter of an hour.' And he was game, so that's exactly what I did. I just played the piano thing and put the drums on that, and it was all one take. And then the guys arrived and we started the Beatles session. But by then I had this demo. I think I might've said, 'D'you mind if I just quickly mix this?' But it sort of mixed itself, you know. That was a nice thing about it - that it was so complete I could just run in and, in fifteen or twenty minutes, make a record just like that.

Afterwards, I said to Badfinger, 'This is how you must do it.' And they said, 'Well, we'll put our spin on it.' I said, 'No, I don't want you to. I want you to do it faithfully, because this is the hit formula. You've got to do it this way.' So they balked a little bit at that, but when you listen to their recording and my demo, they're very similar. You can hear my version on the *Anthology 3* Beatles album and on the fiftieth-anniversary reissue of *Abbey Road*.

I understood that they wouldn't want to slavishly copy something I'd done, and I understood that they'd want to bring their own thing to it, but I was afraid that giving them that freedom could cock it up. Basically, I was

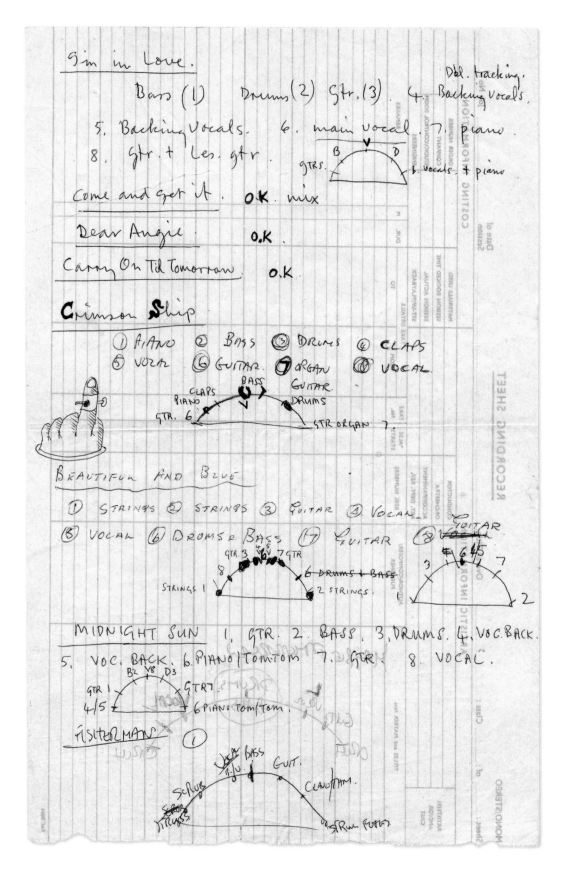

I'm in Love.

Bass (1)   Drums (2) Gtr. (3).   4. Backing Vocals.

5. Backing Vocals.   6. main vocal.   7. piano

8. Gtr. + Les. gtr.

Dbl. tracking.

GTRS.   B   D   8. vocals. + piano

Come and get it.   O.K. mix

Dear Angie.   O.K.

Carry On Til Tomorrow.   O.K.

Crimson Ship

① PIANO   ② BASS   ③ DRUMS   ④ CLAPS
⑤ VOCAL   ⑥ GUITAR.   ⑦ ORGAN   ⑧ VOCAL.

CLAPS   BASS   GUITAR.
PIANO   DRUMS
GTR. 6   STR ORGAN 7.

BEAUTIFUL AND BLUE

① STRINGS   ② STRINGS   ③ GUITAR   ④ VOCAL
⑤ VOCAL   ⑥ DRUMS & BASS   ⑦ GUITAR   ⑧ VOCAL GUITAR

GTR. 3   4 5 6   7 GTR
8   6 DRUMS + BASS
STRINGS 1   2 STRINGS.

3   4 5 6 4   7
2

MIDNIGHT SUN   1, GTR. 2. BASS. 3, DRUMS. 4. VOC. BACK.

5. VOC. BACK. 6. PIANO/TOMTOM 7. GTR. 8. VOCAL.

B2 V8 D3
GTR 1   GTR 7
4/5   6 PIANO TOM/TOM.

FISHERMAN   ①

VOCA BASS   GUIT.
SCRUB   CLAV/TOM.
STR   STRUM FUZZ
STRINGS

31 days   1969   AUGUST

2 SATURDAY (214–151 Week No. 31) s.r 5.24, s.s 8.47

2 gardeners

Emi - Come + get it
Iveys

saying, "This is a finished painting, and if you just do a reproduction, it'll be yours, and I won't bring mine out. You will have painted it."

The song was huge – I think a number one hit for Badfinger in some countries – and the album it was on was also a hit. I also remember they did one or two other things with Apple. Their lead singer was a guy called Pete Ham, who was a terrific guy and a very good writer. With his Badfinger partner, Tom Evans, he co-wrote 'Without You', which was a big hit for Harry Nilsson. God, it's such an emotional song. And I was just thinking, 'Incredible, Pete; that's fantastic. My God, how d'you do that?' Then, sadly, soon after, he committed suicide.

It was such a sad end. He'd written this massive hit, and he gave it to Nilsson. Or maybe it was an album track for Badfinger and Nilsson spotted it and said, 'This would be a great single'; I don't quite know the story. It's a sad irony, though, that I wrote this song for Pete Ham and he said, 'Well . . .' And then he wrote this other song and gave it to someone else, who had the hit. But that's the way the cookie crumbles.

Coming Up

WRITER   Paul McCartney
ARTIST   Paul McCartney
RECORDED   Spirit of Ranachan Studio, Scotland
RELEASED   Single, 1980
     McCartney II, 1980

You want a love to last forever
One that will never fade away
I want to help you with your problem
Stick around, I say

Coming up
Coming up, yeah
Coming up like a flower
Coming up, I say

You want a friend you can rely on
One who will never fade away
And if you're searching for an answer
Stick around, I say

It's coming up
It's coming up
It's coming up like a flower
It's coming up, yeah

You want some peace and understanding
So everybody can be free
I know that we can get together
We can make it, stick with me

It's coming up
It's coming up
It's coming up like a flower
It's coming up for you and me

Coming up
Coming up

It's coming up
It's coming up, I say
It's coming up like a flower
It's coming up, I feel it in my bones

You want a better kind of future
One that everyone can share
You're not alone, we all could use it
Stick around we're nearly there

It's coming up
It's coming up everywhere
It's coming up like a flower
It's coming up for all to share
It's coming up, yeah
It's coming up, anyway
It's coming up like a flower
Coming up

IT'S A VERY POSITIVE SONG. THINGS ARE GOING TO BE GOOD. AND that reflects my very positive attitude. This one started with an urge to just record, to have some fun in the studio. I always kind of likened working solo in the studio to a chemistry professor's laboratory. You can sort of tinker around.

So, I got into my studio in Scotland and started working, doing the drum track. I normally start with the drums. I sometimes use drum machines, but I like to redo it with real drums. I enjoy drumming. Then I put some bass on it. I was just doing an experimental thing. I was messing around and experimenting. Slowing down tapes, or speeding them up.

The song was originally played live by Wings in Glasgow around the time the band was coming to an end. But it was my more experimental studio recording that got released at what turned out to be the start of my solo career. We did a rather nice video for it, directed by Keith McMillan, in which I pretended to be all the people who had played the instruments. Which, as it turns out, I had been.

The phrase 'coming up' works mostly in the sense of a film trailer. 'Coming soon' to a theatre near you. Of course, when you use a word like 'coming', at the back of your mind there's a sexual connotation. Certain words like that are nice to play with for that reason. It doesn't make me go, 'Whoa, I'm being risqué.' But I do like the fact that it can be read in all sorts of ways.

It was nice that 'Coming Up' went to number one in America. A number one is always nice because you can't get much higher. I don't fret if a song doesn't make number one, but that status is an indicator that people like it.

John described 'Coming Up' somewhere as 'a good piece of work'. He'd been lying around not doing much, and it sort of shocked him out of inertia. So it was nice to hear that it had struck a chord with him. At first, after the breakup of The Beatles, we had no contact, but there were various things we needed to talk about. Our relationship was a bit fraught sometimes because we were discussing business, and we would sometimes insult each other on the phone. But gradually we got past that, and if I was in New York I would ring up and say, 'Do you fancy a cup of tea?'

This one started with an urge to just record, to have some fun in the studio. I always kind of likened the studio to a chemistry professor's laboratory. You can sort of tinker around.

COMING UP

i 2 3 4 SAX RIFF

i 2 3 4 RIFF

(1) You want a love   to last forever
One that will never   fade away
I wanna help you with your problems
Stick around I say

CHORUS   Coming up.

i 2

(2)   You want a friend you can rely on
One who will never fade away
+ if your searching for an answer
stick around I say

CHORUS Coming up.   like a flower Hey!!
HARMONY

i 2 3 4   (SOLO) Long (1 2 3 4)

(3) You want some peace + understanding
So everybody   can be free
I know that we can get together
We can make it stick with me

CHORUS   Coming up (like a flower
for you + me
i 2 3 4   i 2 (SOLO)   short (1 2 3 4)

(4) You want a better... kind of future
One that everyone can share
I know if we can get together
Well hear — music everywhere
CHORUS Coming up   BREAK B/D.
i 2 3 4   Hand Claps Coming up ANYWAY.
i 2 3 4
CHORUS Coming up — I say —
like a flower
Feel it in my bones   yea yea yea yea
yea

Satex Danford Limited.

Confidante

WRITER   Paul McCartney

ARTIST   Paul McCartney

RECORDED   Hog Hill Mill, Sussex

RELEASED   *Egypt Station*, 2018

You used to be my confidante
My underneath the staircase friend
But I fell out of love with you
And brought our romance to an end

I played with you throughout the day
And told you every secret thought
Unlike my other so-called friends
You stood beside me as I fought

In your reflected glory I
Could dream of shining far-off lands
Where serpents turn to bits of string
And played like kittens in my hand

In our imaginary world
Where butterflies wear army boots
And stomp around the forest chanting
Long lost anthems
Long lost anthems

You used to be my confidante
My underneath the staircase friend
But I fell out of love with you
And brought our romance to an end

I played with you throughout the day
And told you every secret thought
Unlike my other so-called friends
You stood beside me as I fought
You stood beside me as I fought

You used to be my confidante

T HE GUITAR WAS PROPPED UP ON A WINDOW SEAT IN THE COR-
ner of my living room in the country, in Sussex. It struck me I hadn't
played it for a while, and I looked over and sort of thought, 'Oh my
gosh, there's something wrong with this, I should be playing you, and you
must be lonely.'

I felt quite guilty in a minor way, so I went over and started playing, and
then the song that came out was me talking directly to the guitar and talking
about all the times it had helped me. We always used to say that when you sit
down with your guitar to write a song, you're telling it your secrets, which
then become a song for the world. But at that moment, when you're alone,
the guitar is your confidante. You cradle it. It also looks like a woman. There's
lots of stuff going on there. When you go up to a piano, though, it's almost as
if you're pushing the piano away; they're different actions completely.

'My underneath the staircase friend'. This is a reference to one of the
council houses that we moved to in Liverpool - I think the one in Forthlin
Road that is now a National Trust site, but it may easily be the house before
that, which was in Speke. There was a cupboard underneath the staircase, a
little triangular thing like where Harry Potter grew up. It was normally
where you put your house phone, but it was also a good place if you were
looking for a hideaway cupboard, which I was. I still am; I'm always looking
for my hideaway cupboard. So, I was thinking back and wondering, 'When
did this whole confidante thing start?' There I was underneath the staircase, starting this whole tradition in my life of cradling an instrument and
telling it my troubles. I just liked the idea that with this guitar I could tell
them how grateful I was for having a confidante who could come with me
on far-off journeys. That's how I feel about a guitar.

The song begins with 'You used to be my confidante', but by the time you
get to the end, it's 'But I fell out of love with you / And brought our romance
to an end'. What I like is that you write a lyric, and it suggests different
things to different people. I don't think I was thinking about ending my
relationship with the object of the song - the guitar - but I like using language that can be interpreted in different ways and allows people to attach
their own meaning to a lyric. So, to many listeners this line in the song
could naturally echo the end of a relationship.

At the time I thought, 'Oh, people are going to think this is about the
breakup of The Beatles. About my guitar standing beside me when my band-
mates didn't.' And I suppose at the back of my mind that was true, and sort
of what I was thinking.

'Serpents turn to bits of string'. This is a reference to something that
happened when we were meditating with the Maharishi in Rishikesh back
in 1968. Every evening, people would meet and talk, and the Maharishi
would field questions, and one thing in particular stuck in my mind. People
always used to say, 'Just meditate. Don't worry; it's all cool.' And there was
this guy who said, 'Maharishi, I'm from New York and I have to tell you, I'm
scared of snakes.' The poor guy had a phobia about them. He said, 'I was
meditating, and I saw this snake come towards me in the meditation. I was

CONFIDANTE

Intro.

1. You used to be my confidante
My underneath the staircase friend
But I fell out of love with you
And brought our romance to an end

(CH.) I played with you throughout the day
And told you every secret thoughts
Unlike my other so called friends.
You stood beside me as I fought

2. In your reflected glory I
Could dream of shining far off lands
Where serpents turn to bits of string
And play like kittens in my hand

(CH.) In our imaginary world
The butterflies wear (Army) boots,
And stomp around the forest chanting
long lost Anthems ...

[Instrumental]

Repeat 1. You used to be my confidante
My underneath the staircase friend
But I fell out of love with you
And brought our romance to an end

Repeat
(CH) I played with you throughout the day
I told you every secret thought
Unlike my other so called friends.
You stood beside me as I fought

90

really scared, but I remembered what you said: just look at it and meditate. And it turned into a little piece of string.' I always thought that was a great image, and I remembered it.

'These butterflies wearing army boots'. I now give myself free rein, I'm in an imaginary world, and there are butterflies, but I feel I can imagine anything with these butterflies, so I like the idea of them wearing great big clodhopping army boots. And then once they've got these boots on, they're going to stomp around the forest, chanting long lost anthems. I was imagining them like punks – like punk butterflies, marching around and singing punk songs. And it all started with a guitar.

I don't like to admit this, but I have far too many guitars today. Way too many. This is something I often think about: When you're a kid you have one, and it's your precious guitar, and inevitably that first one's an acoustic. And when you get a little bit of success, you might then go to an electric guitar. And then as you get more success, another electric guitar that does something slightly different might catch your interest. From then on, what happens is you either buy another one because it's lovely and you fancy it, or once you get real acclaim, people start sending them to you. And it's lovely and you can't say no. Someone will send you a guitar which will do this or that – it's an Alvarez and it's very nice, or it's a Taylor – and over the years, companies and individuals have sent me guitars. Recently, I was given the guitar that Scotty Moore, Elvis's great guitarist, played. That one has particular significance.

Of all of them, though, my favourite electric guitar is my Epiphone Casino. I went into the guitar shop in Charing Cross Road in London and said to the guy, 'Have you got a guitar that will feedback, because I'm loving what Jimi Hendrix is doing.' I'm a big admirer of Jimi. I was so lucky to see him at one of his early gigs in London and it was just like the sky had burst. He was a very nice guy, really sweet. We often pay tribute to Jimi in our live show nowadays, jamming on 'Foxy Lady'. Anyway, the guitar shop staff said, 'This is probably the one that will feedback best, because it has a hollow body and they produce more volume than a solid body guitar.' So I took it to the studio, and it had a Bigsby vibrato arm on it, so you could play with the feedback and control it, and it was perfect for that. It was a really good little guitar, a hot little guitar. So that became my favourite electric guitar, and I used it on the intro riff to 'Paperback Writer' and the solo in George's song 'Taxman', as well as quite a number of other pieces through the years. I still play it today. That Epiphone Casino has been a constant companion throughout my life.

I don't like to admit this, but I have far too many guitars today. Way too many. When you're a kid you have one, and it's your precious guitar.

Of all of them, though, my favourite electric guitar is my Epiphone Casino. I went into the guitar shop in Charing Cross Road in London and said to the guy, 'Have you got a guitar that will feed back, because I'm loving what Jimi Hendrix is doing.' I'm a big admirer of Jimi. I was so lucky to see him at one of his early gigs in London and it was just like the sky had burst.

Cook of the House

WRITERS	Linda McCartney and Paul McCartney
ARTIST	Wings
RECORDED	Abbey Road Studios, London
RELEASED	*At the Speed of Sound*, 1976
	B-side of 'Silly Love Songs' single, 1976

Ground rice, sugar, vinegar, Seco salt
Macaroni too
Cook of the house
I'm the cook of the house

No matter where I serve my guests
They seem to like the kitchen best
'Cause I'm the cook of the house
Cook of the house

The salad's in the bowl
The rice is on the stove
Green beans in the colander
And where the rest is heaven only knows

Cinnamon, garlic, salt, pepper
Cornbread, curry powder, coffee too
Cook of the house
I'm the cook of the house

No matter where I serve my guests
They seem to like the kitchen best
'Cause I'm the cook of the house
Cook of the house

And the rest is heaven only knows

Cinnamon, garlic, salt, pepper
Cornbread, curry powder, coffee too
Cook of the house (that's the cook of the house)
I'm the cook of the house (she's the cook
    of the house)

No matter where I serve my guests
They seem to like the kitchen best
'Cause I'm the cook of the house (that's
    cook of the house)

Cook of the house (she's the cook of the house)
Cook of the house (that's the cook of the house)
I'm the cook of the house
Take it, fellow

'NO MATTER WHERE I SERVE MY GUESTS, THEY SEEM TO LIKE THE kitchen best'. That was a sign in the kitchen of a house we were renting somewhere; I seem to remember it was Australia, probably during the *Wings Over the World* tour before our son James was born. So it would have been Linda, Heather, Mary, Stella and me all staying together.

That was a fun thing Linda remembered – and this is basically Linda's song with a bit of help from me. At this time, in Wings, everyone in the band had a song on the album, so this was hers from *At the Speed of Sound*. Sometimes with a song you just look around and you name all the stuff you can see, and in this case she went round all the spices - cinnamon, garlic, curry powder - because, as a family, we spent a lot of time in the kitchen getting our hands dirty. Linda was a very good cook and loved feeding our family and friends, so it was fitting that her song would be 'Cook of the House'.

One of the games we used to play with the kids when they were little was blindfolding them and giving them something to smell, and they'd have to smell it and guess what it was. Coffee and tea were easy, cinnamon was easy, then you'd gradually try and get harder: flour was kind of difficult; salt wasn't easy. That's the kind of thing we would do to amuse ourselves. This was pre-video games. It was pre-pretty much everything.

In any case, this song has a simple, classic rock and roll sound, basically three chords with a fourth thrown in at the turnaround between the chorus and verse. It could have been recorded anytime between 1950 and now. Not everyone would have been inclined to kick off the song with the sound of bacon frying in the key of E-flat. That's what makes it special. Also, the bass I'm playing here used to belong to Bill Black, Elvis Presley's bass player, so that legacy contributes to the vintage feel. I now have two instruments that once belonged to members of Elvis's band!

Above: With family.
Brisbane Zoo, 1975

Left: Linda cooking.
London, 1977

Right: Linda, Heather,
Stella and Lucky in the
kitchen. Scotland,
mid-1970s

2 weeks or days

Goldlocks Xray Lungs
+ Suzie Home tomorrow
x humps 12:30

Dog Next .week

Monkey - Heart
100/-

Mouse .200
Teddy - 300
Badger 4.00 = nose Back
leg

COOK of The House

E
ground rice, Sugar, Vinegar, Sage (saco)
Salt macoroni too
A
The Cook of The House
" ,,

E
no mater were I serve my guests
They seem to like my Kitchen Best
A
The Cook of the House
"   "

D   A
The Salads in the Bowl, The rice is on The
stove, green Beans in the Calender
E
and where the rest is Heaven only Knows
B   E

Cinnamon, garlic, Salt, pepper, corn bread
curry powder coffee too
Cook of The house
I'm the Cook of The house

no matter where I serve my guests
They seem to like my Kitchen Best
oh - macoroni too
COOK of The house
no mater where I serve my guests - Cook of the
house

Country Dreamer

WRITERS   Paul McCartney and Linda McCartney
ARTIST   Paul McCartney and Wings
RECORDED   Abbey Road Studios, London
RELEASED   B-side of 'Helen Wheels' single, 1973

I'd like to walk in a field with you
Take my hat and my boots off too
I'd like to lie in a field with you
Would you like to do it too, May?
Would you like to do it too?

I'd like to stand in a stream with you
Roll my trousers up and not feel blue
I'd like to wash in a stream with you
Would you like to do it too?

You and I, country dreamer
When there's nothing else to do
Me oh my, country dreamer
Make a country dream come true

I'd like to climb up a hill with you
Stand on top and admire the view
I'd like to roll down a hill with you
Would you like to do it too, May?
Would you like to do it too?

You and I, country dreamer
When there's nothing else to do
Me oh my, country dreamer
Make a country dream come true

I'd like to climb up a hill with you
Take my hat and my boots off too
I'd like to lie in a field with you
Would you like to do it too, May?
Would you like to do it too?

Would you like to do it too?

S IMPLICITY. THAT'S THE ONE-WORD DESCRIPTION OF MY philosophy. That was Linda's too. We loved freedom, nature – all the good things in life. To this day I have a really deep feeling for nature. I feel like I'm part of it. Here we all are on this planet – humans, animals, creatures – and the reason I don't eat animals is that I want them to have their shot, like I got my shot. I'm able to bring up kids. I'm able to make love. Why shouldn't they? Mainly because we kill them. I've been vegetarian longer than I was a traditional carnivore.

I think the first line of 'Country Dreamer' is a nod to Ivor Cutler, a brilliant Scottish poet and songwriter who once described himself as an 'oblique musical philosopher'. Like me, he was a sucker for the surreal. I heard him on the radio once, possibly on John Peel's famous programme (although there's also a chance Peel came across him through The Beatles). But anyway, I rang up Ivor and said, 'Do you want to go to dinner?' That's how our friendship started. Ivor was in our film *Magical Mystery Tour* as Buster Bloodvessel, and he wrote a lovely little song called 'I'm Going in a Field'. I love it to this day:

> *I'm going in a field*
> *I'm going in a field*
> *I'm going in a field to lie down*
> *I'll lie beside the grass*
> *I'll lie beside the grass*
> *I'll lie beside the green grass*

So my song starts 'I'd like to walk in a field with you / Take my hat and my boots off too'. It was very much what we were doing in Scotland in the summer, and I like the idea that he's got a hat and boots. In Scotland, it would be raining and muddy a lot, or we'd be on the farm, so you would often have wellies on. They wouldn't be very glamorous boots. But you'd come to a stream, and you'd take them off and get in.

'Would you like to do it too, May?' I'm calling her 'May', and I'm aware that it can be taken as 'would you like to do it to me', so there's an erotic aspect to it. But I'm always doing that – putting in something sort of mildly cheeky. It's allowed, as Linda would've said. That was one of her sayings: 'It's allowed.'

May becomes a country dreamer: 'You and I, country dreamer / When there's nothing else to do'. It's just the very simple things in nature that I actually do like to do. 'I'd like to climb up a hill with you / Stand on top and admire the view / I'd like to roll down a hill with you.' Like Jack and Jill. It's what all kids like to do. It's what you should do on a hill. As we get older we don't do it quite so often. It starts to hurt after a bit.

Here we all are on this planet – humans, animals, creatures – and the reason I don't eat animals is that I want them to have their shot, like I got my shot.

COUNTRY DREAMER

① I'd like to walk through a field with you
Take my hat & my boots off too
I'd like to lie in a field with you
Would you like to do it to ──,
would you like to do it too.

② I'd like to stand in a stream with you
Roll my trousers up & not feel blue
I'd like to wash in a stream with you
Would you like to do it to me,
.. .. TOO.

CHORUS
me oh my COUNTRY DREAMER
When there's nothing else to do
You + I COUNTRY DREAMER
Make a country dream come true.

3.) I'd like to climb up a hill with you
Stand on top + admire the view
I'd like to roll down a hill with you

On the farm. Scotland, 1970

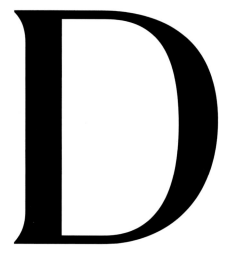

D

A Day in the Life

WRITERS — John Lennon and Paul McCartney
ARTIST — The Beatles
RECORDED — Abbey Road Studios, London
RELEASED — *Sgt. Pepper's Lonely Hearts Club Band*, 1967

I read the news today, oh boy
About a lucky man who made the grade
And though the news was rather sad
Well I just had to laugh
I saw the photograph

He blew his mind out in a car
He didn't notice that the lights had changed
A crowd of people stood and stared
They'd seen his face before
Nobody was really sure if he was from
the House of Lords

I saw a film today, oh boy
The English army had just won the war
A crowd of people turned away
But I just had to look
Having read the book

I'd love to turn you on

Woke up, fell out of bed
Dragged a comb across my head
Found my way downstairs and drank a cup
And looking up, I noticed I was late

Found my coat and grabbed my hat
Made the bus in seconds flat
Found my way upstairs and had a smoke
And somebody spoke and I went into a dream

I read the news today, oh boy
Four thousand holes in Blackburn, Lancashire
And though the holes were rather small
They had to count them all
Now they know how many holes it takes to fill
the Albert Hall

I'd love to turn you on

THE INFLUENCE OF RADIO ON THE BEATLES SIMPLY CAN'T be overstated. You might, indeed, think of *Sgt. Pepper* as a big radio programme. Take something like our use of sound effects as a way of extending our repertoire and range. EMI was such an all-encompassing record company of the old variety that they had a sound library in the same building as the studio. If I wanted to include the sound of blackbirds singing on the song 'Blackbird', I could just find it in the catalogue and order it, and someone would go up and get it from the library and bring it down to the studio. So we started messing around with this library, and it was very liberating.

One of the things that always intrigued me as a kid was how a presenter could be introduced on the radio. Let's say it was Ken Dodd, the great Liverpudlian comedian. He'd come on and go, 'Well,' and then the studio audience would go 'Ooooh' and laugh. My mind would be on fire. What did he do? Did he drop his trousers? Did he make a funny face? Did he produce his trademark tickling stick? What did he do? I really liked that mystery. So I'd say to the other guys, 'Let's use a library sound of an audience laughing when "the one and only Billy Shears" is introduced to sing "With a Little Help from My Friends".' We'd use that effect like Ken Dodd. We really enjoyed titillating the imagination.

And it's your imagination that's the powerful force. With television and the movies it's laid out for you; you can see how a character named Henrietta Gibbs looks. In radio, you make your own Henrietta Gibbs. That was the great thing about *Sgt. Pepper*. They tried to make a movie of it, but it didn't work, because everyone's already got their own picture.

The other big influence on *Sgt. Pepper*, which is certainly very much to the fore in 'A Day in the Life', is that at that time I'd been listening to a lot of avant-garde stuff. Stockhausen. Luciano Berio. John Cage – you know, Cage's silent piece *4'33"*. Being intrigued by all that, I wanted to have an extraordinary instrumental moment in the middle of 'A Day in the Life'. So I talked to George Martin, who was arranging the orchestra. In the same way that choreographer Merce Cunningham would say, 'Pull them across the stage on a rope,' my instruction here was for everybody in the orchestra to start on the lowest note on their instrument and go to the highest note on their instrument over the course of a certain number of bars.

When we got to the session, George Martin had to plan it out for them. Classically trained musicians are thought not to like the idea of improvisation, but I found it interesting that the orchestra split itself into groups. The strings were like sheep: 'If you're going up, I'm going up. I'm not going to be left behind.' But the trumpets and the wind instruments were very receptive to the idea of letting it all hang out, perhaps because they're somewhat overlooked in the orchestra. They were game for anything.

We ourselves were determined to really go for it and find ways of bringing all these other components into what was known as 'popular' music. We liked the idea that what we were attempting was an extension, rather than just a continuation, of the tradition.

So I talked to George Martin, who was arranging the orchestra. In the same way that choreographer Merce Cunningham would say, 'Pull them across the stage on a rope,' my instruction here was for everybody in the orchestra to start on the lowest note on their instrument and go to the highest note on their instrument over the course of a certain number of bars.

Above: Conducting the orchestra. Studio One, Abbey Road Studios, London, February 1967

Right: *Sgt. Pepper's Lonely Hearts Club Band* album cover featuring Karlheinz Stockhausen (back row, fifth from left), 1967

Dear Friend

WRITERS	Paul McCartney and Linda McCartney
ARTIST	Paul McCartney and Wings
RECORDED	Abbey Road Studios, London
RELEASED	*Wild Life*, 1971

Dear friend, what's the time?
Is this really the borderline?
Does it really mean so much to you?
Are you afraid, or is it true?

Dear friend, throw the wine
I'm in love with a friend of mine
Really truly, young and newly wed
Are you a fool, or is it true?

Are you afraid, or is it true?

OFTEN I WOULD THINK OF JOHN, AND WHAT A PITY IT WAS that we'd argued so publicly and so viciously at times. At the time of writing this song, in early 1971, he'd called the *McCartney* album 'rubbish' in *Rolling Stone* magazine. It was a really difficult time. I just felt sad about the breakdown in our friendship, and this song kind of came flowing out. 'Dear friend, what's the time? / Is this really the borderline?' Are we splitting up? Is this 'you go your way; I'll go mine'?

Towards the end of 1969, John had quite gleefully told us it was over. There were a few of us in the Apple boardroom at the time. I think George was away visiting family, but Ringo and I were at the meeting, and John was saying no to every suggestion. I thought we should go back to playing smaller gigs again, but the answer came back: 'No'. Eventually John said, 'Oh, I've been wanting to tell you this, but I'm leaving The Beatles.' We were all shocked. Relations had been strained, but we sat there saying, 'What? Why? Why? Why?' It was like a divorce, and he had just had a divorce from Cynthia the year before. I can remember him saying, 'Oh, this is quite exciting.' That was very John, and I had admired this kind of contrarian behaviour about him since we were kids, when I first met him. He really was a bit loony, in the nicest possible way. But whilst all of us could see what he meant, it was not quite so exciting for those left on the other side.

I'd been keeping largely quiet about John and The Beatles split-up in the press. I didn't really have many accusations to fling, but being John, he was flinging quite a few in interviews. He had accused me of announcing the Beatles breakup to promote the *McCartney* album, but I was just answering Apple's press questions honestly. I didn't want to do interviews to promote it, and Peter Brown at Apple had asked questions like, 'Are you planning a new album or single with The Beatles?' My answer was 'No.' I saw no point in lying.

John would say things like, 'It was rubbish. The Beatles were crap.' Also, 'I don't believe in The Beatles, I don't believe in Jesus, I don't believe in God.' Those were quite hurtful barbs to be flinging around, and I was the person they were being flung at, and it hurt. So, I'm having to read all this stuff, and on the one hand I'm thinking, 'Oh fuck off, you fucking idiot,' but on the other hand I'm thinking, 'Why would you say that? Are you annoyed at me or are you jealous or what?' And thinking back fifty years later, I still wonder how he must have felt. He'd gone through a lot. His dad disappeared, and then he lost his Uncle George, who was a father figure; his mother; Stuart Sutcliffe; Brian Epstein, another father figure; and now his band. But John had all of those emotions wrapped up in a ball of Lennon. That's who he was. That was the fascination.

I tried. I was sort of answering him here, asking, 'Does it need to be this hurtful?' I think this is a good line: 'Are you afraid, or is it true?' - meaning, 'Why is this argument going on? Is it because you're afraid of something? Are you afraid of the split-up? Are you afraid of my doing something without you? Are you afraid of the consequences of your actions?' And the little rhyme, 'Or is it true?' Are all these hurtful allegations true? This song came out in that kind of mood. It could have been called 'What the Fuck, Man?' but I'm not sure we could have gotten away with that then.

Did the three of us – George, Ringo, and I – think of carrying on without John? No, I don't think so. No. We were such a unit, such a foursome. We joked about forming a group called 'The Threetles', but we didn't seriously consider it. It was never anything more than a joke.

We did do a few little bits and pieces together before we all went our separate ways. John and I and Yoko did 'The Ballad of John and Yoko'. He enlisted me for that because he knew it was a great way to make a record. 'We'll go round to Abbey Road Studios. Who lives near there? Paul. Who's going to drum on this record? Paul. Who can play bass? Paul. And who'll do it if I ask him nicely? Paul.' He wasn't at all sheepish about asking. He probably said something like, 'Oh, I've got this song I want to record. Would you come round?' And I probably said, 'Yeah, why not?'

There were still a lot of loose ends to tie up. We still had all the business things to surmount. You have to remember, I sued him in court. I sued my friends from Liverpool, my lifelong friends, in court. But in the end, I think playing on that session with him and Yoko contributed to our having quite a few friendly meetings and conversations later.

I think this song, 'Dear Friend', also helped. I would imagine he heard it. I think he listened to my records when they came out, but he never responded directly to me. That was not his way. We were guys; it wasn't like a boy and girl. In those days you didn't release much emotion with each other.

I was very glad of how we got along in those last few years, that I had some really good times with him before he was murdered. Without question, it would have been the worst thing in the world for me, had he been killed when we still had a bad relationship. I would've thought, 'Oh, I should've, I should've, I should've . . .' It would have been a big guilt trip for me. But luckily, our last meeting was very friendly. We talked about how to bake bread.

Below left: 'The Ballad of John and Yoko' single. Cover photograph by Linda, 30 April 1969

Below right: John Lennon photographed by Linda. Santa Monica, 1974

Opposite: With John Eastman, John Lennon, Yoko Ono, Allen Klein, Ringo Starr, Maureen Starkey and Peter Howard. Apple office, London, 1969

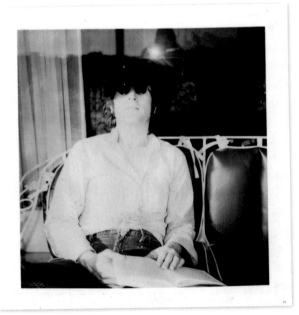

16 TUESDAY (259–106 Week No. 38)

Eg Davis   call agent
Call Davis
Mary's Rice cereal

12:00 Mrs. Meyer

THE · END

Justin + Twiggy's dinner

17 WEDNESDAY (260–105 Week No. 38) Ember Day

Alex   barbara
Print-   agents
              studio

1:00 Lew Grade
     lunch – a-la-deal deli
          by Kathy

3:00 Meeting – Capital EMI agreement

Left: John Lennon and Yoko
Ono in Paul's living room.
London, 1969

Right: London, 1969

Did the three of us - George, Ringo, and I - think
of carrying on without John? No, I don't think
so. No. We were such a unit, such a foursome. We
joked about forming a group called 'The Threetles',
but we didn't seriously consider it.

Despite Repeated Warnings

WRITER   Paul McCartney

ARTIST   Paul McCartney

RECORDED   Henson Studios, Los Angeles;

                  Hog Hill Mill, Sussex; and Abbey Road Studios, London

RELEASED   *Egypt Station*, 2018

Despite repeated warnings
Of dangers up ahead
The captain won't be listening
To what's been said

He feels that there's a good chance
That we have been misled
And so the captain's planning
To steam ahead

What can we do?
What can we do?
What can we do to stop this foolish plan going
    through?
What can we do?
What can we do?
This man is bound to lose his ship and his crew

Despite repeated warnings
From those who ought to know
Well he's got his own agenda
And so he'll go

Those who shout the loudest
May not always be the smartest
But they have their proudest moments
Right before they fall

Red sky in the morning
Doesn't ever seem to faze him
But a sailor's warning signal
Should concern us all

How can we stop him?
Grab the keys and lock him up
If we can do it
We can save the day

The engineer lives with
His wife and daughter Janet
But he misses them so

Although he's working with
The best crew on the planet
They never want him to go

He had a premonition
He senses something's wrong
And by his own admission
He knew it all along

The captain's crazy
But he doesn't let them know it
He'll take us with him
If we don't do something soon to slow it

How can we stop him?
Grab the keys and lock him up
If we can do it
We can save the day

Below decks the engineer cries
The captain's gonna leave us when
    the temperatures rise
The needle's going up
The engine's gonna blow
And we're gonna be left down below
Down below

Yes we can do it
Yeah we can do it now

If life would work out
The way you plan it
That'd be so fine
For the wife and Janet
Sometimes you might
Have to battle through it
But that's the way you learn
How you've got to do it

Yes we can do it, whoa whoa

Despite repeated warnings
Of dangers up ahead
Well the captain wasn't listening
To what was said

So we went to the captain
And we told him to turn around
But he laughs in our faces
Says that we are mistaken

So we gather around him
Now the ropes that have bound him
Prove that he should have listened
To the will of the people
It's the will of the people
It's the will of the people

THERE WAS A PRESIDENT NAMED TRUMP WHO THOUGHT THAT climate change was a hoax - one that the Chinese had created. Sadly, he was not the only one to ignore this existential threat. I recall reading a newspaper article in Japan that stated, 'Nobody's doing anything about it, despite repeated warnings.' I liked that phrase. That was enough to get me started.

The whole climate change issue is hardly new. In fact, when I was a kid back in Liverpool, I remember seeing a very early black-and-white television programme, a children's programme along the lines of *Blue Peter* - a magazine show that would sometimes get into current events. There were three scientists who seemed to me like very old men, and they were talking about the future of the world and what we had to do. They called it the 'Blueprint for the Future,' and I, in my early teens, was very impressed. I thought, 'Well that's a good idea, to start working on it now.'

I've always written songs about what interests me. The subject doesn't have to be important; it can just be a sentimental love song, or it can be a sad song. And then sometimes it can be a song in which I'm actually trying to say something to people, something that I think contains a message worth conveying. Paradoxically, those aren't the ones that people necessarily grab hold of, but I know a few people out there will get the message, and therefore it's worth doing.

As we began recording 'Despite Repeated Warnings', in Henson Studios in Los Angeles, the whole thing started to get a little bit operatic in my mind. I was imagining the words as if they were a scene on stage, like a Gilbert and Sullivan opera with the ship's crew dressed in striped shirts and the mad captain with some kind of gaudy, extravagant gold on his hat.

'Despite Repeated Warnings' is something of an epic, and it goes through a number of changes, both in tempo and in key. It's a form of medley similar

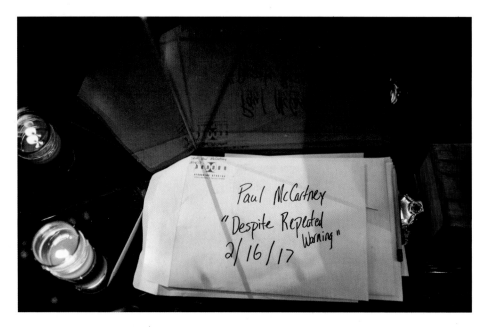

Henson Studios, 2017

116

to 'Band on the Run' and the B-side of *Abbey Road*. I really like the challenge of putting together these songs that go on a journey. And I've always quite fancied actually seeing this song staged. It was almost taking place in a church hall in my head, like a little school production singing in chorus, 'What can we do? / What can we do? / What can we do? / . . . this foolish plan'. This was really, 'What can we do with the drunken sailor?' The tune gets very similar to that.

'The best crew on the planet' is what I call my stage crew, so at a show I will say to the audience, 'And let's hear it for the best crew on the planet.' So that crept in too.

As for the larger picture, we're faced with the political situation, particularly in the US, where a braggart has been in charge and seems quite unstable, to say the least. He's shouting the loudest, but he's not necessarily the smartest. I think some people believe their own myths, which become, in their mind, facts. I often think, 'How can a person get away with some of the things he says?' But then, two days later, the news cycle will have brought us something else he's said, and then that thing we thought the person would never get away with has gone, and it's difficult to bring it back.

It's like when newspapers say something completely wrong about you and you ring them up and say, 'That is complete fabrication; I did not do that.' They'll say, 'Okay, we'll correct it.' The actual story was on the front page, but when you look for your correction, it's on page 29, of course at the bottom: 'Oh, it's been suggested to us that that wasn't true.' Unfortunately, people remember the first bit, and they never see the retraction.

But I am a hopeful person, and that's why we started Meat Free Monday, to remind people that it doesn't take a huge change in your lifestyle to make a positive impact on the environment. Of course, we'd like it if you did it more than just Mondays, but going meat-free one day a week really can make a difference. And if you look at the impact someone like Greta Thunberg has had, it's inspirational. In one year, she went from protesting the climate crisis outside her school by herself to attracting crowds in the tens of thousands listening to her speak. The climate crisis is rightly a huge concern amongst her generation. So, maybe those repeated warnings are starting to get through.

And if you look at the impact someone like Greta Thunberg has had, it's inspirational. In one year, she went from protesting the climate crisis outside her school by herself to attracting crowds in the tens of thousands listening to her speak. The climate crisis is rightly a huge concern amongst her generation. So, maybe those repeated warnings are starting to get through.

The engineer lives with
His wife and daughter Janet
But he misses them so

Although he's working with
The best crew on the planet
They never want him to go

He had a premonition
He senses something wrong
And by his own admission
He knew it all along

The captain's going crazy
But he doesn't know it
He'll take us with him
If we don't do something
Soon to slow it

How can we stop him
Grab the keys & lock him up

If life would work out
The way you plan it
That'd be just fine
For the wife and Janet
Sometimes you might
Have to battle through it
that's the way you learn
How you've got to do it

Yes you can do it whoa - - -

DESPITE

End Section.

So we went to the captain
And we told him to turn round
But he laughs in our faces
Says that we are mistaken

So we gather around him
Now the ropes that have bound him
Prove that he should have listened
To the will of the people
To the will of the people
It's the will of the people

Distractions

WRITER   Paul McCartney
ARTIST   Paul McCartney
RECORDED   Hog Hill Mill, Sussex
RELEASED   *Flowers in the Dirt*, 1989

What is this thing in life
That persuades me to spend
Time away from you?
If you can answer this
You can have the moon

This is the place to be
Any way you can see
There's a lovely view
Why are there always
So many other things to do?

Distractions
Like butterflies are buzzing
Round my head
When I'm alone
I think of you
And the life we'd lead if we could only be free
From these distractions

The postman's at the door
While the telephone rings
On the kitchen wall
Pretend we're not at home
And they'll disappear

I want to be with you
Tell me what I can do
Nothing is too small
Away from all this jazz
We could do anything at all

Distractions
Like butterflies are buzzing
Round my head
When I'm alone
I think of you
And the things we'd do if we could only be through
With these distractions

I'll find a peaceful place
Far away from the noise
Of a busy day
Where we can spend our nights
Counting shooting stars

Distractions
Like butterflies are buzzing
Round my head
When I'm alone
I think of you
And the things we'd do if we could only be through
With these distractions
Like butterflies they're buzzing
Round my head
When I'm alone
I think of you
And the life we'd lead if we could only be free
From these distractions

SOMETIMES I'LL REALISE THAT, HAVING WRITTEN A SONG, IT lacks a certain pizzazz. I'd written 'Distractions' on guitar and could see it needed an arrangement to make it really take off. I'd heard one of Prince's arrangements on *Sign o' the Times*, his album of 1987, and saw that the arranger was someone called Clare Fischer; that was the only name. I assumed it was a very talented woman who had worked such magic for Prince.

When it came to The Beatles, we had started off as a very simple four-piece rock and roll band, so writing arrangements for other musicians was a world we hadn't explored. When we learnt a new song, we would just show each other how to play it: play a G chord here, then change to a C chord, and on it would go. We used to describe ourselves simply as a 'combo'. In fact, I wrote a few letters to people like journalists, trying to get them interested, saying, 'We're a semi-professional rock combo.' And right up until working at Abbey Road Studios, we'd never even considered there being any other instrumentation but ourselves.

The addition of other elements first happened in the mid-sixties, on John's song 'You've Got to Hide Your Love Away'. George Martin suggested we put a flute solo on it, so we thought, 'Well, we'll give it a try.' George was always very good at selecting musicians. He knew the pool, so we always got the top guys, often classical musicians or jazz musicians who were doing sessions to earn a little extra money. That's how we were first coaxed into the idea of having other instrumentation. And, of course, 'Yesterday' was on the same album, *Help!*, and George arranged the string quartet to accompany my acoustic guitar. It was the first time a Beatles song had only one of us on it; it had always been the whole band before that. So, after we'd seen how that was all done and we started broadening our horizons, the sky was the limit.

So, with the help of my wife Linda - who was great at tracking people down - I arranged to meet Clare Fischer in LA, imagining that she'd be some up-and-coming young lady, to talk about the possibility of working together. But the person I'd taken to be a woman turned out to be a man, and a very ordinary-looking, middle-aged gentleman. I guess one should take nothing at face value! I talked to him about maybe having a wind quartet or some-thing. I told him that my dad had attempted to play clarinet when we were kids, and he was always in the upstairs room squeaking away, because if you can't play a clarinet they make an awful bloody noise. Partly because my dad played it - and was persuaded to drop it - I always had an affection for the rich and woody tone of the clarinet. So, we added it to the arrangement, going for more of a Benny Goodman feel than, say, Sidney Bechet.

The meaning of the song is more straightforward than some of my oth-ers. I like this idea that in life, generally, we're always distracted from what we mean to do. This song is saying that life is what happens on your way to doing other things; it's always in transit. I couched it, as I often do, in roman-tic terms: 'What is this thing in life / That persuades me to spend / Time away from you?' But I think it's very true, not just romantically but with mil-lions of things. Even when you meditate, as I do, other things are pushing

With Morris Repass, Hamish
Stuart, Linda, Clare Fischer and
Arne Frager. Los Angeles, 1988

their way into your head. You're lucky if you ever get round to your mantra.
Your head is just swirling with butterflies and, 'Oh, what a good idea; I'll do
that,' and it's very hard to just be still and let a mantra simply roll around in
your head. I think that's the value of meditation. My mind is so active that
it's good to attempt to shut out all those little things that get in your way,
trying to trip you up. Otherwise, as T. S. Eliot wrote, you end up being 'distracted from distraction by distraction'.

DISTRACTIONS.

(1) What is this thing in life $G min7$ $A min7$ $(- mAJ)$
That persuades me to spend $(- mAJ)$ $D min$
Time away from you $G min$
If you can answer this $(A min7 - maj)$
You can have the moon. $D min$

(2) This is the place to be — REPEAT (chords)
Any way you can see
There's a lovely view
Why are there always so many other things to do?

(CHORUS) Distraction B^b —
Like butterflies are buzzing E^b $F.$
round my head $G min$
When I'm alone I think of you E^b $G min$ F
And the life we'd lead if we could only be free $G min$ E^b
from these distractions B^b E^b — F $G min$
,RIFF, (BASS BIT)

(5) I'll find a peaceful place far away from
The noise of a busy day
where we can spend our nights
Counting shooting stars
If you can trust in me (6) AND IF YOU TRUST IN ME
I will soon you'll YOU'LL BE ABLE TO SEE
WHY IS HERE THERE'S ANOTHER WAY.
there always someone
with something else to say . . . . .
" Distractions . " .

Do It Now

WRITER   Paul McCartney

ARTIST   Paul McCartney

RECORDED   Henson Studios, Los Angeles;
                Hog Hill Mill, Sussex; and Abbey Road Studios, London

RELEASED   *Egypt Station*, 2018

Got the time, the inclination
I have answered your invitation
I'll be leaving in the morning
Watch me go

I don't know where the wind is blowing
Got directions to where I'm going
Nothing's certain
That's the only thing I know

Do it now, do it now
While the vision is clear
Do it now
While the feeling is here

If you leave it too late
It could all disappear
Do it now
While your vision is clear

I don't regret the steps I'm taking
The decision that I'm making
Is the right one, or I'm never
Going to know

Got the time, the inclination
   (It's not too late)
I have answered your invitation
   (You've still got time)
I'll be leaving in the morning
   (Follow the beat of your heart)
Watch me go

So do it now, do it now
While your vision is clear
Do it now
While the feeling is here

If you leave it too late
It could all disappear
So do it now
While your vision is clear

Do It Now

IF MY YOUNGER BROTHER MIKE OR I WERE PROCRASTINATING WITH some homework or a job, or if there were some horseshit in the street he wanted us to pick up - and it's hard to imagine now, but there still were horses on the street when I was a kid - my dad would hand us a bucket and a shovel and say, 'Go and collect it.'

He was right; it was a very wise thing to do. He would use the manure in the garden, and it made the flowers grow really well. He loved gardening, and he used to grow flowers like dahlias, snapdragons, and lavender. But it was very embarrassing for two young kids, having to pick up the shit. We'd say, 'Dad, no; the ignominy of it!' If we tried to put things off or say, 'I'll do it tomorrow,' he'd say, 'No, do it now. D-I-N: do it now.' My kids all know the expression. I've told them my dad said it: 'Don't put it off. D-I-N.' Mind you, I always thought 'D-I-N' was a perfect name for a record label. Din. The noise.

'Do it now, do it now / While the vision is clear / Do it now / While the feeling is here'. That's the message my dad was giving us, and it was as true then, when we were kids, as it is today. I think it puts the finger on it exactly: you get rid of the hesitation and the doubt, and you just steamroll through, so the next day you don't have to think, 'Was that the right thing to do?' You've shown your cards, you've spilled your guts onto the page and, like it or not, there it is. I am all for that way of working. When we first started writing songs, we didn't have the luxury of putting it off till tomorrow. Once John and I or I alone started a song, there was nowhere else to go; we had to finish it, and it was a great discipline. There's something about doing it when you have the vision.

It's true in other creative endeavours too. I did a lot of painting in the nineties, and nearly always I would do them in one sitting, so it would be three or four hours at the easel making that painting, because I found that to come back to it was not fun; it was like a problem to solve: 'What was that mood I was in? What was that vision I was having? What was that feeling that got me this far?' Whereas when doing it just in one go, you've solved enough of the problems and you've answered enough of the questions and,

lo and behold, there's your painting, or there's your song. You can mess with it later if you want to, but you don't have to come back to it and think, 'Oh, what was that vision I had for this?' 'Do it now while the vision's clear' is a good piece of advice.

A friend of mine who's a British painter was looking at my paintings, and he said to me, 'Well, that painting style is called *alla prima*, which translates as "at the first time".' When it's applied to painting, I think it means 'in one session'. You don't endlessly paint over it, like a lot of great painters do, which for me would have removed the fun, and I was painting for fun, I was painting to have joy. I've read about the lives of painters, and a lot of it sure ain't fun. They're bloody driving themselves crazy. I read a biography of Willem de Kooning recently and, with at least one of his pictures, he was at it all year. It turned out very well, of course, but it was just endless, endless questions. He was getting drunk, he was going crazy, he was leaving his women, he was just having a crazy life to get this one painting right. That sort of thing doesn't appeal to me, and I'll always hear my father, maybe no longer yelling, but whispering in my ear to get on with it: 'Do it now.'

DO IT NOW

Piano intro

V.1) GOT THE TIME — THE INCLINATION
I HAVE ANSWERED YOUR INVITATION
I'LL BE LEAVING IN THE MORNING
WATCH ME GO

V2) DON'T KNOW WHERE — THE WIND IS BLOWING
GOT DIRECTIONS TO WHERE I'M GOING
NOTHING'S CERTAIN
THAT'S THE ONLY THING I KNOW

CH. DO IT NOW, DO IT NOW
WHILE THE VISION IS CLEAR
DO IT NOW WHILE
THE FEELING'S STILL HERE

IF YOU LEAVE IT TOO LATE
IT COULD ALL DISAPPEAR
(SO) DO IT NOW
WHILE YOUR VISION IS CLEAR

V1) GOT THE TIME — THE INCLINATION
I HAVE ANSWERED YOUR INVITATION
I'LL BE LEAVING IN THE MORNING
WATCH ME GO
V2) DON'T KNOW WHERE etc. ↑

CH. DO IT NOW (SO) DO IT NOW
WHILE YOUR VISION IS CLEAR
DO IT NOW WHILE THE FEELING IS HERE
IF YA LEAVE IT TOO LATE
IT COULD ALL DISAPPEAR
(SO) DO IT NOW WHILE YOUR VISION IS CLEAR

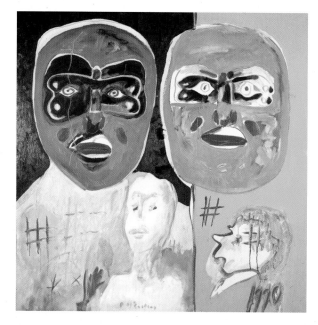

Right: East Hampton, 1990

Left: *Twin Freaks* painting by Paul, 1990

Below: *Egypt Station* painting by Paul, 1988

Dress Me Up as a Robber

WRITER	Paul McCartney
ARTIST	Paul McCartney
RECORDED	AIR Montserrat; and AIR Studios, London
RELEASED	*Tug of War*, 1982
	B-side of 'Take It Away' single, 1982

You can dress me up as a robber
But I won't be in disguise
Only love is a robber
And he lives within your eyes

You can dress me up as a sailor
But I'll never run to sea
As long as your love is available to me
What do I do with a sea of blue?

Dressing me up
It doesn't make a difference
What you want to do
Whichever way you look at it
I'm still in love with you
We go on forever
I may never make a change

Dressing me up
And if I don't convince you
You needn't look too far
To see that I'm not lying
I love you the way you are
What's the point of changing
When I'm happy as I am?

You can dress me up as a soldier
But I wouldn't know what for
I was the one that told you he loved you
Don't wanna go to another war
No no no

THERE'S NO DENYING IT; I REALLY ENJOY DANCING. IF I'M AT A party and some spirited music comes on, I like to dance. It's something my wife Nancy and I are particularly keen on. After a show, when the band and crew get together for a drink, we're always the first ones on the dance floor. Certain songs will just get you dancing, and you also have tracks that become danceable without your ever meaning that to happen.

Certain songs that John and I wrote, like 'I Saw Her Standing There', just have everyone up on their feet. 'Twist and Shout' really gets them going too. Dancing was always a big social thing. It was the way to meet your partner, long before people started meeting online. I remember going dancing once with Nancy, Ringo and his wife Barbara, and we sort of sat there thinking, 'What are we doing here?' You know, we've already got our partners.

When you're trying to write something, you're often looking for a tag to get you started. I wrote this, I think, in the summer of 1980, possibly up in Scotland. And for some reason I just thought, 'You could dress me up as a robber, but it's not gonna change my feelings for you'; that was the basic thing. 'You can dress me up as a soldier / But I wouldn't know what for / I was the one that told you he loved you / Don't wanna go to another war'. That was a little bit of the peacenik in there.

There's a long tradition of songs associated with the soldier going to war. You get fashions in songs, and I think a lot of us had friends who were going to Vietnam - or were trying to avoid going to Vietnam. It was our age group, our peer group; the fact that Americans of our age group were going there brought it home to us.

The whole anti-war thing has been quite a big thing since the sixties. In my case, it started when I met Bertrand Russell, who was already in his nineties, in London. This was, I think, around 1964, and he was staying somewhere in Chelsea - on Flood Street, maybe - and a friend of a friend said, 'You should go and meet him.' I'd seen him on TV and thought he was an interesting speaker. I'd read a few things by him too and had always been impressed by his dignity and how well he put across an idea. So I went along and knocked on the door, and an American student - his assistant or something - came to the door, and I said, 'Oh, hi. Could I meet Mr Russell?' I went just on the off chance, which was how we used to do it. This was the sixties, remember - the freewheeling sixties - when you didn't have to make an appointment or ask someone permission to call them on the telephone. So, even to this day, I'll think, 'Well, if he's in, fine, and if he wants to meet me, if he can spare five minutes, great, and if he wants to go longer, also great.'

Anyway, I went in and met Bertrand Russell, and we talked. At the time he was focusing his energies on the Bertrand Russell Peace Foundation, which he'd set up the year before, and campaigning against the war in Vietnam. He was the first person to tell me about what had been going on in Vietnam, and he explained that it was an imperialist war supported by vested interests. None of us really knew about this at that point. You have to realise, this was still quite early in the war, before the protests really started.

So, I remember going back to the recording studio and telling John about it, and again, he hadn't known there was a war going on in Vietnam either. But I think that was the start of our being more aware of what wars people were involved in, and politics started to become a more regular topic of discussion in the band and amongst our friends and the people we were hanging out with. And so, some of these moments from that time of the fledgling peace movement fed into things like the soldier line in this song.

When it came time to record the song at George Martin's AIR Studios in Montserrat, we had Dave Mattacks play the drums. He's a very fun drummer from England. When I first heard him play, I thought it was John Bonham of Led Zeppelin. I admired Bonham a lot, and I was a friend of his, but then when I inquired, I was told, 'No, it's Dave Mattacks.' It was quite a surprise because Bonham kind of looked the part. He was like a great big farmer, and he bashed the hell out of the kit. He said he always wanted his drums to sound like 'fucking cannons'. But Dave was more like a little primary school teacher, a slight guy. You wouldn't have imagined this big drum sound coming from him. We worked together a little bit, and he was very good. He was also a fun guy. He had drummer jokes: 'How do you know a drummer's come to the door? The knock speeds up.' He would tell you there were certain drum riffs which the drummers at that time had names for. There was a fill known as the 'el-e-phant, el-e-phant, duck-bill plat-y-pus', for example.

'Dress Me Up as a Robber' is great to dance to, but it's also a love song in disguise, a love song in a mask. I think it's a song that should be used at a Venetian masked ball. With the way that 2020 is turning out, the masked ball may be making a bit of a comeback. It should be everywhere now, not just in Venice.

Below left: Dave Mattacks during the *Tug of War* recording sessions. AIR Studios, London, 1982

Below right: With Nancy. Las Vegas, 20 September 2013

DRESS ME UP

(~~DRESSING UP~~)

Intro riff.....

① Well you can dress me up as a robber
But I wont be in disguise,
(EVEN)
(~~Only~~) love is a robber
And he lives within your eyes ooh .... ee oo .....

("harmonies ")

② Well you can dress me up as a sailor
But I'll never run to sea
As long as your love is available to me
What do I do with a sea of blue oo .. ee oo ...

("harmonies ")

③ (Instrumental)

CHORUS) ~~It doesn't~~ make ~~much~~ Dressing me up A difference   DO WHAT YOU WANT TO DO
~~could~~ (IF WE)
Whichever way you look at it   MAYBE) go
I'm still in love with you   on for ever
(I COULD)
Intro riff ....   WANT TO NEVER
~~But~~ ~~I'll never~~ make ~~it~~
A change.

STOP   rythtm
CLAPS (fast music wheel.)

CHORUS (YOU'RE JUST)

④ Well you can dress me up as a soldier
But I wouldn't know what for
I was the one that told you
he loved you
DONT ~~be~~ ~~WANNA~~ g~~o~~ ~~through~~ TO another war?

Intro riff.
END.

("Dressing me up):
If I ~~DONT~~ convince you
you need'nt look too far
to see that I'm not lying

I love you as you are
and whats the point of changing
when (if) I'm happy as I am

Drive My Car

WRITERS   Paul McCartney and John Lennon
ARTIST   The Beatles
RECORDED   Abbey Road Studios, London
RELEASED   *Rubber Soul*, 1965

Asked a girl what she wanted to be
She said, baby, can't you see?
I wanna be famous, a star of the screen
But you can do something in between

Baby you can drive my car
Yes I'm gonna be a star
Baby you can drive my car
And maybe I'll love you

I told that girl that my prospects were good
And she said, baby, it's understood
Working for peanuts is all very fine
But I can show you a better time

Baby you can drive my car
Yes I'm gonna be a star
Baby you can drive my car
And maybe I'll love you
Beep beep, beep beep, yeah

Baby you can drive my car
Yes I'm gonna be a star
Baby you can drive my car
And maybe I'll love you

I told that girl I could start right away
And she said, listen babe, I've got something to say
I got no car and it's breaking my heart
But I've found a driver and that's a start

Baby you can drive my car
Yes I'm gonna be a star
Baby you can drive my car
And maybe I'll love you

Beep beep, beep beep, yeah
Beep beep, beep beep, yeah

THE NEAREST JOHN AND I EVER GOT TO A DRY SESSION was with a song called 'Golden Rings'. I'd brought a version of it out to John's house in Weybridge, and we stalled when we got to the lines 'You can buy me golden rings / Get me all that kind of thing'. We kept singing that over and over and couldn't get beyond it because it was so shockingly bad.

Part of the problem was that we'd already had 'a diamond ring' in 'Can't Buy Me Love'. 'Golden rings' was unoriginal and uninspiring. We couldn't get past it. So we left it, went and had a cup of tea. When we came back, we started thinking of the woman as an LA girl. That improved things a bit. Then she wanted a chauffeur. This is a little like the song 'Norwegian Wood' in the sense that you've got a cast of characters and then, before you know it, you've got a story. You're going to burn someone's house down because she's got a lot of Norwegian wood. So let's burn it and, meanwhile, let's sleep in the bath. Once you get into creating a narrative and storytelling, it's so much more entertaining. It draws you forward so much more easily. Now we were dramatising the interviewing of a chauffeur; we got over that dry moment and finished the song. It became one that didn't get away. And its success had to do with getting rid of 'golden rings' and heading to 'Baby, you can drive my car'.

I know there's a theory that rock and roll couldn't have existed without the guitars of Leo Fender, but it probably couldn't have existed without Henry Ford either. I'm thinking of the relationship between the motorcar and what happens in the back seat. We know that people shagged before the motorcar, but the motorcar gave the erotic a whole new lease on life. Think of Chuck Berry 'riding along in my automobile'. Chuck is one of America's great poets.

'Beep beep, beep beep, yeah'. There you go. It was always good to get nonsense lyrics in, and this song lent itself to 'Beep beep, beep beep, yeah'. We did it in close harmony so it would sound a bit like a horn.

Then there's staying with just two chords for the whole verse. Sometimes you don't even need two; one would do. One of my favourite examples of using just one chord is 'She's Leaving Home', where I fought the chord change. So, it goes 'She' – E major, I think it is. Stays on E – 'is leaving'. Change? No. 'Home'. Change? No. It stays on that E major for a long time. I felt proud of that, because the natural instinct is to change with the opening of every new line. The same is true of the verses of 'Drive My Car'. Two chords are more than enough – maybe even one more than enough.

I know there's a theory that rock and roll couldn't have existed without the guitars of Leo Fender, but it probably couldn't have existed without Henry Ford either. I'm thinking of the relationship between the motorcar and what happens in the back seat. We know that people shagged before the motorcar, but the motorcar gave the erotic a whole new lease on life.

Asked a girl, what she wanted to be
She said, now baby, can't you see?
I wanna be famous, a star on the screen,
but you can do something in between.
You can buy me golden rings
get me all the kind of things
oo, if can buy me rings,
then baby I'd love you.

137

E

Eat at Home

WRITERS   Paul McCartney and Linda McCartney

ARTIST   Paul and Linda McCartney

RECORDED   CBS Studios, New York

RELEASED   *RAM*, 1971

Come on, little lady
Lady, let's eat at home
Come on, little lady
Lady, let's eat at home
Eat at home, eat at home

Come on, little lady
Lady, let's eat in bed
Come on, little lady
Lady, let's eat in bed
Eat in bed, eat in bed

Bring the love that you feel for me
Into line with the love I see
And in the morning you'll bring to me
Love

Come on, little lady
Lady, now don't do that
Come on, little lady
Lady, now don't do that
Do that, do that

Come on, little lady
Lady, let's eat at home
Come on, little lady
Lady, let's eat at home
Eat at home, eat at home

Bring the love that you feel for me
Into line with the love I see
And in the morning you'll bring to me
Love

Come on, little lady
Lady, now don't do that
Come on, little lady
Lady, now don't do that
Do that, do that

L INDA'S GREAT COOKING ULTIMATELY INSPIRED HER OWN
cookbooks. Nobody was writing simple and easy-to-follow recipe
books for meat-free home cooking. So, eating in bed was something
we both really liked to do. There were a couple of other things we really
liked to do, but that's for another day.

It's a very different take on domesticity from that 'Bed-In for Peace' that
John and Yoko had in a hotel room in Amsterdam in 1969. Right from the
start, he and I were always bouncing off each other when it came to subjects
for songs. But the world represented here is certainly much quieter, conducted without the world's press.

You have to remember that Linda and I were newly married, with a baby,
and we were desperately trying to escape the hurly-burly and just find time
to be a family. We were completely cut off on our farm in Scotland, a place
I'd bought a few years before but Linda really fell in love with. So we just
made our own fun. We drew a lot. We wrote a lot. We inspired each other.
Linda took a lot of photographs, and I think Scotland helped her find a new
side to her work, moving away from musicians and capturing nature and
the everyday of family life.

It was a life that might be perceived as idyllic, away from the city and business and the press. In some ways it was quite banal. What I liked about it was
the simplicity. The small scale of things. The paintings I made were small. I
bought only little canvases. I never thought I would be allowed to make visual
art. I always thought that was for 'them'. I would never have dreamt of taking
up horse riding had I not met Linda. Again, that was for 'them'. Horse riding
wasn't for my type. But we really found ourselves in Scotland; it gave us a
wonderful freedom to try new things, just for ourselves.

Apart from riding for fun, there were so many jobs having to do with the farm itself. I actually learnt to shear the sheep with hand clippers - not something one sees much these days, and certainly not something that, when I was a kid in Liverpool, I ever thought I'd end up doing. I was able to shear about fourteen to twenty in a day, and my farm manager, Duncan, would do a hundred. Just getting the sheep on its back is a hard enough trick to pull off. An image of me about to flip a sheep ended up as the cover of *RAM*, the album on which this song appeared. That was part of Linda's record of one shearing session. Linda made an individual portrait of each and every one of our flock.

From a musical perspective, 'Eat at Home' owes much to the example of Buddy Holly, a huge influence on The Beatles when we were growing up and starting to write our own songs. One of the aspects I rather enjoy is that I modified Buddy Holly's tendency to mimic a speech hesitation by introducing a sheep's baa into the phrase 'eat in be-e-e-e-d'. I was proud of that!

Below and right:
At home on the farm.
Scotland, 1970–71

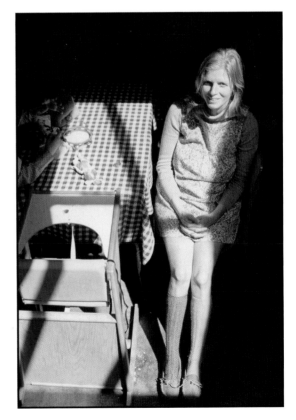

EAT AT HOME

Comeon little **lady**

Lady let's eat at home

Eat at home eat at home

Come on little **lady**

Lady let's eat in bed

Eat in bed eat in bed

Bring the love that you feel for me

Into line with the love I see

And in the morning you'll bring to me love

Come on little **lady**

lady now don't do that

~~Don't~~ do that ~~Don't~~ do that   *INSTRUMENTAL*

Come on little lady

lady let's eat at home

eat at home, eat at home

LADY LET'S EAT AT HOME.

① Come on little lady
lady let's eat at home
come on little lady
lady let's eat at home
eat at home
eat at home .

② Come on little lady
lady let's eat in bed.

   middle   Bring the love that you feel for me
        Into line with the love I see
And every morning you bring   to   me
     love . . . .

③ Come on little lady
lady now don't do that
. . . do that . . do that . .

④ . . lady let's eat at home . . .

145

Ebony and Ivory

WRITER	Paul McCartney
ARTIST	Paul McCartney, with additional vocals by Stevie Wonder
RECORDED	AIR Montserrat
RELEASED	Single, 1982
	Tug of War, 1982

Ebony and Ivory
Live together in perfect harmony
Side by side on my piano keyboard
Oh lord, why don't we?

We all know
That people are the same wherever you go
There is good and bad in everyone
When we learn to live
We learn to give each other
What we need to survive
Together alive

Ebony and Ivory
Live together in perfect harmony
Side by side on my piano keyboard
Oh lord, why don't we?

Ebony, Ivory
Living in perfect harmony
Ebony, Ivory

We all know
That people are the same wherever you go
There is good and bad in everyone
We learn to live
When we learn to give each other
What we need to survive
Together alive

Ebony and Ivory
Live together in perfect harmony
Side by side on my piano keyboard
Oh lord, why don't we?
Side by side on my piano keyboard
Oh lord, why don't we?

Ebony, Ivory
Living in perfect harmony
Ebony, Ivory
Living in perfect harmony

BLACK AND WHITE KEYS LIVE TOGETHER ON A PIANO KEYBOARD, yet Black and white people haven't always lived in harmony. It's an observation Spike Milligan once made.

Spike Milligan was a British-Irish comedian who had written and starred in *The Goon Show*, a BBC radio series in the fifties. The show was a big influence on The Beatles when we were growing up, and it is also where Peter Sellers got his big break. George Martin worked with them for a while too. So, Spike lived very near me in Sussex, and we both liked a laugh, being of Irish origin. I think there is this tradition of funny Irish people which extends to Liverpool. He had gatherings where he would ask you to bring something, and it didn't have to be a bottle; it could just as well be a poem. So I brought him a poem. He lived in a house with a plaque that said, 'Designed by the Blind Architect', and the lane his house was on was called – I'm not kidding – Dumb Woman's Lane. I think it meant a woman who couldn't speak. I wrote a poem about Dumb Woman's Lane and took it round to him, and I read it before dinner.

The poem started like this:

> *The voice of the poet*
> *Of Dumbwoman's Lane*
> *Can be heard across*
> *Valleys of sugar-burned cane,*
> *And nostrils that sleep*
> *Through the wildest of nights*
> *Will be twitching to gain*
> *Aromatic insights.*

'Ebony and Ivory' was written as a response to the problem of racial tension, which had been the cause of a lot of friction in the UK around that time. I wrote it and made a demo in Scotland in my little studio there in 1980; then I rang Stevie Wonder and asked whether he wanted to do something. Stevie and I have known each other for a long time. We first met in 1966, after a show he played at the Scotch of St James club in Mayfair, London. He was only fifteen years old at the time. So, anyway, we were thinking we'd write something together, and I said, 'Well, I've got this song that I'd particularly like to do.' So we went out to Monserrat for the album sessions. George Martin had his studio out there, and Stevie was supposed to show up but he didn't. So there was a lot of phoning, which is the way it is with Stevie. 'We're here. When are you coming out?' It was always 'this Friday'.

Then the weekend would go by, and I'd ring him on Monday. 'Oh, I'll be there on Wednesday.' 'Oh, okay.' So there was a lot of that. He's his own man. He'll show up when he's ready. But it was great when he arrived. It was fascinating because he is such a musical monster; he just *is* music. You had to be super precise, because any mistake he would hear. He asked if we were going to use a drum machine, and I said no, so he got on the drum kit and he was a great drummer with a very distinct style, and that's him playing on the record. The whole song is just me and Stevie.

When we came to do the video, it happened again. It was booked with the team and the studio and technicians, cameramen and everybody, and Ste-

Left and below: With Stevie Wonder during *Tug of War* recording sessions.
AIR Montserrat, 1981

Right: Outtake from 'Ebony and Ivory' photo shoot

vie was supposed to show up on the Monday morning or whatever it was, and he didn't. Getting through to him was a challenge because it would go like this: 'Mr Wonder's in the studio at the moment. I'm sorry, who is this?' 'It's Paul McCartney. We know each other; we've worked together.' 'Oh, well, he's working and he can't be disturbed.' So that went on and on and we were about a week late doing the video when he finally showed up. So yes, it was great to work with him, but there was always this being late thing, not being there. Which I wasn't used to, I must say.

I didn't ever think 'Ebony and Ivory' was going to solve the problems of the world, but I think its heart was in the right place. People made fun of it, of course. Some thought it was too sentimental or simplistic, perhaps. Eddie Murphy did a skit about it on *Saturday Night Live*. It's the sort of thing that's easy to send up.

I've performed it once or twice. I did it at the White House with Stevie when I received the Gershwin Prize a few years after Barack Obama became president. What an honour. Some great people were in attendance. Elvis Costello sang 'Penny Lane', Stevie sang 'We Can Work It Out' and - it was the first time we'd ever played it live together - he and I did 'Ebony and Ivory'.

TO SPIKE, MAN,

THE POET OF DUMBWOMANS LANE.

The voice of the poet
of Dumbwoman's Lane,
Can be heard across
Vallies of sugar - burned cane
And nostrils that sleep
Through the wildest of nights
Will be twitching
To gain aromatic insights.

—

The wife of the farmer
of Poppinghole Lane
Can be seen from the
cab of the Robertsbridge train.
And passengers comments
will frequently turn
To the wages the wife
of a farmer can earn.

The poet of Dumbwoman's Lane
Sallies forth.
He is hoping for no-one to see.

—   with love Paul (YESTERDAYS
                                      MAN.

150

EBONY + IVORY.

CHORUS

Ebony + Ivory
live together in perfect harmony
side by side on my piano keyboard
Oh lord, why don't we?

VERSE 1.

We all know
that people are the same wherever you go
There is good and bad in everyone
We learn to live when we
learn to give each other
what we need to survive, together alive....

CHORUS

MODULATION or KEY CHANGE

VERSE ② We all know

There is right and wrong for everyone

Eight Days a Week

WRITERS	Paul McCartney and John Lennon
ARTIST	The Beatles
RECORDED	Abbey Road Studios, London
RELEASED	*Beatles for Sale*, 1964
	US single, 1965
	Beatles VI, 1965

Ooh I need your love, babe
Guess you know it's true
Hope you need my love, babe
Just like I need you

Hold me, love me
Hold me, love me
I ain't got nothin' but love, babe
Eight days a week

Love you every day, girl
Always on my mind
One thing I can say, girl
Love you all the time

Hold me, love me
Hold me, love me
I ain't got nothin' but love, girl
Eight days a week

Eight days a week
I love you
Eight days a week
Is not enough to show I care

Ooh I need your love, babe
Guess you know it's true
Hope you need my love, babe
Just like I need you

Hold me, love me
Hold me, love me
I ain't got nothin' but love, babe
Eight days a week

Eight days a week
I love you
Eight days a week
Is not enough to show I care

Love you every day, girl
Always on my mind
One thing I can say, girl
Love you all the time

Hold me, love me
Hold me, love me
I ain't got nothin' but love, babe
Eight days a week
Eight days a week
Eight days a week

THE PROBLEM WAS WE ALL LIKED TO DRIVE FAST, AND I myself had been caught one too many times. The police took my licence away, and I was banned from driving for a year. If I wanted to get somewhere, I had to take a bus or train or sometimes hire a driver. By the time I was unbanned, we'd actually earned enough money to get a driver.

I was going out to John's house in Weybridge a lot, and on this particular day I was chatting to the chauffeur and, at the end of the journey, I just happened to ask him what he'd been doing. He said, 'Oh, I've been working eight days a week.' I ran into John's house saying, 'Got the title.'

A lot of what we had going for us was that we were both good at noticing the stuff that just pops up, and grabbing it. And the other thing is that John and I had each other. If he was sort of stuck for a line, I could finish it. If I was stuck for somewhere to go, he could make a suggestion. We could suggest the way out of the maze to each other, which was a very handy thing to have. We inspired each other. So when I arrived with the title, he was just happy that we had a starting point. I mean, I don't think either of us ever thought it was a great song, but it was a cool idea.

Then remembering it - that was the trick. And in order to remember it, we had to write something memorable. You know, if we were writing something that was too clever or too this or that, we probably weren't going to remember it. I always found that by the time I'd got home in the evening and had a drink, I'd completely forgotten it. 'Oh shit,' I would think. 'Well, he'll remember it. But what if he's also had a drink and we've both forgotten it?'

But in the morning, I'd wake up singing it. It would be there, fresh as a daisy. So we had the lyrics for 'Eight Days a Week', and now I'd reinforced them in my brain, and by the time we came to the session, John and I could play it on acoustic guitars for George, Ringo, George Martin, and the engineer. None of them had ever heard it before. John and I were the only two who knew it, but within twenty minutes we'd all learnt it.

Above: With John Lennon during the filming of *Ready Steady Go!* London, 1964

Then remembering it – that was the trick. And in order to remember it, we had to write something memorable. You know, if we were writing something that was too clever or too this or that, we probably weren't going to remember it. I always found that by the time I'd got home in the evening and had a drink, I'd completely forgotten it.

Eleanor Rigby

WRITERS	Paul McCartney and John Lennon
ARTIST	The Beatles
RECORDED	Abbey Road Studios, London
RELEASED	*Revolver*, 1966
	'Eleanor Rigby'/'Yellow Submarine' double A-side single, 1966

Ah look at all the lonely people
Ah look at all the lonely people

Eleanor Rigby
Picks up the rice in the church where a wedding
   has been
Lives in a dream
Waits at the window
Wearing the face that she keeps in a jar by the door
Who is it for?

All the lonely people
Where do they all come from?
All the lonely people
Where do they all belong?

Father McKenzie
Writing the words of a sermon that no
   one will hear
No one comes near
Look at him working
Darning his socks in the night when
   there's nobody there
What does he care?

All the lonely people
Where do they all come from?
All the lonely people
Where do they all belong?

Ah look at all the lonely people
Ah look at all the lonely people

Eleanor Rigby
Died in the church and was buried
   along with her name
Nobody came
Father McKenzie
Wiping the dirt from his hands as
   he walks from the grave
No one was saved

All the lonely people
   (Ah look at all the lonely people)
Where do they all come from?
All the lonely people
   (Ah look at all the lonely people)
Where do they all belong?

Me – those were
the days – shorts.
Behind me is
the "Local."

M Y MUM'S FAVOURITE COLD CREAM WAS NIVEA, AND I
love it to this day. That's the cold cream I was thinking of in the
description of the face Eleanor keeps 'in a jar by the door'. I was
always a little scared by how often women used cold cream.

Growing up I knew a lot of old ladies – partly through what was called Bob-
a-Job Week, when Scouts did chores for a shilling. You'd get a shilling for cleaning out a shed or mowing a lawn. I wanted to write a song that would sum them
up. Eleanor Rigby is based on an old lady that I got on with very well. I don't
even know how I first met 'Eleanor Rigby', but I would go around to her house,
and not just once or twice. I found out that she lived on her own, so I would go
around there and just chat, which is sort of crazy if you think about me being
some young Liverpool guy. Later, I would offer to go and get her shopping.
She'd give me a list and I'd bring the stuff back, and we'd sit in her kitchen. I
still vividly remember the kitchen because she had a little crystal radio set.
That's not a brand name; it actually had a crystal inside it. Crystal radios were
quite popular in the 1920s and '30s. So I would visit, and just hearing her stories enriched my soul and influenced the songs I would later write.

She may actually have started with a quite different name. Daisy Hawkins,
was it? I can see that 'Hawkins' is quite nice, but it wasn't right. Jack Hawkins
had played Quintus Arrius in *Ben-Hur*. Then there was Jim Hawkins from
one of my favourite books, *Treasure Island*. But it wasn't right. This is the
trouble with history, though. Even if you were there, which I obviously was,
it's sometimes very difficult to pin down.

Above: Early 1950s

It's like the story of the name 'Eleanor Rigby' on a marker in the grave-yard at St Peter's Church in Woolton, which John and I certainly wandered around, endlessly talking about our future. I don't remember seeing the grave there, but I suppose I might have registered it subliminally.

St Peter's Church also plays quite a big part in how I come to be talking about many of these memories today. Back in the summer of 1957, Ivan Vaughan (a friend from school) and I went to the Woolton Village Fête at the church together, and he introduced me to his friend, John, who was playing there with his band The Quarry Men.

I'd just turned fifteen at this point and John was sixteen, and Ivan knew we were both obsessed with rock and roll, so he took me over to introduce us. One thing led to another - typical teenage boys posturing and the like - and I ended up showing off a little by playing Eddie Cochran's 'Twenty Flight Rock' on the guitar. I think I also played Gene Vincent's 'Be-Bop-a-Lula' and a few Little Richard songs too.

A week or so later, I was out on my bike and bumped into Pete Shotton, who was The Quarry Men's washboard player - a very important instrument in the skiffle band. He and I got talking, and he told me that John thought I should join them. That was a very John thing to do - have someone else ask me so he wouldn't lose face if I said no. John often had his guard up, but that was one of the great balances between us. He could be quite caustic and witty, but once you got to know him, he had this lovely warm character. I was more the opposite: pretty easy-going and friendly, but I could be tough when needed.

I said I would think about it and a week later said yes. And after that John and I started hanging out quite a bit. I was on school holidays and John was

With Ivan Vaughan and
George Harrison.
Liverpool, late 1950s

158

Ah, look at all the lonely people

Eleanor Rigby, picks up the rice
in the church where a wedding
has been
lives in a dream.
Waits at the window, wearing the face
that she keeps in a jar by the door
who is it for?
All the lonely, — — — — etc.

Father McKenzie, writing the words of a
sermon that no-one will hear
no-one comes near.
Look at him working, darning his
socks in the night when there's
nobody there, what does he care?
All the lonely people . . . . .

Ah look at all the lonely people

Paul McCartney

about to start art college, usefully next door to my school. I showed him how to tune his guitar, he was using banjo tuning – I think his neighbour had done that for him before – and we taught ourselves how to play songs by people like Chuck Berry. I would have played him 'I Lost My Little Girl' a while later, when I'd got my courage up to share it, and he started showing me his songs. And that's where it all began.

I do this 'tour' when I'm back in Liverpool with friends and family. I drive around the old sites, pointing out places like our old house in Forthlin Road, and I sometimes drive by St Peter's too. It's only five or ten minutes away by car from the old house. And I do often stop and wonder about the chances of The Beatles getting together. We were four guys who lived in this city in the north of England, but we didn't know each other. Then, by chance, we did get to know each other. And then we sounded pretty good when we played together, and we all had that youthful drive to get good at this music thing.

To this very day, it still is a complete mystery to me that it happened at all. Would John and I have met some other way, if Ivan and I hadn't gone to that fête? I'd actually gone along to try and pick up a girl. I'd seen John around – in the chip shop, on the bus, that sort of thing – and thought he looked quite cool, but would we have ever talked? I don't know. As it happened, though, I had a school friend who knew John. And then I also happened to share a bus journey with George to school. All these small coincidences had to happen to make The Beatles happen, and it does feel like some kind of magic. It's one of the wonderful lessons about saying yes when life presents these opportunities to you. You never know where they could lead.

And as if all these crazy coincidences weren't enough, it turns out that someone else who was at the fête had a portable tape machine – one of those old Grundigs. So there's this recording (admittedly of pretty bad quality) of The Quarry Men's performance that day. You can listen to it online. And there are also a few photos around of the band on the back of the truck. So, this day that proved to be pretty pivotal in my life still has this presence and exists in these ghosts of the past.

I always think of things like these as being happy accidents. Like when someone played the tape machine backwards in Abbey Road and the four of us would stop in our tracks and go, 'Oh! What's that?' So then we'd use that effect in a song, like on the backwards guitar solo for 'I'm Only Sleeping'. It happened more recently too, on the song 'Caesar Rock' from *Egypt Station*. Somehow this drum part got dragged accidentally to the start of the song on the computer, and we played it back and it's just there in those first few seconds and it doesn't fit. But at the same time it does.

So, my life is full of these happy accidents, and coming back to where the name 'Eleanor Rigby' comes from, my memory has me visiting Bristol, where Jane Asher was playing at the Old Vic. I was wandering around, waiting for the play to finish, and saw a shop sign that read 'Rigby', and I thought, 'That's it!' It really was as happenstance as that. When I got back to London, I wrote the song in Mrs Asher's music room in the basement of 57 Wimpole Street, where I was living at the time.

Around that same time, I'd started taking piano lessons again. I took lessons as a kid, but it was mostly just practising scales, and it seemed more like homework. I loved music, but I hated the homework that came along with learning it. I think, in total, I gave piano lessons three attempts – the first time when I was a kid and my parents sent me to someone they knew locally. Then, when I was sixteen, I thought, 'Maybe it's time to try and learn to play properly.' I was writing my own songs by that point and getting more serious about music, but it was still the same scales. 'Argh!! Get outta here!!' Then again, when I was in my early twenties, Jane's mum Margaret organised lessons for me with someone from Guildhall School of Music, where she worked. I even played 'Eleanor Rigby' on piano for the teacher, but this was before I had the words. At the time, I was just blocking out the lyrics and singing 'Ola Na Tungee' over vamped E minor chords. I don't remember the teacher being all that impressed. They just wanted to hear me play even more scales, so that put an end to the lessons.

When I started working on the words in earnest, 'Eleanor' was always part of the equation, I think, because we had worked with Eleanor Bron on the film *Help!* and we knew her from The Establishment, Peter Cook's club

With George Martin,
George Harrison and John
Lennon. Abbey Road
Studios, London, circa 1968

Above: With George
Harrison, John Lennon and
Dennis Littler at Auntie Jin
and Uncle Harry's.
Liverpool, 1958

Left: Eleanor Bron during
the filming of *Help!*
Bahamas, 1965

on Greek Street. I think John might have dated her for a short while, too, and I liked the name very much. Initially, the priest was 'Father McCartney', because it had the right number of syllables. I took the song out to John at around that point, and I remember playing it to him, and he said, 'That's great, Father McCartney.' He loved it. But I wasn't really comfortable with it because it's my dad – my father McCartney – so I literally got out the phone book and went on from 'McCartney' to 'McKenzie'.

The song itself was consciously written to evoke the subject of loneliness, with the hope that we could get listeners to empathise. Those opening lines – 'Eleanor Rigby / Picks up the rice in the church where a wedding has been / Lives in a dream'. It's a little strange to be picking up rice after a wedding. Does that mean she was a cleaner, someone not invited to the wedding, and only viewing the celebrations from afar? Why would she be doing that? I wanted to make it more poignant than her just cleaning up afterwards, so it became more about someone who was lonely. Someone not likely to have her own wedding, but only the dream of one.

Allen Ginsberg told me it was a great poem, so I'm going to go with Allen. He was no slouch. Another early admirer of the song was William S. Burroughs who, of course, also ended up on the cover of *Sgt. Pepper*. He and I had met through the author Barry Miles and the Indica Bookshop, and he actually got to see the song take shape when I sometimes used the spoken-word studio that we had set up in the basement of Ringo's flat in Montagu Square. The plan for the studio was to record poets – something we did more formally a few years later with the experimental Zapple label, a subsidiary of Apple. I'd been experimenting with tape loops a lot around this time, using a Brenell reel-to-reel – which I still own – and we were starting to put more experimental elements into our songs. 'Eleanor Rigby' ended up on the *Revolver* album, and for the first time we were recording songs that couldn't be replicated on stage – songs like this and 'Tomorrow Never Knows'. So, Burroughs and I had hung out, and he'd borrowed my reel-to-reel a few times to work on his cut-ups. When he got to hear the final version of 'Eleanor Rigby', he said he was impressed by how much narrative I'd got into three verses. And it did feel like a breakthrough for me lyrically – more of a serious song.

George Martin had introduced me to the string quartet idea through 'Yesterday'. I'd resisted the idea at first, but when it worked I fell in love with it. So I ended up writing 'Eleanor Rigby' with a string component in mind. When I took the song to George, I said that, for accompaniment, I wanted a series of E minor chord stabs. In fact, the whole song is really only two chords: C major and E minor. In George's version of things, he conflates my idea of the stabs and his own inspiration by Bernard Herrmann, who had written the music for the movie *Psycho*. George wanted to bring some of that drama into the arrangement. And, of course, there's some kind of madcap connection between Eleanor Rigby, an elderly woman left high and dry, and the mummified mother in *Psycho*.

The End

WRITERS   Paul McCartney and John Lennon

ARTIST   The Beatles

RECORDED   Abbey Road Studios, London

RELEASED   *Abbey Road,* 1969

Oh yeah, alright
Are you gonna be in my dreams tonight?

And in the end the love you take
Is equal to the love you make

This poure widwe.
"With face pale of drede and bisy thought,
She hath at scole and elleswhere hem sought,"
With modres pitee in hir brest enclosed
... as she were half out of hir mynde.
~~Hir litel child.~~
...on Cristes mooder, meeke + kynde [She cryde.
She frayneth + she preyeth pitously
His mooder swowninge
This newe Rachel

J OHN NEVER HAD ANYTHING LIKE MY INTEREST IN LITERATURE, though he was very keen on Lewis Carroll and, in particular, Winston Churchill. His Aunt Mimi had lots of books by Churchill in the front parlour. Not a bad basis for an education.

In my case, I was always fascinated by the couplet as a form in poetry. When you think about it, it's been the workhorse of poetry in English right the way through. Chaucer, Pope, Wilfred Owen. I was particularly fascinated by how Shakespeare used the couplet to close out a scene, or an entire play. Just taking a swing through Macbeth, for example, you'll find a few humdingers, like

> *Receive what cheer you may:*
> *The night is long that never finds the day.*

or

> *I go, and it is done; the bell invites me.*
> *Hear it not, Duncan; for it is a knell*
> *That summons thee to heaven or to hell.*

This was Shakespeare's way of saying, 'That's it, folks,' and 'The End' was our way of saying the same.

> *And in the end the love you take*
> *Is equal to the love you make*

This is one of those couplets that can keep you thinking for a long time. It may be about good karma. What goes around comes around, as they say in America.

I often muse upon what might have happened, had I not ended up in a band that rather took over my life. I wonder about the path I thought I was on with my A level in English literature and where that might have led me.

Above: Copying 'The Prioress's Tale' lines from Geoffrey Chaucer's *The Canterbury Tales*. From Paul's English Literature schoolbook

And in the end
The love you take
is equal to
The love you make.

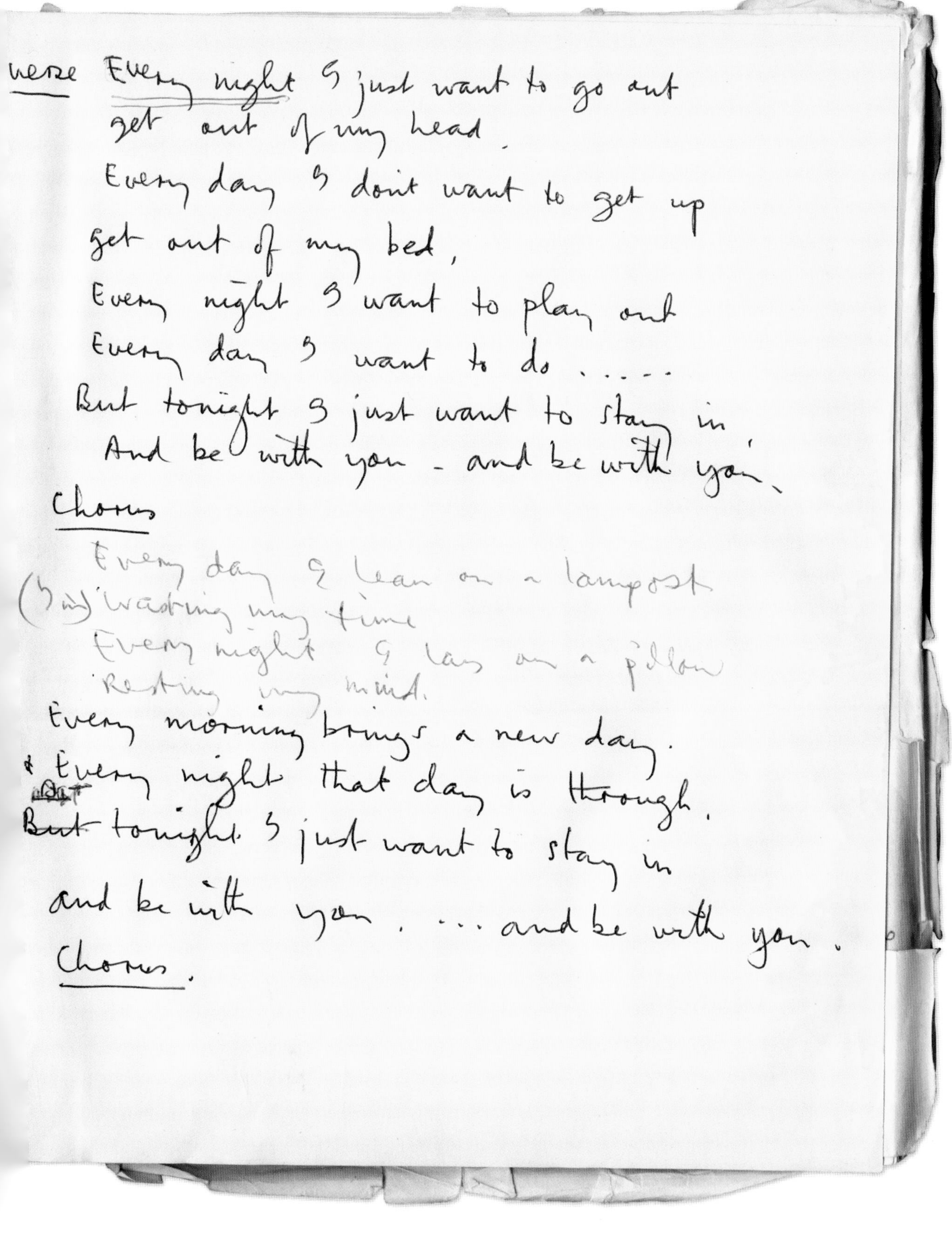

Every night I just want to go out
get out of my head.
Every day I don't want to get up
get out of my bed,
Every night I want to play out
Every day I want to do . . . . .
But tonight I just want to stay in.
And be with you - and be with you.

Chorus

Every day I lean on a lampost
(Bis) wasting my time
Every night I lay on a pillow
Resting my mind.
Every morning brings a new day.
& Every night that day is through.
But tonight I just want to stay in
and be with you . . . . and be with you.

Chorus.

167

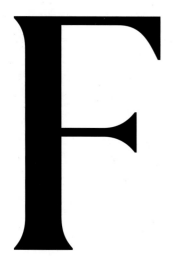

Fixing a Hole

WRITERS   Paul McCartney and John Lennon
ARTIST   The Beatles
RECORDED   Regent Sound Studio, London; and Abbey Road Studios, London
RELEASED   *Sgt. Pepper's Lonely Hearts Club Band*, 1967

I'm fixing a hole where the rain gets in
And stops my mind from wandering
Where it will go

I'm filling the cracks that ran through the door
And kept my mind from wandering
Where it will go

And it really doesn't matter if I'm wrong I'm right
Where I belong I'm right
Where I belong
See the people standing there
Who disagree and never win
And wonder why they don't get in my door

I'm painting the room in a colourful way
And when my mind is wandering
There I will go

And it really doesn't matter if I'm wrong I'm right
Where I belong I'm right
Where I belong
Silly people run around
They worry me and never ask me
Why they don't get past my door

I'm taking the time for a number of things
That weren't important yesterday
And I still go

I'm fixing a hole where the rain gets in
And stops my mind from wandering
Where it will go
Where it will go

B EFORE I WRITE A SONG, THERE'S A BLACK HOLE AND THEN I get my guitar or piano and fill it in. The notion that there is a gap to fill is no less honourable a basis for an inspiration than a bolt of lightning coming down out of the sky. One way or another, it's a miracle. I sit down and there's a blackness. There's nothing in this hole. Maybe I start conjuring and at the end of three hours I have a rabbit to pull out of what had looked like a hole but was actually a top hat. Or, at the end of the session there's not a black hole anymore but a coloured landscape.

On the subject of coloured landscapes, I was the last in the group to take LSD. John and George had urged me to do it so that I could be on the same level as them. I was very reluctant because I'm actually quite straitlaced, and I'd heard that if you took LSD you would never be the same again. I wasn't sure I wanted that. I wasn't sure that was such a terrific idea. So I was very resistant. In the end I did give in and take LSD one night with John.

I was pretty lucky on the LSD front, in that it didn't screw things up too badly. There was a scary element to it, of course. The really scary element was that when you wanted it to stop, it wouldn't. You'd say, 'Okay, that's enough, party's over,' and it would say, 'No it isn't.' So you would have to go to bed seeing things.

Around that time, when I closed my eyes, instead of there being blackness there was a little blue hole. It was as if something needed patching. I always had the feeling that if I could go up to it and look through, there would be an answer. Now, I could go on about how the wordplay in Bing Crosby's song 'Please' - 'Oh, Please / Lend your little ear to my pleas' - might be informing the wordplay in 'And it really doesn't matter if I'm wrong I'm right / Where I belong'. The fact is that the most important influence here was not even the metaphysical idea of a hole, which I mentioned earlier, but this absolutely physical phenomenon - something that first appeared after I took acid. I still see it occasionally, and I know exactly what it is. I know exactly what size it is.

Some people take 'Fixing a Hole' to be about heroin. That's most likely because they're visualising needle holes. At the point the song was written, the drug was more likely than not to be marijuana. As it happens, I was living pretty much on my own in London and enjoying my new house. So the whole world of home improvements was beginning to impinge on me in a quite literal way.

I was the last in the group to take LSD. John and George had urged me to do it so that I could be on the same level as them. I was very reluctant because I'm actually quite straitlaced, and I'd heard that if you took LSD you would never be the same again.

The Fool on the Hill

WRITERS   Paul McCartney and John Lennon
ARTIST   The Beatles
RECORDED   Abbey Road Studios, London
RELEASED   *Magical Mystery Tour*, 1967

Day after day
Alone on a hill
The man with the foolish grin
Is keeping perfectly still
But nobody wants to know him
They can see that he's just a fool
And he never gives an answer

But the fool on the hill
Sees the sun going down
And the eyes in his head
See the world spinning round

Well on the way
Head in a cloud
The man of a thousand voices
Talking perfectly loud
But nobody ever hears him
Or the sound he appears to make
And he never seems to notice

But the fool on the hill
Sees the sun going down
And the eyes in his head
See the world spinning round

And nobody seems to like him
They can tell what he wants to do
And he never shows his feelings

But the fool on the hill
Sees the sun going down
And the eyes in his head
See the world spinning round

Round, round, round, round, round

He never listens to them
He knows that they're the fools
They don't like him

The fool on the hill
Sees the sun going down
And the eyes in his head
See the world spinning round

Round, round, round, round, round

MAHARISHI MAHESH YOGI WAS THOUGHT BY SOME TO BE THE Beatles' spiritual advisor. And I think it's fair to say he was. This song was written around the time of our involvement with the Maharishi, and it certainly deals with that kind of experience.

I remember starting to work on it up in Heswall, on the Wirral peninsula, where my dad was living at the time. He had a piano in the house because he himself was a musician. And it was perhaps partly because he was a musician and had his own jazz band that he was so very appreciative of our success. He was so proud of me. He was tickled by the fact that his son was recognised. We'd go into a restaurant, and we'd be sitting there or in a bar, and he'd be looking around at all the people. He'd spot someone who had recognised me, and he'd go, 'They've got you, they've got you.'

In a strange way, it's precisely because people had 'got' us, that we were no longer able to be quite ourselves, which then left The Beatles so open to the possibilities the Maharishi offered. We needed to recentre ourselves. To get back to basics. We were introduced to the Maharishi in 1967 by George Harrison, who had gone to see him talk at the Hilton on Park Lane in London. Shortly after, we all went to study with him in Bangor in Wales. Then, in early 1968, we went to Rishikesh, in India, for what was meant to be an extended period. Ringo and his wife Maureen left after ten days. Jane Asher and I left after five weeks. George and John and their wives left about a fortnight after that. But the Maharishi had made a mark on all of us.

I know some people think that my description of the Maharishi as a 'fool' is disparaging. That's not the case at all. I often get 'The Fool' card during a tarot reading, for example. Maybe it's from my tendency to try and see the positive side of things, or keeping an eye out for new ideas and adventures. In the song, I'm simply describing how the Maharishi was perceived by so many people - as the 'giggling guru'. That was not my own perception. I'm fascinated by how much trouble people have in recognising irony.

So, all in all, I think 'The Fool on the Hill' is a very complimentary portrait

Above: Jim Mac's Jazz Band (dad Jim is third from right from the drum kit), circa 1920s

and represents the Maharishi as having the capacity to keep perfectly still in the midst of the hurly-burly. He's admirably self-contained and doesn't pay much attention to popular opinion. He's a person who is open to ridicule because of his beliefs, but his beliefs may well be right. I think he may be related somehow to the truth-telling Fool in *King Lear*.

With Maharishi Mahesh Yogi. Wales, 1967

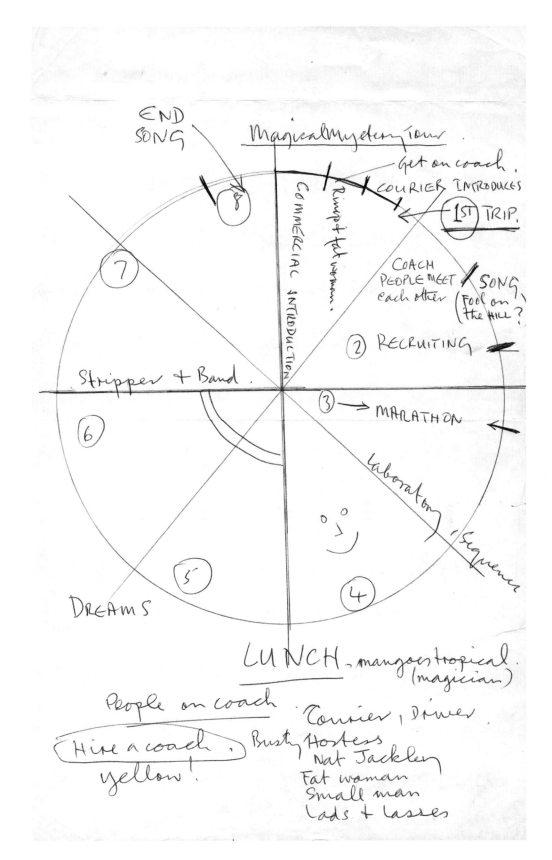

Paul's notes for the *Magical Mystery Tour* film

For No One

WRITERS   Paul McCartney and John Lennon
ARTIST   The Beatles
RECORDED   Abbey Road Studios, London
RELEASED   *Revolver*, 1966

Your day breaks
Your mind aches
You find that all her words of kindness linger on
When she no longer needs you

She wakes up
She makes up
She takes her time and doesn't feel
    she has to hurry
She no longer needs you

And in her eyes you see nothing
No sign of love behind the tears cried for no one
A love that should have lasted years

You want her
You need her
And yet you don't believe her when
    she says her love is dead
You think she needs you

And in her eyes you see nothing
No sign of love behind the tears cried for no one
A love that should have lasted years

You stay home
She goes out
She says that long ago she knew someone
    but now he's gone
She doesn't need him

Your day breaks
Your mind aches
There will be times when all the things
    she said will fill your head
You won't forget her

And in her eyes you see nothing
No sign of love behind the tears cried for no one
A love that should have lasted years

Above: 'For No One' was written in the Austrian Alps during the filming of *Help!* March 1965

I T'S A SONG ABOUT REJECTION. THE BREAKUP, OR MARKING THE end of a relationship that didn't work, has always been quite a rich area to explore in a song. Having been through it a few times - as I suppose a lot of people have - it was an emotion I could relate to, and it seemed like a good idea to put into a song because probably a lot of other people could relate to it too. In the song, I'm talking about two people who've broken up, but obviously, as with any writer, it all comes from your own experience, and inevitably you're talking about yourself.

There are two short lines: 'She wakes up / She makes up'. Then you have long lines after the two short ones. 'She takes her time and doesn't feel she has to hurry / She no longer needs you'. Then this: 'And in her eyes you see nothing / No sign of love . . .' It's a horrible moment when you've broken up with someone, and you look at them - this person you used to be in love with, or *thought* you were in love with - and none of that old feeling is there. It's like it just switched off too, and it's not great to be on the receiving end of that.

At the time, you think any love affair could or should or would or will last forever, unless it's a really quick 'wham, bam, thank you ma'am' one-night stand. But when you're going out with someone, when it's your girlfriend and you've been with her for a reasonable amount of time, it's very different. Jane Asher and I were together for around five years, so at the back of my mind I expected to marry her, but as the time got closer, I think I also realised it wasn't right. You can't ever put your finger on it, but when Linda came along, shortly after Jane and I broke up, I just thought, 'Oh, I dunno, maybe this is more right.' And then when Linda and I got to know each other, I felt, 'This is more me; I'm more her.' And there were little things with Jane where we just didn't quite match up. I loved a lot of things about her, and I will

179

always admire a lot of things about her. She's a wonderful woman, but little bits of the jigsaw weren't quite fitting.

If I'm lucky with these songs, they just come out of the blue. It's not so much that I compose them; they arrive. You'll hear a lot of composers saying that. I was meditating this morning, and I was thinking that the whole point of meditation is to try and stop thoughts arriving, because your brain is so active that a word will suggest another word, and that other word will send you off on a trail of thought, and then you've got to work your way back. You're always thinking, even in sleep, so there's always some sort of activity going on, and it's very handy when you're coming to write because you can just plug in to that activity and use it as an opener for a song. What usually comes to you is your first verse, which sets up some sort of rhyming pattern, some sort of rhythmic pattern, and normally your second verse will follow that pattern. It's probably going to have the same melody because you're coming back to the verse again. 'Your day breaks' works on the level of both 'your day begins' and 'your day is broken', and 'She makes up' is working in a couple of ways: putting on makeup and making up after an argument.

I think that's one of the nice things about the English language – that you can take things in multiple ways. I always feel very sorry for people trying to learn the language, when there are so many ambiguous words, but it's a lucky thing for a songwriter. You're writing and it's coming in to you and you're just grabbing the bits you like. And what are you grabbing? It's something magical, and sometimes there's more meaning in it than even you thought there was, but the cosmos wants you to put these words down because they will explain something to someone. Starting with yourself.

① Your day breaks,
    your mind aches
You find that all her words of kindness
linger on when she no longer
                    needs you.

② She wakes up
    she makes up
She takes her time and doesn't feel she
                    has to hurry, she no
                        longer needs
                            you

And in her eyes you see nothing,
    no sign of love behind the tears,
        cried for no-one,
    A love that should have lasted years.

③ You want her, you need her
and yet you don't believe her
when she says ~~her love~~ is dead
    - you thinks she needs you.

SOLO

And in her eyes you see nothing
    no sign of love behind the tears
    Cried for no-one
    A love that should have lasted years

④ You stay home
she goes out
she says that long ago she knew
                    someone
    but now he's gone, she doesn't need him

Middle. And in her eyes you see n....
        etc......

⑤ Your daybreaks
    Your mind aches
There will be times when all the things
                    she said
will fill your head
        You won't forget her.

Middle. Fine.

Paul McCartney
Paul
Paul McCartney
Paul M.

From Me to You

WRITERS   John Lennon and Paul McCartney

ARTIST   The Beatles

RECORDED   Abbey Road Studios, London

RELEASED   Single, 1963

If there's anything that you want
If there's anything I can do
Just call on me and I'll send it along
With love from me to you

I've got everything that you want
Like a heart that's oh so true
Just call on me and I'll send it along
With love from me to you

I got arms that long to hold you
And keep you by my side
I got lips that long to kiss you
And keep you satisfied

If there's anything that you want
If there's anything I can do
Just call on me and I'll send it along
With love from me to you

From me
To you
Just call on me and I'll send it along
With love from me to you

I got arms that long to hold you
And keep you by my side
I got lips that long to kiss you
And keep you satisfied

If there's anything that you want
If there's anything I can do
Just call on me and I'll send it along
With love from me to you
To you
To you
To you

JOHN AND I WERE STILL LIVING AT HOME WHEN THE BEATLES started making records, and it occurred to us we should try and reach out to our fans. We were just trying to get more and more people to like us. It was still a thrill that people liked us and would go to great lengths to show us that, like writing letters to us. Our efforts at reaching out to the fans were summed up in one of our early songs, called 'Thank You Girl', which Chrissie Hynde (later of The Pretenders), heard in Akron, Ohio.

All our early stuff had personal pronouns in the titles. First single 'Love Me Do', second single 'Please Please Me', next one 'From Me to You' - we managed to get two of them in on that one! Then came 'She Loves You' and 'I Want to Hold Your Hand'. It was all very personal, so that we were reaching whoever was listening to the song.

'Love Me Do' was making a very personal plea: 'Love, love me do / You know I love you'. And 'Please Please Me' was our first number one hit in England. So, after that came this song, 'From Me to You'. We used every trick in the book. There was a catchy sing-along intro; you didn't even have to know the words and you could sing along with that. We were fore-grounding the sound of John's harmonica on these songs. It had been on 'Love Me Do', and now it was on 'From Me to You'. The idea of sending a letter was always a big thing in rock and roll. Just think 'Please Mr. Post-man' and 'Return to Sender'.

We were on tour with Roy Orbison at the time we wrote this. We were all on the same tour bus, and it would stop somewhere so that people could go for a cup of tea and a meal, and John and I would have a cup of tea and then go back to the bus and write something. It was a special image to me, at twenty-one, to be walking down the aisle of the bus and there on the back seat of the bus is Roy Orbison, in black with his dark glasses, working on his guitar, writing 'Pretty Woman'. There was a camaraderie, and we were inspiring each other, which is always a lovely thing. He played the music for us, and we said, 'That's a good one, Roy. Great.' And then we'd say, 'Well, listen to this one,' and we'd play him 'From Me to You'. That was kind of a historic moment, as it turned out.

We'd always had basic chords. If you were in C, it would be C, A minor, F and G; those would be the chords, and you didn't really vary them; you didn't need to, because there were so many permutations that you could write lots of songs and they'd all sound quite different, just by shifting the sequence. It's endlessly fascinating. But in this song, when we go to the middle eight - 'I got arms that long to hold you' - that chord moves out of the C, A minor, F, G sequence and into G minor. After writing that, I remember thinking, 'Now we're getting somewhere.'

The Beatles on tour with
Roy Orbison and Gerry and
the Pacemakers. UK, 1963

THE NORTH'S OWN ENTERTAINMENTS PAPER

MERSEY BEAT

Vol. 2. No. 45. APRIL 11—25, 1963 Price THREEPENCE

THE BEATLES STORY
PUBLISHED FOR THE FIRST TIME – SEE PAGE SEVEN

THE BEATLES: GEORGE HARRISON, JOHN LENNON, RINGO STARR, PAUL McCARTNEY. (Photo: Peter Kaye)

INSIDE: LEE CURTIS ★ GERRY AND THE PACEMAKERS

ONLOOKER ★ DANCE DATE ★ MERSEY ROUNDABOUT

★ WIN THE BEATLES L.P. COMPETITION ★

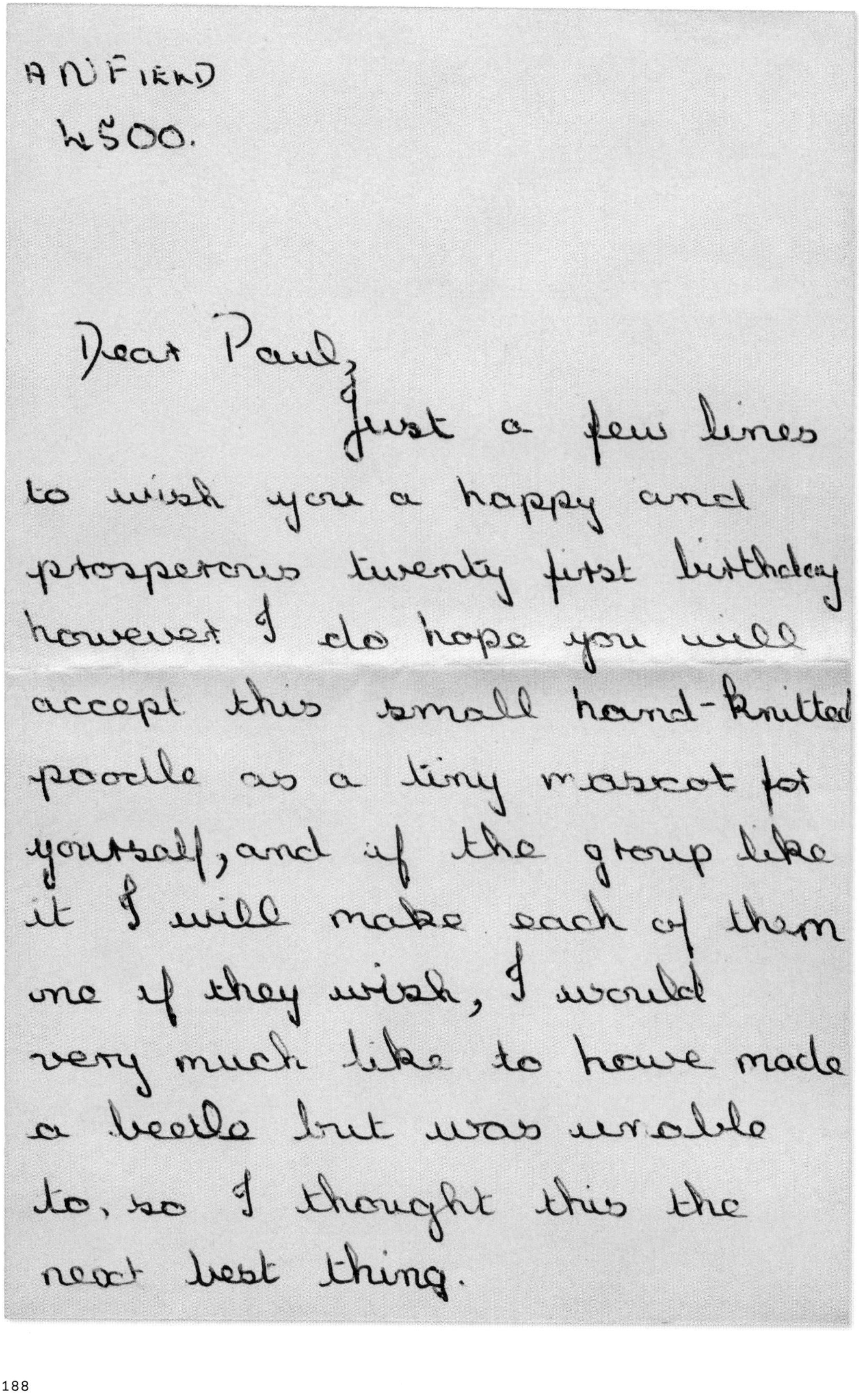

ANFIELD
4500.

Dear Paul,
                Just a few lines
to wish you a happy and
prosperous twenty first birthday
however I do hope you will
accept this small hand-knitted
poodle as a tiny mascot for
yourself, and if the group like
it I will make each of them
one if they wish, I would
very much like to have made
a beetle but was unable
to, so I thought this the
next best thing.

Fan mail, 1963

I sincerely hope you had
a wonderful time tonight
your 21st birthday. Hoping
you will let me know if
you received same O.K and
if you liked it, I hope so
very much

I Remain
Yours sincerely
Marjorie

x x x x x x x x x

x x x x x x x x

x x x x x x.
(21).

G

Get Back

WRITERS   Paul McCartney and John Lennon
ARTIST   The Beatles
RECORDED   Apple Studio, London
RELEASED   Single, 1969
Let It Be, 1970

Jo Jo was a man who thought he was a loner
But he knew it couldn't last
Jo Jo left his home in Tucson, Arizona
For some California grass

Get back
Get back
Get back to where you once belonged
Get back
Get back
Get back to where you once belonged
Get back, Jo Jo

Go home

Get back
Get back
Get back to where you once belonged
Get back
Get back
Get back to where you once belonged
Get back, Jo

Sweet Loretta Martin thought she was a woman
But she was another man
All the girls around her say she's got it coming
But she gets it while she can

Get back
Get back
Get back to where you once belonged
Get back
Get back
Get back to where you once belonged
Get back, Loretta

Get back
Get back
Get back to where you once belonged
Get back
Get back
Get back to where you once belonged

Get back, Loretta
Your mommy's waiting for you
Wearing her high-heel shoes
And a low-neck sweater
Get back home, Loretta

Get back
Get back
Get back to where you once belonged

THE THING ABOUT THE BEATLES WAS, WE WERE A DAMN GOOD little band. The four of us just knew how to fall in with each other and play, and that was our real strength. That made it all the more sorrowful to think that our breaking up was almost inevitable.

So there's a wistful aspect to 'Get Back'. The idea that you should get back to your roots, that The Beatles should get back to how we were in Liverpool. And the roots are embodied in the style of the song, which is straight-up rock and roll. Because that was definitely what I thought we should do when we broke up - that we should 'get back to where we once belonged' and become a little band again. We should just play and do the occasional little gig.

The others laughed at that - quite understandably - because by then it was not really a practical solution. John had just met Yoko, and he clearly needed to escape to a new place, whereas I was saying we should escape to an old place. Reviving the old Beatles just wasn't on the cards. It was too late to be recommending that we not forget who we were and where we once were from. If my dream at the time really was to get back to where we once belonged, John's dream was to go beyond where we once belonged, to go somewhere we didn't yet belong.

I've already mentioned how in September 1969 we were in a meeting and talking about future plans, and John said, 'Well, I'm not doing it. I'm leaving. Bye.' In the ensuing moments, he was giggling and saying how this felt really thrilling, like telling someone you're going to divorce them and then laughing. At the time, obviously, that was wildly hurtful. Talk about a knockout blow. You're lying on the canvas, and he's giggling and telling you how good it feels to have just knocked you out.

It took a while, but I suppose I eventually got with the programme. This was my best mate from my youth, the collaborator with whom I'd done some of the best work of the twentieth century (he said, modestly). If he fell in love with this woman, what did that have to do with me? Not only did I have to let him do it, but I had to admire him for doing it. That was the position I eventually reached. There was nothing else I could do but be cool with it.

Pages 194–195: The Beatles and Yoko Ono. Twickenham Studios, London, 1969

Getting Closer

WRITER	Paul McCartney
ARTIST	Wings
RECORDED	Abbey Road Studios, London
RELEASED	*Back to the Egg,* 1979
	Single, 1979

Say you don't love him
My salamander
Why do you need him
Oh no don't answer
Oh no

I'm getting closer
I'm getting closer to your heart

Keeping ahead of the rain on the road
Watching my windscreen wipers
Radio playing me a danceable ode
Cattle beware of snipers

When will you see me
My salamander
Now don't try to tell me
Oh no don't answer
Oh no

I'm getting closer
I'm getting closer to your heart

Hitting the chisel and making a joint
Gluing my fingers together
Radio play me a song with a point
Sailor beware of weather

I'm getting closer
My salamander
Well when will we be there
Oh no don't answer
Oh no

I'm getting closer
I'm getting closer to your heart

Closer, closer

L YMPNE CASTLE IS A GRAND OLD BUILDING IN KENT, IN THE SOUTH-
east of England. It was owned by two rather aristocratic people – Harry
and Deirdre Margary. They were very posh. We would write and record,
and then they'd invite me in for a drink in the evening, and I'd go and have a
little whisky before I went home. I remember working on this song there,
even though we ended up finishing and recording it at Abbey Road.

We recorded a whole bunch of stuff at Lympne Castle. Why? I don't know.
I suspect because it was nearish to where we lived, on the way to Folkestone
on the south coast. We took a mobile truck there, and we more or less went
in and recorded the album *Back to the Egg*, so you'd get these kinds of slightly
oddball things happening and oddball songs coming out. I'm a bit more pur-
poseful these days than I was then. I was probably smoking a little too much
wacky baccy at the time.

One of the things about Wings was this freedom to not make sense. Sometimes I just liked the words and I wasn't bothered about making sense. 'Say
you don't love him' – that's not from any real experience, it's not like I was
being jilted or cuckolded or anything; it was a device to get me into the song.
'I'm getting closer to your heart.' I'm also arriving, driving towards where
you are. 'Keeping ahead of the rain on the road / Watching my windscreen
wipers / Radio playing me a danceable ode'. 'Hitting the chisel and making a
joint' . . . You knew your audience would be amused by those little references,
because rolling joints was still a little bit underground at that time.

Sometimes you just like a word, so you try and find an excuse to put it in.
I remember Linda telling me a story about how when she was a kid, she was
a fan of nature, just like I was, and she would look under stones to find a liz-
ard or a newt, which she would call a 'salamander'. I loved the idea that in

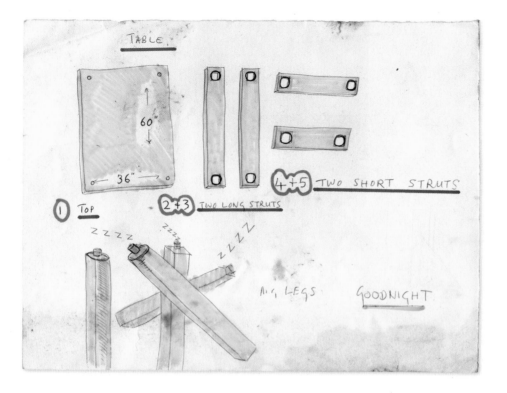

her world it was 'salamander' – much more exotic. Salamanders have a mythical aspect, born in fire, so that's how the salamander made its way in.

A song like this might be thought of as a collage. I put things together that I'd seen or heard, and it had been around for a few years before we recorded it. I seem to remember there being a sign along the road somewhere: 'Beware Cattle'. And there might have been bullet holes in the signs, because guys sniped at them for target practice, so I thought, 'Cattle beware . . . Gluing my fingers together / Radio play me a song with a point.' You know, not everything needs to have a point. A song is kind of a construction job, so I've done my usual thing of just sort of assembling it all and taking it somewhere.

It's no accident that one of my hobbies at school was woodworking. When we lived in Scotland, I made a table with glue only, no nails. It was very basic; I drew it and I bought the wood. I would sit at the kitchen table when the kids were playing or getting ready for bed, and I would be chiselling, making these little dovetail joints. I'd finish each piece, a leg or a corner, and eventually I had a pile of them. One day I thought, 'I've actually got to dare to put this together with glue.' I got my Evo-Stik woodworking glue, put it all together, and it all worked except the last piece, which didn't seem to fit. It was the cross-brace underneath, so I turned it upside down and it all fitted together. The table's still standing.

Right: Wings photo shoot. Lympne Castle, Kent, 1978

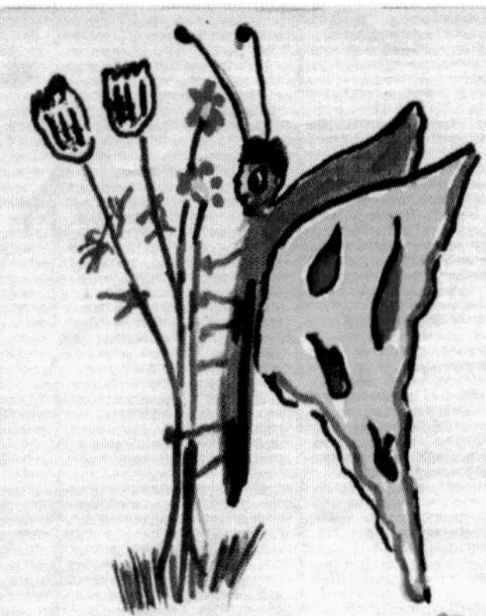

CAMPBELTOWN
x∞ SCOTLAND ∞x

① I've been sent to tell you...

. . . .

CHORUS. he didn't mean it ...

② . . . . . . (descant))/
. . . . guitars etc !..

CHORUS he didn't mean it .. A ...

tempo up. A . . . .

(I'm getting closer)

Say you don't love him
my salamander
do you still need him? ah no dont answer
I'm getting closer .. to your heart.

Instrumental verse
oh no don't answer, my salamander
oh no . . . .

I'm getting closer

E — Waterspout drums.

A D E
La BAMBA
up to — E —

1 st verse
love comes in
2nd verse —
— Only love —
3rd verse
4th verse.
love comes in — etc. (4 times)

we're open tonight
— TEMPO UP —Emin)
well you can
Dress me up as a
robber —
OPEN TONIGHT ORCHESTRA
ROCKESTRA
OPEN TONITE
VACAS

GETTING CLOSER

(1) I'M GETTING CLOSER
~~TRAMPLE THE RUSHES~~

MY SALAMANDER
WHEN WILL WE BE THERE
~~AH~~ NO DON'T ANSWER OH NO

I'm getting closer .... to your heart

(2) THEY
DO ~~THEY~~ TAKE PRISONERS
MY ~~SALAMANDER~~ ? SALAMANDER
WHEN WILL THEY ~~YOU~~ FREE ME ?
~~AH~~ NO DON'T ANSWER OH NO

I'm getting closer ... to your heart.

(3) CRASH THROUGH THE MOUNTAINS
TEAR THEM ASUNDER
HOW WILL IT BE THERE ?
WHY DO WE WONDER ?   OH — OH

I'm getting closer .... to your heart

Ghosts of the Past Left Behind

WRITERS   Paul McCartney and Carl Davis
ARTIST   Royal Liverpool Philharmonic Orchestra
RECORDED   Liverpool Cathedral
RELEASED   *Paul McCartney's Liverpool Oratorio*, 1991

BOYS
Ghosts of the past left behind

MEN'S CHORUS (GHOSTS)
You're sleeping
Amongst us
We're in your dream

NURSE
You're dreaming
Try to rest, my child

MEN'S CHORUS (GHOSTS)
You called us
We heard you
And we are here

NURSE
To save your child
You must be still

MEN'S CHORUS (GHOSTS)
We're ready
To listen
To what you ask

NURSE
Go to sleep

WOMEN'S CHORUS (GHOSTS)
You're crossing
The water
The tide is strong

MARY DEE
No

WOMEN'S CHORUS (GHOSTS)
Your child is
Drawn to us
Into our throng

SHANTY
No

FULL CHORUS (GHOSTS)
This child is
Most welcome
Soon one of us

MARY DEE
No I tell you
You'll never get through
I'll never let you
No one is stealing this child
I'm not afraid of
Ghosts that the past left behind

SHANTY
Let her recover
Then let me love her
Until we run out of time
And in the future
I will promise to be the man
She had in mind

NURSE
Be still
Be calm
Your child is safe

IT WAS IN 1991 THAT WE PERFORMED THE *LIVERPOOL ORATORIO* AT Liverpool Cathedral, one of the largest in Europe. It was a bittersweet occasion because it was also at Liverpool Cathedral that, as a child, I had failed an audition as a chorister.

It's strange that I still felt that sting, since it had been nearly forty years, but everyone I'm sure can recall that disappointment from a setback in childhood that never quite disappears. The idea then was that if you became a chorister, you got free books as a prize, and my parents were keen for me to have free books. But I failed the audition. The guy may have liked some other boys more than me. Who knows what he was looking for? But the sad reality was that I didn't live up to his expectations.

Even though I didn't pass muster as a chorister, I've always liked the architecture of big cathedrals, churches, sacred spaces of any kind, so I go into them wherever I can. Liverpool Cathedral was designed by Sir Giles Gilbert Scott, who also did the iconic red telephone box. He designed Battersea and Bankside power stations; the latter is now Tate Modern. There are a couple of churches in New York, like St Patrick's or St Thomas, that I don't pass without going in. They have this quiet majesty, which is funny, considering that they're situated in the middle of a very busy city.

My interest in classical music was never that great, though I did acquire a bit of a collection in the 1960s. I had an uncle, called Jack Ollie, who would come down to stay with us in London. He was a working-class Liverpool guy, but he had a cultural side to him. I had a big vinyl collection, and I would go out to work at the studio or what have you, and he would stay at our house with his wife and go through all the records. He loved *Scheherazade* by Rimsky-Korsakov which he used to call 'Sherazio'. 'I love that Sherazio, Paul.' 'Yeah, good.'

When, decades later, I was invited to write something for the Royal Liverpool Philharmonic for their 150th anniversary, I thought, 'Yeah, great!' as I always do. I worked with Carl Davis on the arrangement. He had written the scores for films like *The French Lieutenant's Woman* and *Scandal*, and right back at the start of his career he did music for the David Frost satirical TV show *That Was the Week That Was*, which had an incredible set of writers, like John Cleese, Peter Cook, Dennis Potter – all also at the start of their careers. So, I would drive up to Carl's house in Barnes, near Richmond upon Thames. We'd spend three hours at his piano. I did that for weeks and weeks and weeks while we were writing it.

I loved the drives out to these houses for writing sessions – to Carl Davis for this or, back in the sixties, over to John Lennon, or indeed to George Martin. I found it actually quite heartwarming to go up to Carl's to work. For a project as long as this, I like the idea of going to what seems to me a neutral space. I'm going to work, so I'm leaving home – 'See you darling, I'll be in later.' I still do that; my recording studio is twenty minutes away from where I live. People say, 'Why don't you get a home studio, Paul?' And I say, 'Well, I did that once and it was terrible, because you're never out of the studio. You've no life.' It's nice to have that separation between 'the office' and home.

Sometimes, if I got to Carl's a bit early, I would go to the local pub. One day I was chatting with this Irish guy at the bar, and I'm having only a little half beer or something like that (you don't want to get wasted), and the subject came up. He asked, 'What are you doing? What are you up to?' And I replied, 'Well, I'm writing a classical piece for the Liverpool Philharmonic.' He said, 'God, don't you find that daunting?'

And I'll tell you the truth, it had not occurred to me that it was daunting.

With Carl Davis.
Liverpool, 1991

I said, 'No, I don't think so; I'm having fun with it.' But that often happens with me. I'll bite off something and I'll be halfway through chewing it and enjoying it, when someone will say, 'Do you know how to do this?' I think, 'Oh no, I'd forgotten about that aspect. You have to know how to do things in order to do them?'

Anyway, at Carl's house I'd just give him an idea or sing a tune to him or pick a key, and we would just make it up as we went along. It was a fabulous exercise for me because as I had my ideas, he wrote them down. Carl is a few years older than me, I think he was in his mid-fifties at this point, and his background was totally different to mine. He'd grown up in New York and gone to university to study composition, so he knew all this musical theory that I hadn't come across before, and it was a very interesting experience. He would have reams of manuscript paper on the piano, and he'd say, 'Oh, wait a minute, wait a minute, wait a minute. Let me get that. Wait . . .' He would transcribe it, and to make sure it was correct I'd ask him to play it back. Then I'd say, 'Great. Okay, moving on.'

The men's chorus in the Royal Liverpool Philharmonic Choir, I would discover, was this bunch of Liverpool guys, and when there was a break you'd get talking to them and you'd say, 'What do you do?' They'd say things like, 'I'm a plumber. I've got a little plumbing business, but I like singing.' Or 'I'm a gynaecologist,' and so on. I love that about choirs, that they're nearly always composed of people from different walks of life. And then they come together as one because of their love of music. They become one walk of life: the choir. I find that fascinating.

The soloists were extraordinary. Again, I didn't know what I was doing, so I just said, 'Can we get so-and-so? Can we get Kiri Te Kanawa to sing the soprano?' Even though she was then one of the greatest opera stars in the world, we got her, so this was a great cast. The kids were also great, and there was a part for a boy soloist, and we found a boy who could do it really well, so he was flown in from London.

I found it all very exciting, not at all daunting. The only time I thought, 'This is daunting,' was while talking about it on radio, when they would throw little curve balls at me. I remember a rather posh BBC Radio 4 programme, and there was a posh lady, a jolly, middle-aged lady, who said, 'Well, an "oratorio"?' I said, 'Yeah, I asked Carl, "Is this like a symphony or a concerto? What is it we're writing? What do you call it?" And Carl said, "Well, the form is that of an 'oratorio'." And I said, "Great! Nice word. We'll call it the 'Liverpool Oratorio'."'

Then she said, 'Well, why Carl Davis?' And I said, 'He's very good, isn't he?' 'Yes,' she replied, 'but there are many other conductors who are considered better than him.' So, suddenly, with one blow, I was daunted.

The critics were more daunting than actually writing it was. And you know, they just had a good sharpen of their pencils and scratched me off their list. But then I got a letter from Neil Kinnock, the leader of the Labour Party at that time, who wrote, 'Don't worry Paul, they'll always say that. They're bound to say it's no good, but it's damn good, and I love it.'

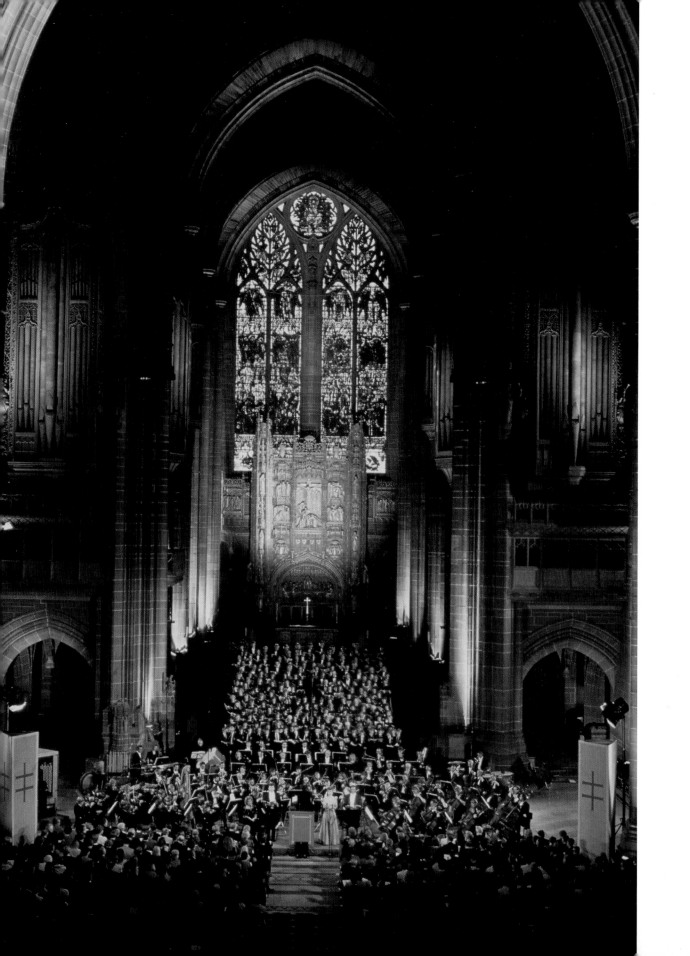

Left: Performance of *Liverpool Oratorio*. Liverpool Cathedral, June 1991

Above: With Dame Kiri Te Kanawa, Jerry Hadley, Carl Davis, Sally Burgess and Sir Willard White

Right: With Dame Kiri Te Kanawa and Carl Davis

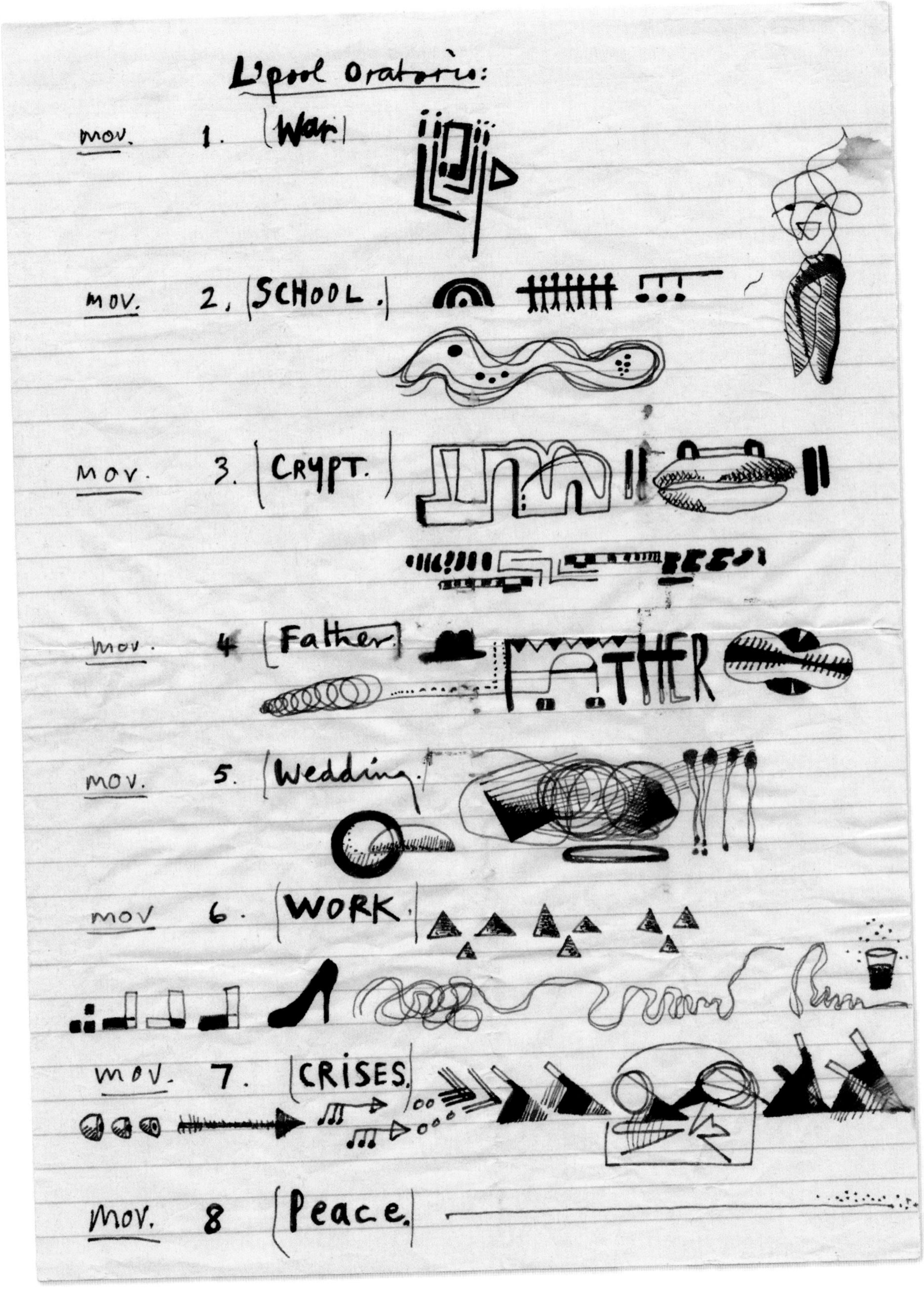

L'pool Oratorio:

mov. 1. [War]

mov. 2. [SCHOOL.]

mov. 3. [CRYPT.]

mov. 4 [Father]

mov. 5. [Wedding.]

mov. 6. [WORK.]

mov. 7. [CRISES.]

mov. 8 [Peace.]

She sleeps the GHOSTS
re'appear. The nurse is
Comforting...

The GHOSTS
are ready to
take the
child as it
Crosses into "their throng."
SHE cries "NO!"....
HE too, and promises to be
the man she had in mind.

The nurse says the child is safe.
and SHE sings a song of HOPE
              WE MUST
and FAITH. Save the child!
HE joins in. All join them..
        They are together...

Girls' School

WRITER   Paul McCartney
ARTIST   Wings
RECORDED   Abbey Road Studios, London
RELEASED   'Mull of Kintyre'/'Girls' School' double A-side single, 1977

Sleepyhead kid sister
Lying on the floor
Eighteen years and younger, boy
Well she knows what she's waiting for

Yuki's a cool school mistress
She's an Oriental princess
She shows films in the classroom, boy
They put the paper on the windows

Ah what can the sisters do?
Ah girls' school

Head nurse is Sister Scala
Now she's a Spanish doll
She runs a full-body outcall massage parlour
From the teachers' hall

Ah what can the sisters do?
Ah girls' school

Well now Roxanne's a woman trainer
She puts the kids to bed
She gives them pills in a paper cup
And she knocks them on the head

Ah what can the sisters do?
Ah girls' school

She shows the films in the classroom, boy
Where they put the paper on the windows yeah

Ah what can the sisters do?
Ah girls' school

SOMETIMES, WHEN YOU LOOK BACK, IT HELPS TO PUT CERTAIN lyrics into context. The Beatles had been initiated into sex thanks to our stay in Hamburg, spending time on the Reeperbahn. We were professional musicians hanging out with professional dancers. So, we were just members of the entertainment business getting together for what you might call social reasons.

But America was like going to a different planet. When we went over there, the girls were throwing themselves at us. As teenagers, we'd had a pretty tough time getting girls, so this was new, and totally different. And then, of course, when the pill came along, all hell broke loose. Or maybe heaven.

The sexual revolution, when you think of it, was part of our revolt against our parents' generation, which was perhaps a little more prudish. It certainly changed a lot for our generation, and we Beatles got to experience more of it maybe than others. But I'm glad to have had that slightly outrageous part of my life, some of which filtered into the lyrics. By the time this song was written, of course, things were much more settled, and I had a family and was focused on other things. But, as with every revolution, some people will push things further than others. And the sexual revolution didn't stop in the sixties; throughout the seventies there continued to be an atmosphere of wanting to push or break the sexual boundaries. The hangover from the free love, 'all you need is love' period is that sometimes things got a little seedy, and porn became pretty widespread. On the flip side, there was also the tongue-in-cheek, seaside postcard type of things like the *Carry On* films and *The Benny Hill Show*. So, all of these elements found their way into this song.

If you're in a rock and roll group, you're always trying to write songs that are going to work live. I think this one came from seeing an ad for a porn film called *Girl School*. It might even have said something like (I'm trying to recall from forty years ago), 'See Yuki and so-and-so romp to your delight'. So I thought, 'Right, I'm going to imagine this school into a song.' I thought, 'It's a girls' school, like St Trinian's - which had been a comic book and a series of films set in an all-girls school when I was growing up. But now it would be a kind of grown-up St Trinian's. I just started to imagine all the characters and what they were all up to, and it was all a little bit racy.

So here we are: 'Sleepyhead kid sister / Lying on the floor / Eighteen years and younger, boy / Well she knows what she's waiting for'. The MeToo movement is really what she was waiting for, but no one knew this at the time. 'She's an Oriental princess / She shows films in the classroom, boy / They put paper on the windows' and 'Head nurse is Sister Scala' - these might have actually been from the film, or I might have seen them in the ad. The song is a series of vignettes, all tied together. That's something I like to do across a lot of my lyrics. If you think about it, the vignette is really my stock-in-trade.

A lot of the guitar bands who came along in the eighties - the glam metal bands - took this kind of risqué lyric and ran with it. But for us, it was really just a one-off reflection of what was happening at the time.

I'm not sure how I knew about the idea of a full-body outcall massage parlour. Normally, one just gets a massage, but some massage parlours offered so-called happy endings. So, I used to do a bit on stage because I had a keyboard that sounded like massage music. I'd play this instrument in sound check for a bit of fun and to loosen everyone up. I'd say, 'It's time for your massage. Please lie facedown. Would you rather have oil or cream?'

And there were a few massage stories that I used to tell in concert, because I've had some pretty wild massages, and when I say 'wild' I mean funny wild, not sexual. There was one in Japan where the girl came in and said, 'Please lie on floor,' so I lay on the floor, and she was giving me a massage. I started relaxing, but then suddenly she started to sing, 'Yesterday, all my troubles seemed so far away.' I'm going, 'Oh shit, where do I put myself now. Can't I escape this anywhere?' Thank God she didn't know the middle eight.

And then there was one in New Orleans, totally different, with a big guy, quite rotund, and he said, 'Just sit up on the table.' Once I'd complied - and how could you not - he said, 'Now imagine your leg is hollow.' And I'm thinking, 'Okay.' And then he said, 'Imagine your neck is long and made of bronze,' and I'm thinking, 'Where is this going?' And he asked, 'How do you feel?' and I said, 'I'm feeling like a bronze-necked giraffe,' which in hindsight is a great song title.

The song is a series of vignettes, all tied together. That's something I like to do across a lot of my lyrics. If you think about it, the vignette is really my stock-in-trade.

MULL OF KINTYRE

WINGS DOUBLE A

GIRLS SCHOOL

GIRLS SCHOOL

(1) Sleepy Sue/Roxanne the woman trainer
Puts the kids to bed
She gives them thrills in a paper cup
And she knocks them on the head

(2) Yukis the cool school mistress
— (she's an) oriental princess
She shows films in the classroom
Happy put paper over the windows (windess!) ✓
Ah oo what can the (sisters) do?
— ah oo — girls school

(3) Head nurse is Sister Scala
She's a Spanish doll
She runs a full body out call
massage parlour from the teachers hall
(C) Sleepy heads the kid sister
lying on the floor
18 years and younger
Dreaming at night with the boys
Knows what she's waiting for.

GTR. TUNING.   (E A⁺ E B E E)

Give Ireland Back to the Irish

WRITERS	Paul McCartney and Linda McCartney
ARTIST	Paul McCartney and Wings
RECORDED	Abbey Road Studios, London
RELEASED	Single, 1972

Give Ireland back to the Irish
Don't make them have to take it away
Give Ireland back to the Irish
Make Ireland Irish today

Great Britain, you are tremendous
And nobody knows like me
But really what are you doing
In the land across the sea?

Tell me how would you like it
If on your way to work
You were stopped by Irish soldiers?
Would you lie down, do nothing?
Would you give in or go berserk?

Give Ireland back to the Irish
Don't make them have to take it away
Give Ireland back to the Irish
Make Ireland Irish today

Great Britain and all the people
Say that people must be free
And meanwhile back in Ireland
There's a man who looks like me

And he dreams of God and country
And he's feeling really bad
And he's sitting in a prison
Say should he lie down, do nothing?
Should he give in or go mad?

Give Ireland back to the Irish
Don't make them have to take it away
Give Ireland back to the Irish
Make Ireland Irish today

BANNED EVERYWHERE

New
McCartney
single

MY MOTHER'S FATHER, OWEN MOHAN, WAS FROM TULLYNAM-alra in County Monaghan. At some point he moved to Liverpool, where he worked as a coalman. The family was Catholic. I'm not quite sure precisely where my paternal grandfather was born in Ireland, but I do know his family were Protestants. My brother and I were baptised Roman Catholic at the insistence of my mother, but we were raised nondenominationally. So, our household represented in microcosm the Irish political and religious divide.

On 30 January 1972 British soldiers opened fire on a peaceful protest in Derry, as anyone who was alive in Great Britain can recall. Twenty-eight unarmed civilians were shot, and fourteen people died as a result of their wounds. This shocking event became known as Bloody Sunday. As it happened, I was in New York that day, having met with John the day before. It was a meeting at which we more or less agreed to stop sniping at each other.

It was deeply troubling to me to see footage of a perfectly peaceful demonstration that had gone wrong. It looked as if our army boys had acted indiscriminately and fired on innocent people. There was immediately a cover-up, claiming that the protesters weren't innocent but had rifles. But it seemed to me a reasonable demonstration, the kind that had been happening in Black communities throughout recent history. So, I was shocked by the idea that our soldiers had perpetrated this horror because up till that point, I had thought our boys were all great. Then I imagined Irish soldiers on the streets of Liverpool when I was growing up, telling me I couldn't go here or I couldn't go there – 'Tell me how would you like it / If on your way to work / You were stopped by Irish soldiers?' The idea of armed soldiers stopping me from going down the street seemed so wrong to me that, even though I wasn't a writer of protest songs, I just felt I had to say something about this.

We made the record, and I sent it over to EMI. I immediately got a phone call from Sir Joseph Lockwood, the head of EMI, with whom I always got on well; he was a very clever and charming man, and I liked him a lot. He said we couldn't put this record out, because of the delicacy of the Irish situation. I told him this particular event had affected me very deeply, and I felt I must respond to it. He asked me to reconsider. So, I gave it a couple of days and rang back and said I had to put it out. He said the record would be banned by the BBC, and no good would come of it for me. I told him I didn't care. This was a big enough event in my history - in my country's history - for me to take some kind of a stand. So we put it out, and Sir Joe was right. It was banned. But it was also number one in Ireland and in Spain, though not in the US.

Henry McCullough was a member of Wings at the time, and he got a bit of flak because he was a Northern Ireland boy. Henry was Protestant, so some people were a bit upset by his involvement in this song. It really was that bad at the time. Then there were others who perceived the song as a rallying cry for the IRA. It certainly wasn't written to be one. For better or worse, this was a moment where I had a sense that art could, and should, respond to a situation. Unfortunately, it's a situation that still hasn't quite been resolved - and perhaps never will.

He said the record would be banned by the BBC, and no good would come of it for me. I told him I didn't care. This was a big enough event in my history - in my country's history - for me to take some kind of a stand. So we put it out, and Sir Joe was right. It was banned. But it was also number one in Ireland and in Spain, though not in the US.

Vinyl label artwork
mock-ups, 1972

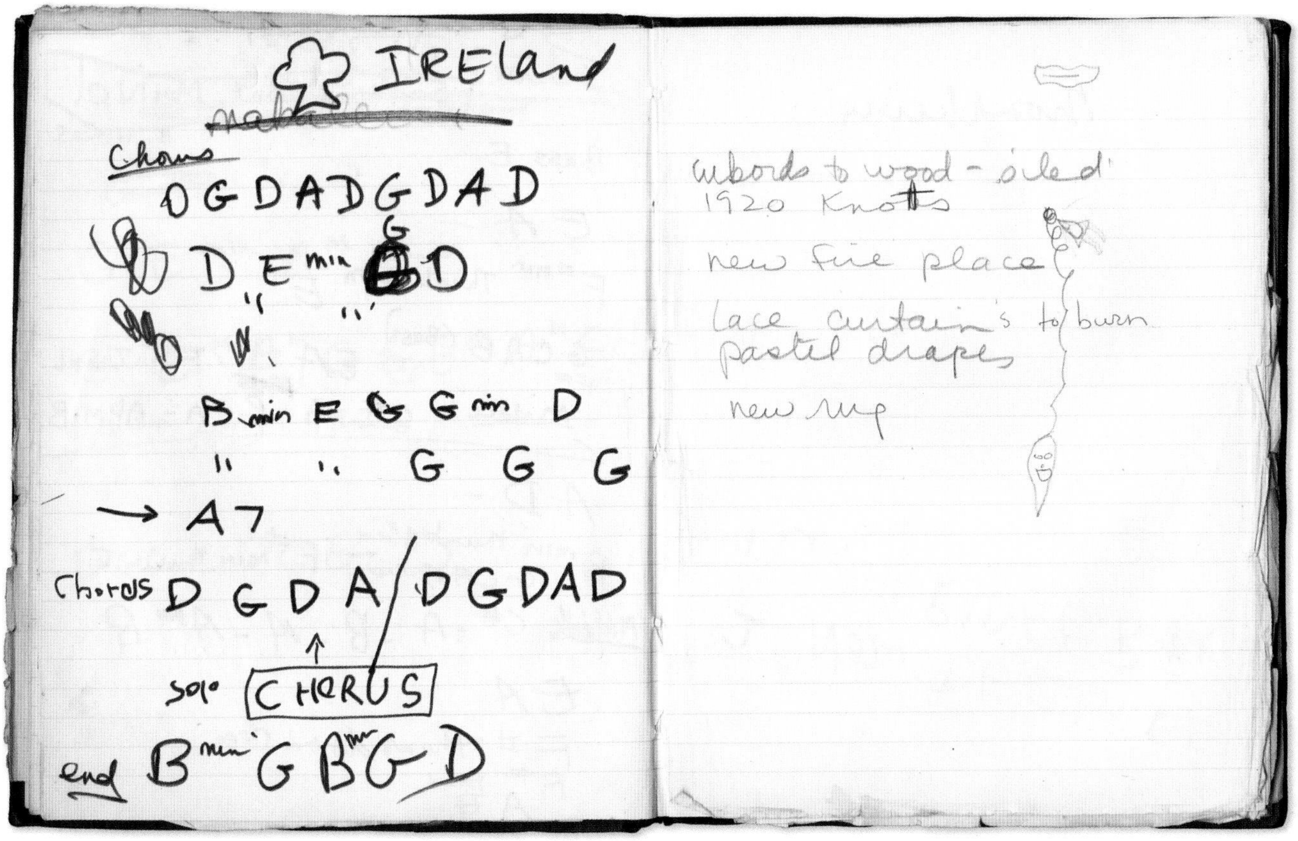

IRELAND

Chorus

D G D A D G D A D

D E min G G D

B min E G G min D
G G G

→ A7

Chorus D G D A / D G D A D

solo CHORUS

end B min G B min G D

w/words to wood – oiled
1920 Knots

new fire place

Lace curtain's to burn
pastel drapes

new rug

Above: Linda's handwritten chords for 'Give Ireland Back to the Irish', circa 1972

Left: With Henry McCullough. Wings *UK Tour*, 1973

Golden Earth Girl

WRITER   Paul McCartney
ARTIST   Paul McCartney
RECORDED   Hog Hill Mill, Sussex
RELEASED   *Off the Ground*, 1993

Golden earth girl, female animal
Sings to the wind, resting at sunset
In a mossy nest
Sensing moonlight in the air
Moonlight in the air

Good clear water, friend of wilderness
Sees in the pool her own reflection
In another world
Someone over there is counting

Fish in a sunbeam
In eggshell seas
Fish in a sunbeam
Eggshell finish

Nature's lover climbs the primrose hill
Smiles at the sky, watching the sunset
From a mossy nest
As she falls asleep she's counting

Fish in a sunbeam
In eggshell seas
Fish in a sunbeam
Eggshell finish

THOUGH THIS SONG IS PRIMARILY AN ODE TO LINDA, WHO REALLY was a 'golden earth girl', and my wife of twenty-four years by the time this was released, it also gives a little bit of a nod towards John and Yoko. Yoko often said things like, 'Look at that cloud,' or used words connected with nature. I'd always liked that about her work, and then John picked up on it later with his surreal way of swapping things around.

I'd known Yoko since she'd arrived in London in the mid-sixties. In fact, I met her before John met her. I remember that she arrived at my house and said, 'We're collecting manuscripts for John Cage's birthday. Do you have a manuscript we can have?' I said, 'We don't really have manuscripts. We have sort of words on paper, a piece of paper with lyrics on it.' She said, 'Yeah, well, that'd be good.' I told her I really hadn't got anything like that myself, but I said John might. And so I directed her to him. I'm not even sure whether she ever picked up on that invitation, because the next thing I heard, she was having an exhibition at a little gallery that some friends and I had helped set up. It was called the Indica Gallery and was in the basement of their bookstore in Mason's Yard, London. John went to the exhibition, and I think that was when he and Yoko met, towards the end of 1966. He climbed up a ladder to see what she'd written on the ceiling, and got close enough to it to read it, and it said, 'Yes.' So he thought, 'That's a sign; this is it,' and they fell madly in love.

Once they were an item, there was the whole Beatles recording thing, where she would be there too. I think this started at the beginning of the 'White Album' sessions - so, around the end of spring in 1968. And at first we all - all of us except John - found it pretty intrusive, but we went along with it and worked around her. And eventually I came to the realisation that, look, if John loves her, we've just got to let it be, and we've got to support this relationship. That was basically my feeling.

Then, a year or two later, The Beatles broke up, and it was a bad period, a real low point, where everyone was taking potshots at everyone. And I felt that John and Yoko were particularly good in the potshot department, saying things in interviews, or comments that would make their way to you. They would say not always very pleasant things, and looking back on it, I sort of think, 'Why? You're annoyed, so say something unpleasant?'

Over time, the situation eased off and my relationship with John got better, and I used to see him in New York or speak to him on the phone. Then in 1975 he and Yoko had a baby boy, Sean, so we had even more in common, and we'd often talk about being parents. So that was all good, until he was killed. And of course, from then on really, I was very sympathetic to Yoko. I'd lost my friend, but she'd lost her husband and the father of her child.

In his lyrics, John would include allusions to Yoko and nature, like using 'ocean child' in the song 'Julia', which, I understand, is how her name translates into English, and I'm using similar sort of imagery here for Linda – 'Good clear water, friend of wilderness'. Funnily enough, John wrote a song for the 'White Album', called 'Child of Nature', that didn't end up on the record, and he rewrote it as 'Jealous Guy'. As I've said, Linda really helped me find another side of myself. If anyone deserves the title 'Child of Nature', it's her.

Golden earth girl, female animal
Sings to the wind, resting at sunset
In a mossy nest

In his lyrics, John would include allusions to Yoko and nature, like using 'ocean child' in the song 'Julia', which, I understand, is how her name translates into English, and I'm using similar sort of imagery here for Linda – 'Good clear water, friend of wilderness'.

Golden Slumbers

WRITERS   Paul McCartney and John Lennon
ARTIST   The Beatles
RECORDED   Abbey Road Studios, London
RELEASED   *Abbey Road*, 1969

Once there was a way to get back homeward
Once there was a way to get back home
Sleep, pretty darling, do not cry
And I will sing a lullaby

Golden slumbers fill your eyes
Smiles awake you when you rise
Sleep, pretty darling, do not cry
And I will sing a lullaby

Above: Auntie Jin, Angela, Heather, dad Jim and Linda. Heswall, 1968

'**G**OLDEN SLUMBERS', AS COMPARATIVELY FEW PEOPLE KNOW, IS an old Victorian song based on a poem by the Elizabethan drama- tist Thomas Dekker. I happened to find the words on a piece of piano sheet music when I was in Liverpool. My dad had married again, to a woman who had a daughter; and my stepsister Ruth, or maybe her mother, played a bit of piano. Even then, I always looked inside the piano seat because a lot of people have their sheet music in there. That's where I first discov- ered 'Golden Slumbers'.

The original song was written before records were easily available, and people had to make their own entertainment. You can imagine a Victorian parlour with the pretty young girl standing up to sing as the handsome young man accompanies her. Or sometimes it was the other way round. That tradition morphed into many houses having a piano, and there were incredibly successful sheet music songs, like Irving Berlin's 'Alexander's Ragtime Band', that sold in the millions. For a long time, the way people heard new songs was through sheet music around the family piano.

My dad Jim was our family pianist, and funnily enough, he got our upright piano from Harry Epstein's North End Music Store - also known as NEMS - in Everton. Harry's son grew up to be Brian, The Beatles' manager. That upright piano lived in our front parlour in Forthlin Road and was where I wrote things like 'When I'm Sixty-Four'. Dad wouldn't teach me the piano, though; he wanted me to take lessons. He didn't think he was good enough and, because my parents had aspirations for us, he wanted me to learn the 'real stuff'. I took a few lessons from time to time but ended up being pretty much self-taught, just like him. I found lessons to be too restricting and boring. It was much more interesting to make up songs than to practise scales.

Dad only ever wrote one song – to my knowledge – called 'Walking in the Park with Eloise'. We recorded it with Wings in Nashville in the seventies so that I could play it to him, and we put it out as a single under the name The Country Hams. I had friends like Chet Atkins and Floyd Cramer play on it. So, I told him about it afterwards: 'Dad, you know that song you wrote?' And he said, 'I didn't write a song, son.' So I said, 'But, you did. You know, "Walking in the Park with Eloise"?' And he said, 'No, I didn't write it. I made it up.'

Music was a big thing in our house. Dad's friend at the cotton exchange, Freddie Rimmer, was the pianist for his family. So there was always someone around who could play the piano, and it was a wonderful thing because it meant people broke into song a lot, like in musicals. When records came in after the first war, when my dad was young, that changed how people listened to music. Except whenever there was a gathering, or a New Year's Eve 'do' – the Liverpool word for a get-together – at the McCartney home. That's when the booze started flowing and the piano was wheeled out. Everyone would be gathered around it, and the children would be running around the house.

I remember as a boy that that was always a very wonderful thing because the piano would be banging out these old songs that everyone knew, particularly the aunties; the aunties had them down and knew all the verses. And the camaraderie of people all standing around in a room, getting drunk and singing these songs, was something very special, sort of like something out of James Joyce's *The Dead*. I always thought the McCartney family was ordinary when I was growing up, but I realise now how lucky I was to have that kind of a family, where people were decent, good and friendly. Not rich; nobody had any money, but that was almost an advantage, because they had to do everything themselves.

I liked the 'Golden Slumbers' lyrics on that sheet music a lot, and I noodled around and came up with a tune for them. It's what we might generously call sampling, or possibly stealing. But because I don't read music, I didn't know what the melody was, so I put my own to it. It's very possible that I'd been feeling down in London. I was back in the solace of family and Liverpool, and what with the Beatles troubles down south, I was likely thinking, 'Wouldn't it be nice to get home and have that comfortable feeling again?' So, there may have been some of that in the background. I wouldn't rule it out.

When I wrote the song, I hadn't been back home to Liverpool for a long time. But now I was at my dad's house, which wasn't quite home because it was a house I'd bought him when I got some money – a five-bedroomed mock Tudor place in Heswall near the River Dee. But it was still Liverpool, and it was 'homeward'. So I added, 'Once there was a way to get back homeward / Once there was a way to get back home'. The song turned out to be quite soulful, and I think that's what attracted me to those lyrics in the first place – that notion of consoling a baby or reading kids a bedtime story.

'Sleep, pretty darling, do not cry / And I will sing a lullaby'. Those are lines – or something with a similar sentiment – that most parents probably say to their children to soothe them when they're growing up. One of the things I love about writing songs, and including lines like that, is, when you're

Dad Jim, Mary and Martha.
Heswall, 1971

watching a film or listening to the radio or something, to have the song pop up with someone else singing it. I just love that it's touched that nerve. A recent film - an animated film called *Sing* - uses 'Golden Slumbers' to open the film, and it's very powerful, and the song comes up again right at the end when you've heard the whole story and everything's worked out.

People sometimes ask me whether I mind if they do different versions of my songs, or whether I'm worried that the original meaning will be distorted. And I say 'No; far from it. I love to hear another interpretation of one of my songs.' It's a compliment that someone thought enough of the song to want to cover it. What's great is that the next generation, if they're watching a kids' animated film, now know 'Golden Slumbers'.

Even more, it's good to know that my dad got to hear this song. I didn't know it at the time, but he'd be dead only seven years later. He lived long enough, though, to know what a great effect he had on my life.

④

Golden slumbers fill your eyes
Smiles awake you when you rise
sleep pretty darling do not cry
and I will sing a lullaby,

Boy, you're going to carry that weight
carry that weight a long time
Boy you're gonna carry that weight
carry that weight a long time.

I never give you my pillow
I only send you my invitations
And in the middle of the celebrations
I break down,

Boy you're gonna carry that weight
carry that weight a long time.

Repeat.....

Apple Corps Ltd., 3 Savile Row, London, W.1. 01-734 8232. Cables Apcore London, W.1. Director, N. S. Aspinall.

You never give me your money.

Out of college....

One sweet dream.

The sun king.
Mean mister mustard.
Her majesty.

Polythene Pam.

She came in through the bathroom window.

Once there was a way......

Golden Slumbers,...

Carry that weight.

I never give you my pillow...

Carry that weight.

Good Day Sunshine

WRITERS	Paul McCartney and John Lennon
ARTIST	The Beatles
RECORDED	Abbey Road Studios, London
RELEASED	*Revolver*, 1966

Good day sunshine
Good day sunshine
Good day sunshine

I need to laugh, and when the sun is out
I've got something I can laugh about
I feel good in a special way
I'm in love and it's a sunny day

Good day sunshine
Good day sunshine
Good day sunshine

We take a walk, the sun is shining down
Burns my feet as they touch the ground

Good day sunshine
Good day sunshine
Good day sunshine

Then we'd lie beneath a shady tree
I love her and she's loving me
She feels good, she knows she's looking fine
I'm so proud to know that she is mine

Good day sunshine
Good day sunshine
Good day sunshine

A LOVELY SUNNY SUMMER DAY. ONCE AGAIN, I WAS OUT AT John's house in Weybridge. I'd driven myself there from my home in London in my beautiful sierra-blue Aston Martin, ejector seat and all. I love to drive, and an hour's drive is a good time to think of things; if you've got half an idea, you can flesh it out on the way.

I would often arrive at John's place with a fully formed idea. Sometimes I would have to wait, if John was late getting up; he was a lazy bastard, whereas I was a very enthusiastic young man. Mind you, if I did have to wait there was a little swimming pool I could sit beside. Bought with our song-writing money. We used to joke about that. Once we realised the monetary value of what we were doing, we would joke, 'Let's write a swimming pool.'

Around that time there was quite a spate of summer songs. 'Daydream' and 'Summer in the City' by The Lovin' Spoonful, The Kinks' 'Sunny After-noon' – I think all those came out during the same year, 1966. We wanted to write something sunny. Both John and I had grown up while the music hall tradition was still very vibrant, so it was always in the back of our minds. There are lots of songs about the sun, and they make you happy: 'The Sun Has Got His Hat On' or 'On the Sunny Side of the Street'.

It was now time for us to do ours. So we've got love and sun, what more do we want? 'We take a walk, the sun is shining down / Burns my feet as they touch the ground' – that was a nice memory of summer. 'Then we'd lie beneath a shady tree / I love her and she's loving me'. It's really a very happy song.

I have talked to classical composers who puzzle over the time signature, but we never laid out the time signature. We just went, 'It goes like this . . .' Classical people can't say, 'It goes like this', because they're invested in formalised notation - they've got to know whether it's 3/4 time or 5/4 or something else - and that was definitely the tradition with all the groups. Sure, we'd all had piano lessons, but none of us had enjoyed them. I was talking to Jeff Lynne, of ELO fame, about this kind of thing many years later, and he said, 'Well we just made it all up, didn't we?' If George Harrison wrote, 'Here comes the sun, de-de-de-de', we would all just have to remember that.

It's worth recalling that there was no sheet music to look at. It's quite tricky, but our method was just to listen to a song and learn it, and that was where our investment came from. If someone is just reading off the notes - 'one two three, one two three four' - I always feel as if they don't enjoy it as much. It's a job.

It's worth recalling that there was no sheet music to look at. It's quite tricky, but our method was just to listen to a song and learn it, and that was where our investment came from. If someone is just reading off the notes - 'one two three, one two three four' - I always feel as if they don't enjoy it as much. It's a job.

INTRO.
(BREAKS ETC;) then GOOD DAY SUNSHINE.

(1) I NEED TO LAUGH, AND WHEN THE SUN IS OUT
I'VE GOT SOMETHING I CAN LAUGH ABOUT

(2) I FEEL GOOD IN A SPECIAL WAY
I'M IN LOVE AND IT'S A SUNNY DAY

CHORUS GOOD DAY SUNSHINE, ...

(3) WE TAKE A WALK, THE SUN IS SHINING DOWN
BURNS MY FEET AS THEY TOUCH THE GROUND
BREAK — B CHORD.
VERSE   IN B.   SOLO (guitar.)

GOOD DAY SUNSHINE (BREAKS ETC..)

(4) THEN WE LIE BENEATH A SHADY TREE,
I LOVE HER, AND SHE'S LOVING ME

SHE FEELS GOOD, SHE'S KNOWS SHE'S LOOKING
FINE.

I'M SO PROUD TO KNOW THAT SHE IS MINE.

GOOD DAY SUNSHINE . (FORTE
FORTAS
FORTISSIMOS)
repeat - end
Length. 2·10

235

Goodbye

WRITERS   Paul McCartney and John Lennon
ARTIST   Mary Hopkin
RECORDED   Morgan Studios, London
RELEASED   Single, 1969

Please don't wake me up too late
Tomorrow comes and I will not be late
Late today when it becomes tomorrow
I will leave to go away

Goodbye
Goodbye
Goodbye, goodbye
My love, goodbye

Songs that lingered on my lips
Excite me now and linger on my mind
Leave your flowers at my door
I'll leave them for the one who waits behind

Goodbye
Goodbye
Goodbye, goodbye
My love, goodbye

Far away my lover sings a lonely song
And calls me to his side
When a song of lonely love invites me on
I must go to his side

Goodbye
Goodbye
Goodbye, goodbye
My love, goodbye

I T WAS TWIGGY, OF ALL PEOPLE, WHO HAD COME ROUND FOR DIN-ner with her manager, Justin de Villeneuve, and said, 'Have you seen this girl on the television?' She was talking about a young Welsh singer named Mary Hopkin. I said, 'No,' and she said, 'Well, watch her next week.' I did, and I thought, 'Wow, terrific voice.'

Mary Hopkin was appearing in a competition called *Opportunity Knocks* – a kind of prototype for shows like *American Idol* – which she won. After seeing her on the show, I thought, 'Okay, I've got an idea of a couple of things I could do that she could sing, and I could produce the session.'

So Mary and I spoke on the phone a few times – I had to speak with her parents too, as she was only eighteen and I didn't want them to think I was up to no good – and she and her mum agreed to come to London for a meeting. I suggested I could produce her for The Beatles' Apple record label, and could find songs that I thought would be successful.

I started off with a version of an old Russian song someone else had written: 'Those Were the Days'. I got an arrangement from an arranger I knew, booked a studio, and helped Mary learn the song. It's important to learn a song before recording begins, because then you can do it without looking. I think if you do that, you feel it more when you're performing it, and Mary was very good at that. She was a quick study. I would just send her round a little demo or something, and she'd learn the song from that, and then we would go in and do it. I was putting it all together, literally putting the package together. Going into the studio and listening to the sounds that were being produced, and encouraging Mary to do a good take, which she did really quite easily, and then mixing it.

'Those Were the Days' was her most successful song, and it was a song I knew would be a hit. In fact, it was a big hit. Number one in several countries. Then I was looking for something to follow that, so I thought, 'Well, I'll just write something in the same whimsical tone.'

Even today, over fifty years later, what interests me in this lyric - and I don't think I've ever done it before or since - is the use of the same word over and over, in each line. So 'Please don't wake me until *late* / Tomorrow comes and I will not be *late* / *Late* today when it becomes tomorrow.' I would normally shy away from that and try and find another word that isn't just a repeat, but I think repetition, sometimes, is effective. '*Leave* your flowers at my door / I'll *leave* them for the one who waits behind'. The word 'lonely' is used in the same way in the third verse.

'Goodbye' was in the tradition of the 'I'm leaving, but I'll be back soon' kind of song you used to hear when you were a kid. They'd be requested on the radio, because it'd be going out to some military people who would be stationed in Bahrain or Christmas Island or Hong Kong or somewhere. Or there was a tradition in Liverpool of joining the Merchant Navy. 'What are you doing?' you'd ask someone, and they'd say, 'I've joined the merch.' And then they'd be going off on the seas. Or there were people emigrating to Canada and Australia, and they'd be missing home. I was always influenced by situations like these, and I would imagine myself into the position of the person listening to the song far away from home. I'd imagine I was one of the home crowd, thinking, 'Gosh, they're missing this with all the uncles and aunties and all the fun of being at home.' It would be sad.

Funnily enough, years later the family and I were on a boat going from the northernmost tip of Scotland to the Shetland Islands. It was the only boat we could get. We were supposed to be on a ferry, but we'd missed it, so we got this small fishing boat to take us. It was quite an interesting bit of sea, surrounding a bit of land quite appropriately called Cape Wrath, and we felt the wrath of the sea that day; I threw up. But it was delightful coming into the Orkney Islands and seeing loads of puffins along the cliffs. I'd never seen a puffin. The captain was called Captain George. He was almost Norwegian; they sort of cross over a bit up there, a little bit Scottish but sort of Norwegian. And he told me that 'Goodbye' was his favourite song of all time. I understood, because he was always going off on his fishing trips, so he understood that 'don't worry, I'll be back' sentiment.

I was very happy to produce Mary, but she wanted to be a folk singer pure and simple. I said, 'Well, that's great, you go and be a folk singer, and I can recommend all sorts of good producers to work with' - she ended up working with and marrying Tony Visconti, David Bowie's producer - 'but I myself wouldn't be that into it.' So I did an album with her, but it wasn't folk; it was songs we agreed we liked, but it wasn't the style she wanted to follow.

Twiggy had been right to talk to me about her. These two songs - 'Those Were the Days' and 'Goodbye' - did well, and the album *Post Card* did well too, but then after that Mary did, indeed, go back to her folk-singing roots.

Right: With Mary Hopkin working on *Post Card*. Abbey Road Studios, London, 1969

Please don't wake me up too late,
Tomorrow comes
And I will not be late.
Late today when it becomes tomorrow
I will leave & go away
Goodbye . . . .
     Songs that lingered on my lips
Exite me now
And linger on my mind
Leave your flowers at my door
I leave them for the one who waits behind,
Goodbye . . . . .
     Far away my lover sings
A ~~lonely~~ lonely song
and calls me to his side
where the sound of heavy drums
     invites me on,
          I must be by his side . . . . .
               Goodbye . . . . . —

Apple Corps Ltd 3 Savile Row London W1 Gerrard 2772/3993 Telex Apcore London

240

Furthermore in the country I will
lay my burden down,

GOODBYE.

Please don't wake me up too late
Tomorrow comes,
and I will not be late.
Late today when it becomes tomorrow
I will leave to go away.
goodbye ...
Songs that linger on my lips
excite me now
and linger on my mind.
Leave your flowers at my door
I leave them for the
one who waits behind.
goodbye ...

Right: Paul's original
acetate demo of 'Goodbye'

Got to Get You Into My Life

WRITERS   Paul McCartney and John Lennon
ARTIST   The Beatles
RECORDED   Abbey Road Studios, London
RELEASED   *Revolver*, 1966

I was alone, I took a ride
I didn't know what I would find there
Another road where maybe I
Could see another kind of mind there

Ooh then I suddenly see you
Ooh did I tell you I need you
Every single day of my life?

You didn't run, you didn't lie
You knew I wanted just to hold you
And had you gone, you knew in time
We'd meet again, for I had told you

Ooh you were meant to be near me
Ooh and I want you to hear me
Say we'll be together every day

Got to get you into my life

What can I do, what can I be?
When I'm with you I want to stay there
If I am true, I'll never leave
And if I do, I know the way there

Ooh then I suddenly see you
Ooh did I tell you I need you
Every single day of my life?

Got to get you into my life

W HAT WE HAD TO GET INTO OUR LIVES, IT SEEMED, WAS marijuana. Until we happened upon marijuana, we'd been drinking men. We were introduced to grass when we were in the US, and it blew our tiny little minds.

I've touched on this before, but exactly what happened is that we were in a hotel suite, maybe in New York around the summer of 1964, and Bob Dylan turned up with his roadie, the kind of guy who was more than a roadie - an assistant, friend, sidekick. He'd just released *Another Side of Bob Dylan*. We were just drinking, as usual, having a little party. We'd ordered drinks from room service - scotch and Coke and French wine were our thing back then - and Bob had disappeared into a back room. We thought maybe he'd gone to the toilet, but then Ringo came out of that back room, looking a bit strange. He said, 'I've just been with Bob, and he's got some pot,' or whatever you called it then. And we said, 'Oh, what's it like?' and he said, 'Well, the ceiling is kind of moving; it's sort of coming down.' And that was enough.

After Ringo said that, the other three of us all leapt into the back room where Dylan was, and he gave us a puff on the joint. And you know how a lot of people take a puff and think it's not working? We expected something instantaneous, so we kept puffing away and saying, 'It's not working, is it?' And suddenly it was working. And we were giggling, laughing at each other. I remember George trying to get away, and I was sort of running after him. It was hilarious, like a cartoon chase. We thought, 'Wow, this is pretty amazing, this stuff.' And so it became part of our repertoire from then on. How did we get our pot? To tell you the truth, it just showed up. There were certain people you could get it from. You just had to know who had some.

So, this song is my ode to pot. It was something that entered our lives, and I thought it would be a good idea to write a song with 'Got to get you into my life', and only I would know that I was talking about pot. Many years later I told people what it was about, but when we made the record it was just, 'I was alone, I took a ride / I didn't know what I would find there'. It was very joyous at that time. The scene turned darker a few years later, as the whole drug thing did, but it started off as a rather sunny-day-in-the-garden type of experience.

'Got to Get You Into My Life' is off *Revolver*, and we were having fun trying out different instruments in the arrangements. Earlier on that record there's 'Eleanor Rigby', which is just violins, viola and cellos. 'Love You To' has George playing the sitar. Then here we have the brass section. I'd been listening to a lot of American R & B and soul, and there were horn sections on those records - Joe Tex, Wilson Pickett, Sam & Dave, people like that. That was enough impetus for me to think, 'I'll have a go at that.' That's often how things happen with me. I'll hear something on the radio and think, 'Oh wow, I'm going to do my version of that.' So we got some horn players - trumpets and saxophones, I think - into Abbey Road Studio Two, and I explained to them how I wanted it, and they got it immediately.

A version of this song was done by Cliff Bennett and The Rebel Rousers. The way it normally happened was that we'd write a song and record it with The Beatles, and then decide whether or not it was going to be a single. If we then wrote something that we thought was an even better song, that would become the single, and this other song would then maybe make it onto the B-side. Or, if not, it would become an album track. And then sometimes people would say, 'Hey, you got any songs, man?' Their producer and manager might say, 'This is a good Beatles song, and they're not putting it out. You should do this as a single.'

Cliff Bennett was someone we knew. We'd met him a few years before in Hamburg. We admired him; he admired us. He was one of the first people to notice a song, called 'If You Gotta Make a Fool of Somebody', that Freddie and the Dreamers covered, and he said, 'Wow, that's the first rock and roll song I've ever heard in 3/4 time.' He was very astute to notice something like that. He was a good singer, and he became a friend, and he wanted to do a cover of 'Got to Get You Into My Life', so I produced it for him.

It's interesting to work with another artist recording one of my songs, as it makes me ask questions about how it should sound. Should his be exactly the same as ours, or should things be changed around a bit? Some songs have more breathing room than others, and the question comes up about whether to improvise in a song like this. If your aim in doing a concert is to please people, it's probably best to leave the song alone. Somebody might say, 'We should do it faster' or 'We should do it slower,' and there were one or two times when that really worked.

I read recently that Bob Dylan thinks he does his songs pretty much as they sound on his records, but I don't agree. We went to one of his concerts recently, and it was sometimes difficult to recognise the songs. And in the *New York Times* he was quoted as saying he doesn't improvise. I laughed my head off when I read that. I thought it was the funniest thing I've read for a while. He's a great guy, but you just don't know whether he's being tongue-in-cheek.

Left and right: The Beatles in Los Angeles and Las Vegas, 1964

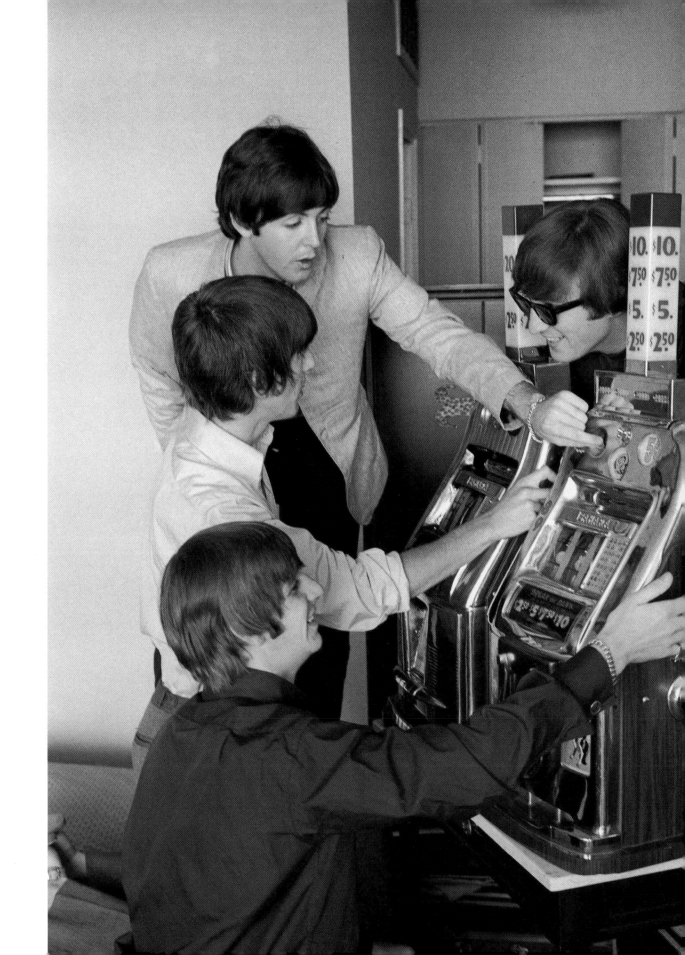

Great Day

WRITER   Paul McCartney
ARTIST   Paul McCartney
RECORDED   Hog Hill Mill, Sussex
RELEASED   *Flaming Pie*, 1997

When you're wide awake
Say it for goodness sake
It's gonna be a great day
While you're standing there
Get up and grab a chair
It's gonna be a great day

And it won't be long (oh no it won't be long)
It won't be long (no no it won't be long)
It won't be long (oh no it won't be long)
It won't be long, oh

Ooh oh yeah
Gonna be a great day

And it won't be long (oh no it won't be long)
It won't be long (no no it won't be long)
It won't be long (oh no it won't be long)
It won't be long, ooh yeah

When you're wide awake
Say it for goodness sake
It's gonna be a great day
While you're standing there
Get up and grab a chair
It's gonna be a great day

AFTER THE BREAKUP OF THE BEATLES, I WOULD OFTEN JUST SIT around a lot. Sometimes I sat in the kitchen while the kids were playing. Maybe they were drawing. Maybe they were doing bits and pieces of homework.

In this case, I came across the chords and I just felt optimistic, and I liked the idea of a song saying that help is coming and there's a bright light on the horizon. I've got absolutely no evidence for this, but I like to believe it. It helps to lift my spirits, to move me forward, and hopefully it might help other people move forward too.

One of the strengths of songs is that, if you're really lucky, they reach people. And I'm often conscious that there might be a lot of people out there who aren't having a great time, or are just worried, and could really use some good luck. And so, if I can be a reassuring voice, then I think that's very important. I think a lot of music I listened to as a kid, or even the music of my dad's generation, was uplifting. A song could make you feel better. Uplifting music is very valuable, so I like the idea of creating that, and I think that's been a lot of what I do. But this song was just very simple, almost like a nursery rhyme: 'When you're wide awake / Say it for goodness sake / It's gonna be a great day'.

The fact that the lyrics are very close to the Beatles song 'It Won't Be Long' has been pointed out, but I remember once talking to John about something we were writing, and there was a situation like that. I can't remember what the line was, but let's say it was from a Dylan song, and I was pretty much stealing it for my song. John said, 'Well, no, it's not stealing. It's a quote.' And that made me feel better.

This was the last song on the *Flaming Pie* album. It was added at the end, a bit like my song 'Her Majesty' showing up at the end of *Abbey Road*. I think it's kind of good, when you have a collection of songs that have clearly been

Above: With Stella and Mary. Scotland, 1977

247

thought out, to then finish with something that's a little throwaway. It reminds us that not everything is thought out, and it can put you in a good mood for the rest of the night.

In understanding how lyrics come about, you have to appreciate the stage of life of the writer. Today, I might write totally differently, but when you have little kids, as I did at this time, you're often composing ditties like 'Her Majesty' or 'Hey Diddle' or something like this.

You're just not sitting there always trying to be too meaningful. I used to do these little songs just to amuse the kids. But the truth is I still write for kids. Maybe it means I've never fully grown up, but I've got one that's called 'The Bouncy Song', and one, I confess, called 'Running Around the Room', which is another family classic. Then we have one that goes, 'Fishes, fishes, fishes swimming in the sea'. There are quite a few of them from when the kids were growing up – songs I didn't release. So, I suppose this is in that tradition; it's a little song that says a lot.

John and I used to write our songs in pretty much three hours. It wasn't that we set a strict time limit; it was just that by three hours, we'd had enough, and we learnt that by then we could polish it off. That two to three hours is a kind of natural period. It's why most classes or seminars and most recording sessions are two to three hours. After that your brain goes a bit.

This time period carried over to our family life. If I knew Linda was downstairs doing something – a photo session or a cookery programme – then I would abscond and try to write something, with part of the thought being to surprise her, to give her a little gift at the end of those two hours and be able to say, 'Guess what I was doing!'

Even now, I'm still disappearing into little rooms. It's about finding a quiet place to think, creating private space for one to imagine. You don't particularly want to let anyone in on that process, though. So if there's someone in the next room, within earshot, doing the dishes and they've got half an ear on me, and after I've reappeared they say, 'That sounded nice,' I'll think, 'You weren't supposed to hear it. But it's okay, now that it's done.'

Right: Working lyrics, early 1970s

Left: Arizona, 1995

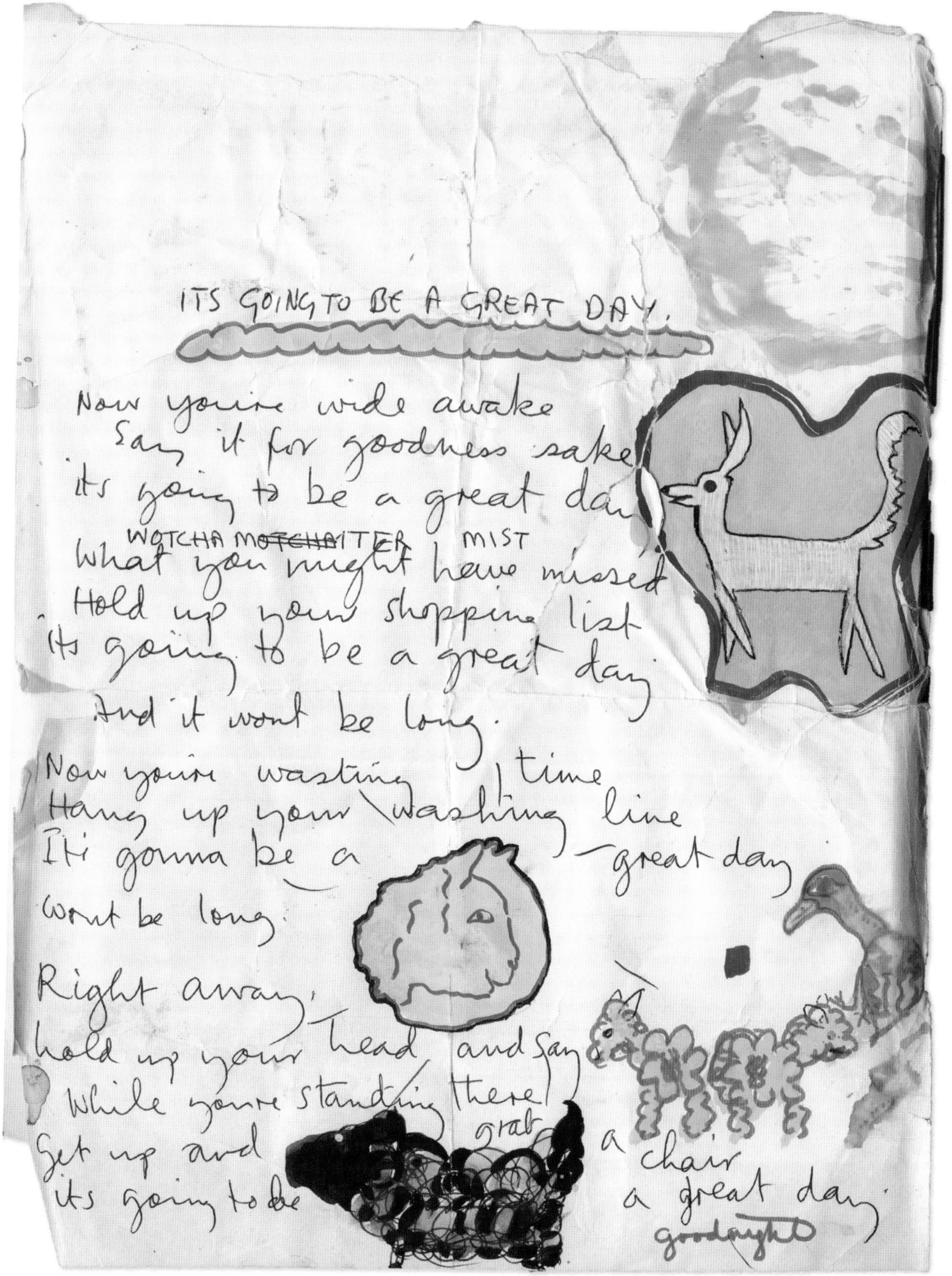

ITS GOING TO BE A GREAT DAY.

Now you're wide awake
  Say it for goodness sake
Its going to be a great day
  WOTCHA ~~MITCHAITER~~ MIST
What you might have missed
  Hold up your shopping list
Its going to be a great day.

  And it wont be long.

Now you're wasting time
Hang up your washing line
Its gonna be a ———— great day

Wont be long.

Right away,
hold up your head and say
  While you're standing there
Get up and   grab   a chair
its going to be   a great day.
                                         goodnight.

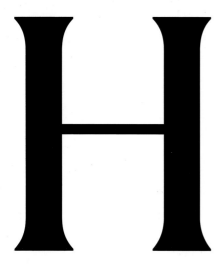

H

A Hard Day's Night

WRITERS   John Lennon and Paul McCartney
ARTIST   The Beatles
RECORDED   Abbey Road Studios, London
RELEASED   *A Hard Day's Night*, 1964
               Single, 1964

It's been a hard day's night
And I've been working like a dog
It's been a hard day's night
I should be sleeping like a log
But when I get home to you
I find the things that you do
Will make me feel alright

You know I work all day
To get you money to buy you things
And it's worth it just to hear you say
You're gonna give me everything
So why on earth should I moan
'Cause when I get you alone
You know I feel okay

When I'm home
Everything seems to be right
When I'm home
Feeling you holding me tight, tight, yeah

It's been a hard day's night
And I've been working like a dog
It's been a hard day's night
I should be sleeping like a log
But when I get home to you
I find the things that you do
Will make me feel alright

So why on earth should I moan
'Cause when I get you alone
You know I feel okay

When I'm home
Everything seems to be right
When I'm home
Feeling you holding me tight, tight, yeah

It's been a hard day's night
And I've been working like a dog
It's been a hard day's night
I should be sleeping like a log
But when I get home to you
I find the things that you do
Will make me feel alright
You know I feel alright
You know I feel alright

PART OF WHAT LIES BEHIND THIS SONG IS, OF COURSE, EUGENE O'Neill's play *Long Day's Journey Into Night*. It was playing at the time in London. So, we were kind of aware of that phrase. The great thing about Ringo is that he would come up with these malapropisms. He would say things that were just ever so slightly out of whack, but genius. I think the difference between us and a lot of other people is that not only did we hear these out-of-the-ordinary phrases, but we paid attention to them. One day Ringo said, 'Gosh, it's been a hard day's night,' and we went, 'What? Hard day's night? That's brilliant.'

The title is certainly a commentary on the craziness of our lives. I would say it was predominantly John's commentary on things. But we were all knackered, so it was the perfect phrase for our state of being.

We were still young lads. We were twenty-two, twenty-three. But we were world famous already. After a while, we got a bit tired of it. Too much screaming, too many autographs, too much lack of privacy. It wore you down a bit. But early on, when we were in the first throes of fame, it couldn't help but be very exciting. We'd been hoping beyond hope that people would ask us for an autograph. I practised. We all practised. And my autograph is virtually the same today, except it's now 'Paul' instead of 'JP'. All my school exercise books look like my autograph now.

So, you know, you'd always been looking for this to happen. To get a great guitar, to be able to buy your dad a house - all that sort of stuff. There we were, all in our little button-down shirts, our little ties, our little nifty tie-pins, the three-button jackets. And all smoking those ciggies, Rothmans or Peter Stuyvesant - or in Ringo's case, Lark, 'cause he was always, you know, Mr Suave. Anyway, it was very exciting to be young, rich and famous.

Much has been made of the opening chord of the song. I still don't know what it is. If you asked me to play it, I couldn't; I'd have to work it out. I think there may be two chords in there, a G and an F. John basically wrote the song, and I think I probably helped with the middle eight – 'When I'm home / Everything seems to be right'. I got to sing that bit, so that probably means I helped with it. Generally, I took the higher part.

By that time our records were already getting a little bit more sophisticated, more experimental, so we were using a certain amount of jiggery-pokery. The solo that George Harrison was to play, say, was a bit too fast, so George Martin would slow it down and record it at half speed. We always referred to George Martin as the grown-up behind the glass window, and we were the kids in the studio. He helped with song arrangements and could play the piano, and we learnt a lot of technical tricks from him.

I don't think we were trying to be particularly suggestive with the lyrics; I think we were just young guys. Peter Sellers did a nice version of it, where he did really milk the double entendre: '*Feeling you holding me tight*'.

Pages 254–255: Script for
A Hard Day's Night

253

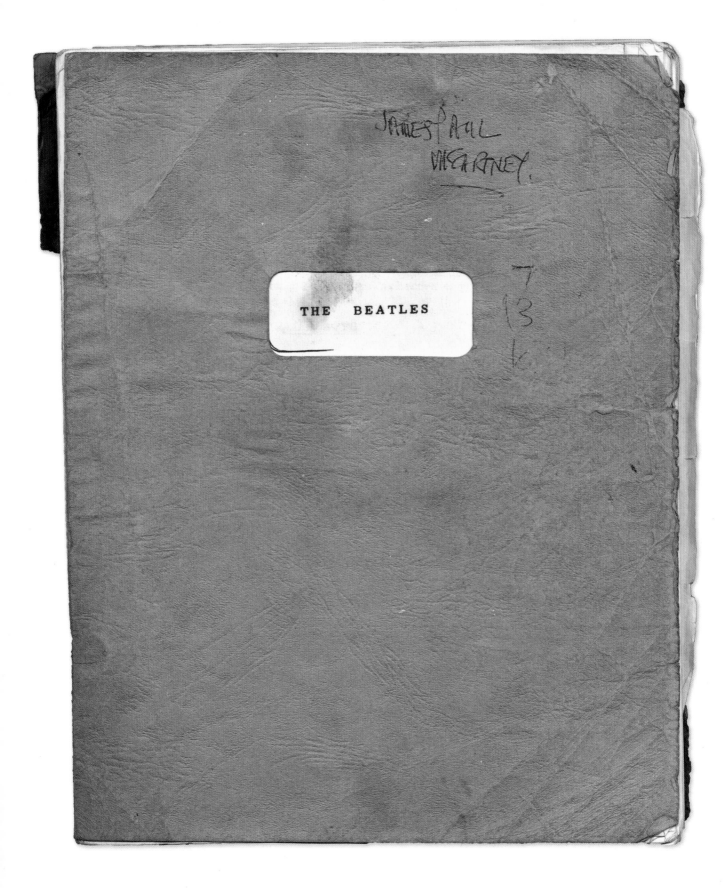

THE BEATLES

Below: Practising signatures on a coaster from the Casbah Coffee Club, an early venue played by The Quarry Men

Right: Fans at the premiere of *A Hard Day's Night*. London Pavillion, 6 July 1964

Helen Wheels

WRITERS	Paul McCartney and Linda McCartney
ARTIST	Paul McCartney and Wings
RECORDED	EMI Studios, Lagos
RELEASED	Single, 1973
	Band on the Run US release, 1973

Said farewell to my last hotel
It never was much kind of abode
Glasgow town never brought me down
When I was heading out on the road
Carlisle city never looked so pretty
And the Kendal freeway's fast
Slow down driver, want to stay alive
I want to make this journey last

Helen, hell on wheels
Ain't nobody else gonna know the way she feels
Helen, hell on wheels
And they never gonna take her away

M6 south down to Liverpool
Where they play the West Coast sound
Sailor Sam, he came from Birmingham
But he never will be found
Doing fine when a London sign
Greets me like a long lost friend
Mister Motor, won't you check her out
She's got to take me back again

Helen, hell on wheels
Ain't nobody else gonna know the way she feels
Helen, hell on wheels
And they never gonna take her away

Got no time for a rum and lime
I wanna get my right foot down
Shake some dust off of this old bus
I gotta get her out of town
Spend the day upon the motorway
Where the carburettors blast
Slow down driver, wanna stay alive
I want to make this journey last

Helen, hell on wheels
Ain't nobody else gonna know the way she feels
Helen, hell on wheels
And they never gonna take her away

HELEN WHEELS IS THE NAME OF MY LAND ROVER. SHE WAS JUST a little Land Rover when I bought her in Scotland. I needed something to get around all that rugged countryside. The four-wheel drive made her perfect for going up and down steep hills.

I'd always wanted to do a road song, but all the ones we knew were American – 'Take It Easy,' 'Sweet Home Alabama,' 'Route 66' above all. I loved the versions by both Nat King Cole and Chuck Berry. Wings were playing live a lot at this point. In fact, the year before, we'd been touring around Europe in an open-top double-decker bus. In the summer of 1973, when I was writing songs for what would become the *Band on the Run* album, Wings had been travelling all over the UK on tour, which probably also influenced this song.

What's interesting about 'Route 66', as my wife Nancy and I discovered about ten years ago, is that the place-names in the song are actually in the correct order. We used the song as a map of sorts.

There's a humorous aspect built into the very idea of a UK road song. Because the US is three thousand miles across, it allows for some latitude, whereas you could almost spit across the UK. So you need a longer journey. As luck would have it, I had an eight-or-nine-hour journey from Scotland to London. It's a journey I used to make a lot, in both directions.

From London it took four hours to get to Liverpool. We would sometimes stop over in Liverpool to break up the trip. Another four or five hours up to Glasgow, then turn left. Starting in Scotland, it was always fun to go south through Cumbria, particularly in daylight. Kendal is in the Lake District, but the 'Kendal freeway' is meant to be a joke because Kendal is a total bottleneck, as anyone who's tried to drive through it will confirm.

We used to have a roadie, called Mal, who claimed he liked that moment on any journey when there were still two hundred miles to go. The lines 'M6

Above: With Mary and Helen Wheels. Scotland, 1970

south down to Liverpool / Where they play the West Coast sound' are meant to be an amusing reference to the interaction of The Beach Boys and The Beatles. 'Sailor Sam' represents another form of interweaving. With 'Sailor Sam' I was initially just wanting a rhyme for Birmingham, and then I thought, 'Wait a minute; Sailor Sam's in "Band on the Run".' He makes a little guest appearance here, a cameo as in a film. And then I put the lid on it by saying Sailor Sam 'never will be found'. That seals the deal with the 'Band on the Run' overlap. Intertextuality, as they call it in posh circles. The songs are talking to each other.

The conversations are transatlantic. 'Spend a day upon the motorway / Where the carburettors blast / Slow down driver, wanna stay alive / I want to make this journey last'. The carburettor comes indirectly from Chuck Berry, who pioneered what you might call the 'erotics' of the automobile, particularly in 'No Particular Place to Go'. I suppose what I'm saying is that, for some people, 'carburettor' isn't a word they'd expect to find in a song. It's a nice word, though, isn't it? Car-bur-ett-or. I'm not particularly mechanical, so it's probably the only part of an engine I've ever heard of! And it has the English 'car' in it.

In any case, the idea of doing an English road song was challenging but rewarding. I like the idea that a song like this still has legs. And I actually still have Helen Wheels. She's still running. They're built to last, those things.

Left: *Band on the Run* recording sessions. Lagos, Nigeria, 1973

Right: Sitting in Helen Wheels, photographed by daughter Mary. At home, Sussex, 2020

HELEN WHEELS.

① Said farewell to my last hotel
It never was much kind of abode,
Glasgow town never brought me down
When I was heading out on the road
  Carlisle city never ~~seemed~~ looking so pretty
And the Kendal freeway's fast.
  Slow down driver, want to stay
                            alive
  I want to make this journey last
                      hell on
CHORUS.   Helen — ~~Helen~~ Wheels
Aint nobody else gonna know the
way she feels
  · Helen — hell on Wheels
And they never gonna take her away
② M6 south down to Liverpool
where they play the West coast sound
Sailor Sam "he" came from Birmingham
But he never will be found.
Doing fine when a London sign
greets me like a long lost friend,
  Mr. Motor wont you check her
out, she's got to take me back
                      again.

CHORUS
Helen Wheels

and they never gonna take her away...
③ Got no time for a rum + lime
I wanna get my right foot down
Shake some dust off of this
old bus
I gotta get her out of town
Spend the day upon the motorway
Where the carburettors blast
Slow down driver, wanna stay
alive,
I want to make this journey
last

Chorus HELEN —

Helter Skelter

WRITERS	Paul McCartney and John Lennon
ARTIST	The Beatles
RECORDED	Abbey Road Studios, London
RELEASED	*The Beatles*, 1968

When I get to the bottom I go back to the top
　of the slide
Where I stop and I turn and I go for a ride
Til I get to the bottom and I see you again
Yeah, yeah, yeah

Do you, don't you want me to love you?
I'm coming down fast but I'm miles above you
Tell me, tell me, tell me, come on, tell me the
　answer
Well you may be a lover but you ain't no dancer

Helter Skelter
Helter Skelter
Helter Skelter

Will you, won't you want me to make you?
I'm coming down fast but don't let me break you
Tell me, tell me, tell me the answer
You may be a lover but you ain't no dancer
Look out

Helter Skelter
Helter Skelter
Helter Skelter
Look out, 'cause here she comes

When I get to the bottom I go back to the top
　of the slide
And I stop and I turn and I go for a ride
And I get to the bottom and I see you again
Yeah, yeah, yeah

Well do you, don't you want me to make you?
I'm coming down fast but don't let me break you
Tell me, tell me, tell me your answer
You may be a lover but you ain't no dancer
Look out

Helter Skelter
Helter Skelter
Helter Skelter

Look out
Helter Skelter
She's coming down fast
Yes she is

PETE TOWNSHEND HAD BEEN TALKING IN THE MUSIC PRESS ABOUT how The Who had just recorded the loudest, the dirtiest, the rockiest thing ever. I loved that description, so I came into the studio and said to the guys, 'Let's just see how loud we can get and how raucous. Let's try to make the meters peak.'

A lot of people in the US still don't know what a helter skelter is. They think it's a roller coaster. It's actually another fairground fixture - conical, with a slide around the outside. We went on them loads of times as kids. You'd walk up the stairs inside, and you'd take a mat - just like a doormat - and you'd sit on it and slide down, and then you'd walk up again. I used that as a symbol of life. One minute you're up, next minute you get knocked down. You're feeling euphoric, then you're feeling miserable. Such is the nature of life. The verses are based on the Mock Turtle's song from *Alice in Wonderland*:

> *'Will you walk a little faster?' said a whiting to a snail,*
> *'There's a porpoise close behind us, and he's treading on my tail.*
> *See how eagerly the lobsters and the turtles all advance!*
> *They are waiting on the shingle - will you come and join the dance?*
> *Will you, won't you, will you, won't you, will you join the dance?*
> *Will you, won't you, will you, won't you, won't you join the dance?'*

John and I both adored Lewis Carroll, and we often quoted him. Lines like 'She's coming down fast' have a sexual component, perhaps a little drug component too. A little darker.

But things really got dark when Charles Manson, a year later, hijacked the song. He thought The Beatles were the Four Horsemen of the Apocalypse, and he was reading all this stuff into the lyrics. All sorts of secret meanings. Apparently, he read hell into '*Helter Skelter*'. I didn't perform the song for years after Manson and the Sharon Tate murders. It was all too twisted.

The distortion we continued to be interested in was the sound distortion we could create by using techniques we developed with the brilliant engineers at Abbey Road. The recording process for 'Helter Skelter' was endless, a feat of endurance. So much so that Ringo, at the end of it, shouted out something about having blisters on his fingers. It was that kind of session. We had played the hell out of it, so maybe Manson did detect something infernal in it. The song has sometimes been credited as the start of heavy metal. I don't know whether that's the case, but it's certainly true that the music preceding rock, the gentle and romantic dance music, was kicked over. We were kicking that out of the way with this song.

Over the years I've looked for the Who track that Pete Townshend was referring to. I've even asked Pete about it, and he can't remember. Maybe it was 'I Can See for Miles'. The loudest, the dirtiest, the rockiest thing ever? I never heard anything by The Who that was as loud and dirty as it was in my imagining of it.

HELTER SKELTER.

DO YOU DONT YOU WANT ME TO LOVE YOU
I'M COMING DOWN FAST BUT I'M MILES ABOVE YOU
                      COME ON TELL ME
TELL ME TELL ME TELL ME ^ THE ANSWER
WELL YOU MAY BE A LOVER BUT YOU AINT NO DANCER
  LOOK OUT   HELTER SKELTER   HELTER SKELTER
              "   "   YEAH

WHEN I GET TO THE BOTTOM I GO BACK TO THE TOP OF THE
AND I STOP AND I TURN AND I GIVE YOU A THRILL   HILL
      TILL I SEE YOU A GAIN

DO YOU DONT YOU WANT ME TO MAKE IT
I'M LOVING YOU BABY AND I CANT FAKE IT
TELL ME TELL ME TELL ME THE ANSWER
YOU MAY BE A LOVER BUT YOU AINT NO DANCER
LOOK OUT HELTER SKELTER. + +

Working lyrics
transcribed by Mal Evans
with notes by Paul, 1968

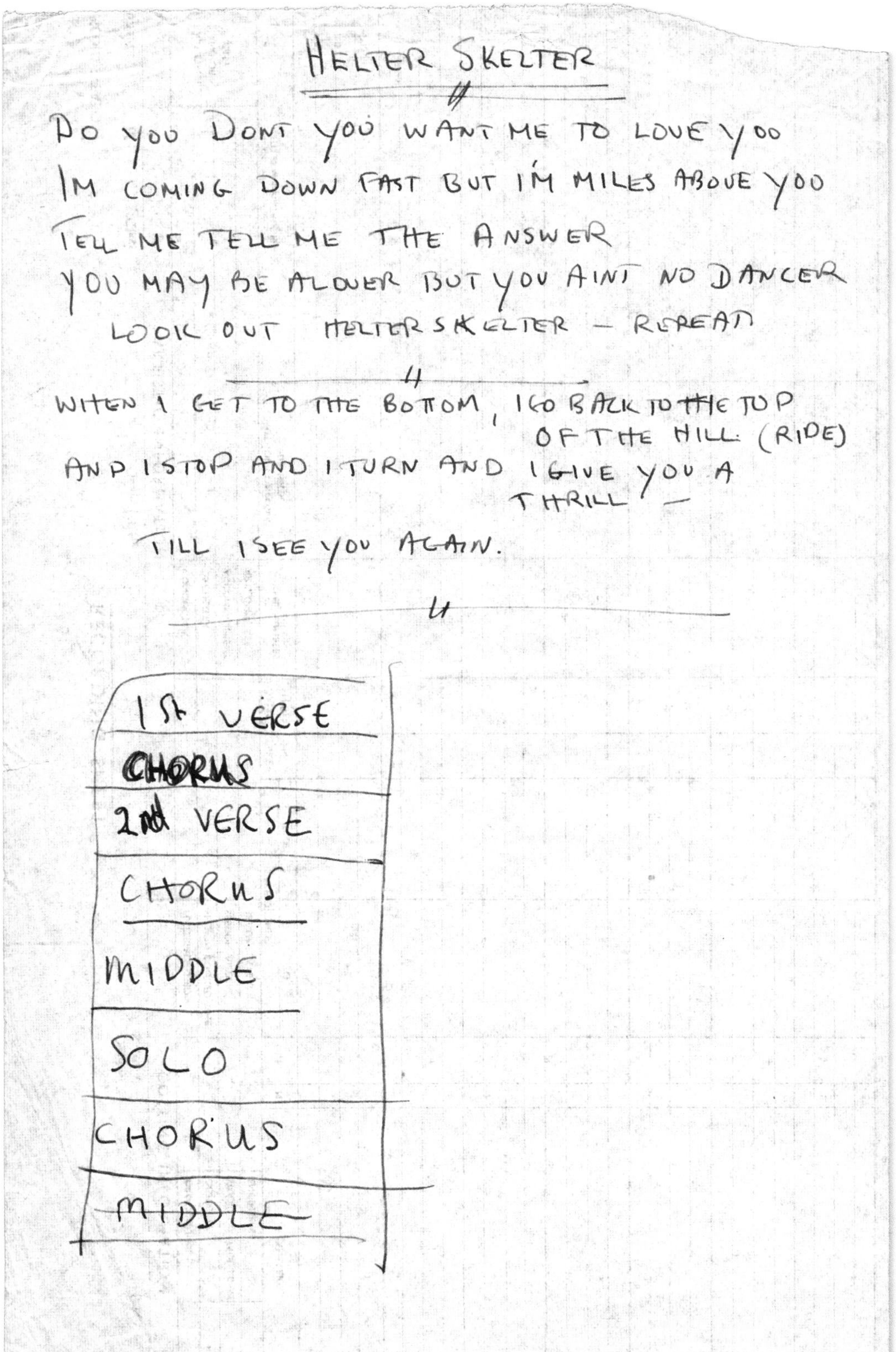

HELTER SKELTER

Do you Dont you want me to love you
I'm coming down fast but I'm miles above you
Tell me tell me the answer
You may be a lover but you aint no dancer
    Look out   Helter Skelter — Repeat

When I get to the bottom, I go back to the top
                    of the hill (ride)
And I stop and I turn and I give you a
                    thrill —

    Till I see you again.

1 st   verse
CHORUS
2 nd verse
CHORUS
MIDDLE
SOLO
CHORUS
MIDDLE

267

Her Majesty

WRITERS   Paul McCartney and John Lennon

ARTIST   The Beatles

RECORDED   Abbey Road Studios, London

RELEASED   *Abbey Road*, 1969

Her majesty's a pretty nice girl
But she doesn't have a lot to say
Her majesty's a pretty nice girl
But she changes from day to day

I wanna tell her that I love her a lot
But I gotta get a belly full of wine
Her majesty's a pretty nice girl
Someday I'm gonna make her mine
Oh yeah someday I'm gonna make her mine

YOU'RE SITTING AROUND WITH AN ACOUSTIC GUITAR, JUST FOR your own fun, and then you get a little idea, and sometimes it's enough to finish up as a 'big' song. 'Her Majesty' was just a little fragment really, and I didn't know what to do with it. It's tongue-in-cheek, treating the queen as if she were just a nice girl and not bothering with the fact that she would become the longest-reigning monarch ever in the UK, or that she was queen of the nation. It's just being cheeky. 'Her majesty's a pretty nice girl / But she doesn't have a lot to say' - that seemed to be true. She doesn't say much - only the annual Queen's Speech at Christmas and the opening of Parliament.

However slight the song might be, I liked it, so I brought it to the session. I think it was the second side of what would become *Abbey Road*, and we didn't know where to place it. It was just by accident that it found its way onto the end of something, and we thought, 'Well, actually, that's a good idea.' It would be a nice little afterthought, a little irreverent look at the monarchy by a young man in his late twenties.

As it turns out, I have had the pleasure of meeting the queen over the years. I think part of the secret behind her popularity, at least for my generation, was that she was quite a babe. I was ten in 1953 when she was crowned, which made her twenty-seven or something. And so, in our boyish ways, we rather fancied her. She was a good-looking woman, like a Hollywood film star.

Later, when we became The Beatles, we met her in a line-up somewhere; I think it would have been the Royal Command Performance at the London Palladium in 1963. They tell you that if she stops, you can talk, but if she doesn't stop, don't try and stop her. You're supposed to call her 'ma'am'. 'Yes, ma'am.' So she stopped and said, 'Where are you playing next?' I said,

'Slough, ma'am.' She said, 'Oh, that's just near us.' She made a little joke like that. It's near Windsor Castle.

Later, she came up to officially open LIPA – the Liverpool Institute for the Performing Arts – which is the performing-arts school I'd helped set up in my old grammar school. She very kindly cut the ribbon. So, when I meet her nowadays, she asks me about that. 'How's your school in Liverpool?' And I say, 'It's doing rather well, ma'am.'

I think she's great. I have a lot of admiration for her. I think she's sensible, intelligent. Unlike some of the monarchs you read about in history, she's fairly straightforward. And she's got a good sense of fun too. The Olympics opening ceremony with the Bond thing was great. Daniel Craig picks her up at the palace, they get in a car, then a helicopter, and then, live at the Olympics, you see this person dressed in the same outfit come hurtling out in a parachute. It was funny. She loves a bit of showbiz.

I think she's the glue that often holds the nation together. The Commonwealth is not the empire anymore, but it's a gathering of people, and they all like her. I was very happy when she became the longest-reigning British monarch. She's an excellent role model, holding down the job, being sensible. Loads of challenges, but she seems to manage.

I did once perform this song for the queen. I don't know how to break this to you, but she didn't have a lot to say.

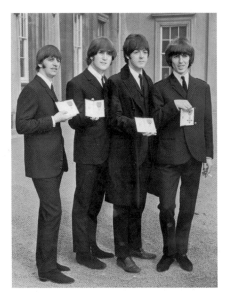

Far left: *The Queen Getting a Joke* painting by Paul, 1991

Left: The Beatles with their MBEs. Buckingham Palace, London, 26 October 1965

Right: Receiving the Companion of Honour from the queen. Buckingham Palace, London, 4 May 2018

Here, There and Everywhere

WRITERS	Paul McCartney and John Lennon
ARTIST	The Beatles
RECORDED	Abbey Road Studios, London
RELEASED	*Revolver*, 1966

To lead a better life
I need my love to be here

Here, making each day of the year
Changing my life with a wave of her hand
Nobody can deny that there's something there

There, running my hands through her hair
Both of us thinking how good it can be
Someone is speaking, but she doesn't know
   he's there

I want her everywhere
And if she's beside me I know I need never care
But to love her is to need her

Everywhere, knowing that love is to share
Each one believing that love never dies
Watching her eyes and hoping I'm always there

I want her everywhere
And if she's beside me I know I need never care
But to love her is to need her

Everywhere, knowing that love is to share
Each one believing that love never dies
Watching her eyes and hoping I'm always there

I will be there and everywhere
Here, there and everywhere

T HINK OF 'ANYTHING GOES'. THERE'S A PRELIMINARY SECTION TO
that Cole Porter song that seems to have absolutely nothing to do
with it:

> *Times have changed*
> *And we've often rewound the clock*
> *Since the Puritans got the shock*
> *When they landed on Plymouth Rock . . .*

In coming up with lyrics to 'Here, There and Everywhere', we were trying
to emulate the openings of some of our favourite old songs that had a completely rambling preamble. That's what lies behind the lines 'To lead a better
life / I need my love to be here'.

What I like most about this song is that we think we're on a path on the
moors and we're going for a walk, and then suddenly we've arrived where
we started. It's not quite that we've gone around in a circle. It's more magical than that. We've come to another beginning of the path. You can see
back to where you came from, and you're definitely not there. You're in a
new place, though it's got the same scenery. I've always liked that trick.

In terms of circularity, though, it's hard to beat the fact that 'Here, There
and Everywhere' was influenced most immediately by The Beach Boys' 'God
Only Knows' from *Pet Sounds*. What's really interesting is that 'God Only
Knows' was itself inspired by Brian Wilson's repeated listening to our songs
on *Rubber Soul*.

My favourite line is 'Changing my life with a wave of her hand'. I look at
that line now and wonder where it came from. What was it? Was I thinking
of the queen waving from the royal carriage? Or just the power of the little
thing. The power of doing hardly anything. She waves her hand and she's
changed my life. It summons up a lot.

So now when I sing it, I look back at it and think, 'The boy's not bad.' In
fact, if pushed, I would say that 'Here, There and Everywhere' is my own
favourite of all my songs.

HERE, THERE, and EVERYWHERE.

To lead a better life, I need my love to be ~~here~~ HERE

Here,
Making each day of the year
Changing my life with a wave of her hand,
Nobody can deny that there's something there

there
Running my hands through her hair,
Both of us thinking how good it can be
Someone is speaking, but she ~~doesn't seem to care~~ know he's there

want
I ~~need~~ her everywhere

AND IF
(as long as) She's beside me, I know I need

But   never care
~~For~~to love her is to need her everywhere

Knowing that love is to share.
~~Each one~~ believing that love never dies
Watching her eyes and (hoping She's always
                                        here [NEAR]
        hoping I'm always there) [THERE]

ETC.

BEATLE PLANS FOR NINETEEN SIXTY-SIX

During early April the Beatles wrote and rehearsed no less than sixteen new songs. The rest of the month and part of May were spent in their London recording studio putting them on tape ready to be made into a new single record and new L.P. album. The album - as yet untitled - is not likely to be issued before August. The single "PAPERBACK WRITER" + "RAIN" - will be in the shops on Friday June 10. To hear it before this date you should send a request on a postcard to at least one of the Radio request programmes or Radio Stations as they are issued with a copy in advance.

"PAPERBACK WRITER" has Paul singing the main verses and John and George joining him on the chorus segments.

"RAIN" is a very simple song featuring John with Paul and George joining in on falsetto chorus parts.

The Beatles will play a short series of concerts in Germany during the final week of June. The schedule is as follows:

June 24 - Munich - Circus Kroner   )
June 25 - ESSEN - Grughalle   ) - two performances each date
June 26 - HAMBURG - Ersst Merk Halle   )

Appearing with the Beatles on each of these dates in Germany will be Cliff Bennett & The Rebel Rousers.

On June 27 the Beatles will fly direct from Hamburg to Tokyo for further concert dates in Japan and then on to the Phillippines for two concerts in Manila. The dates are as follows:

June 30)
July 1) -- Budo Kan Theatre Tokyo -- one performance on each date
July 2)

July 4)--- National Football Stadium Manila - two performances

In the middle of August the Beatles will depart from London for a slightly extended repeat of last year's concert tour of America and Canada. The tour will open on Friday August 12 at the International Amphitheatre in Chicago. Then the rest of the schedule reads like this

August 13 : Detroit Olympic Stadium Michigan
August 14 : Louisville Fairground Stadium
August 15 : Washington Stadium
August 16 : Philadelphia Stadium
August 17 : Toronto Maple Leaf Gardens
August 18 : Boston Fenway Park
August 19 : Memphis Coliseum
August 20 : Cincinatti Crosley Field
August 21 : St. Louis Busch Stadium
August 23 : New York Shea Stadium
August 25 : Seattle Municipal Stadium
August 28 : Los Angeles Dodge Stadium
August 29 : San Fransisco

The above details are included so that if you have a pen-pal living in a country mentioned you can send them on. The club is unable to give information of where tickets may be obtained for overseas performances.

For flight details please ring the fan club at COVent Garden 2332 nearer the time of the tours.

It is unlikely that the Beatles' third film will go into production until the group returns from America. To date The Beatles and their producer Walter Shenson have not chosen a script.

Towards the end of the year Brian Epstein has confirmed that the Beatles will definately undertake a British concert tour, but dates and cities will not be announced until much nearer the time.

Here Today

WRITER   Paul McCartney
ARTIST   Paul McCartney
RECORDED   AIR Studios, London
RELEASED   *Tug of War*, 1982

And if I said
I really knew you well
What would your answer be?
If you were here today
Here today

Well knowing you
You'd probably laugh and say
That we were worlds apart
If you were here today
Here today

But as for me
I still remember how it was before
And I am holding back the tears no more
I love you

What about the time we met?
Well I suppose that you could say that
We were playing hard to get
Didn't understand a thing
But we could always sing

What about the night we cried?
Because there wasn't any reason left
To keep it all inside
Never understood a word
But you were always there with a smile

And if I say
I really loved you
And was glad you came along
Then you were here today
For you were in my song
Here today

A LOVE SONG TO JOHN, WRITTEN VERY SHORTLY AFTER HE DIED. I was remembering things about our relationship and about the million things we'd done together, from just being in each other's front parlours or bedrooms to walking on the street together or hitchhiking - long journeys together which had nothing to do with The Beatles. I was thinking of all these things in what was then my recording studio in Sussex. Before it was made into a studio, it was just a little house with a small room upstairs with bare, wooden plank floors and bare walls, and I had my guitar with me, so I just sat there and wrote this.

It started, as it so often does, with finding something nice on the guitar, in this case a lovely chord. I just found that chord and pushed on from that; that was the dock, and I could push the boat out and finish the song.

There's one line in the lyric I don't really mean: 'Well knowing you / You'd probably laugh and say / That we were worlds apart'. I'm playing to the more cynical side of John, but I don't think it's true that we were so distant.

'But you were always there with a smile' - that was very John. If you were arguing with him, and it got a bit tense, he'd just lower his specs and say, 'It's only me,' then put them back up again, as if the specs were part of a completely different identity.

'What about the night we cried?' That was in Key West, on our first major tour to the US, when there was a hurricane coming in and we couldn't play a show in Jacksonville. We had to lie low for a couple of days, and we were in our little Key West motel room, and we got very drunk and cried about how we loved each other. I was talking to someone yesterday who was telling me that if he cried, his father would say, 'Boys don't cry. You mustn't do that.' My dad wasn't like that, but that was the attitude: male people do not cry. I

think now it's acknowledged that it's a perfectly good thing to do, and I say, 'God wouldn't have given us tears if he didn't mean us to cry.'

I heard somewhere recently, 'Why can't men say "I love you" to each other?' I don't think it's as true now as it was back in the 1950s and '60s, but certainly when we were growing up you'd have had to be gay for a man to say that to another man, so that blinkered attitude bred a little bit of cynicism. If you were talking about anything soppy, someone would have to make a joke of it, just to ease the embarrassment in the room. But there's a longing in the lines 'If you were here today' and 'I am holding back the tears no more', because it was very emotional, writing this song. I was just sitting there in that bare room, thinking of John and realising I'd lost him. And it was a powerful loss, so to have a conversation with him in a song was some form of solace. Somehow I was with him again. 'And if I say / I really loved you' – there it is, I've said it. Which I would never have said to him.

It's a very charged experience to perform this song in concert. It's just me and a guitar. In the current show, I do 'Blackbird' and then 'Here Today', and I'm stuck in the middle of a great big arena with all these people, and a lot of them are crying. It's always a very sentimental, nostalgic, emotional moment.

Left: John Lennon during *The Beatles* recording sessions. Abbey Road Studios, London, 1968

Above: Leicester Square Tube Station, London, 9 December 1980

And its always the same hard luck story.
~~Just take~~ If your Mother was here....
~~Get~~ ~~Her and~~
Mother: Now, now, thats enough. Are ~~you~~
seeing Abie tonight ~~?~~?
Norma: Yes, he's picking me up at half
Seven.
Mother: I don't know where he gets ● the
money from, what with the car, and all
these little presents.
Norma: His dad's a wholesale.
Mother: A wholesale what?
Norma: He never told me, he's not a one
for talking.
[Enter Tony] (Exit Mother laughing) car, Tony
~~...~~ Did you see Abies ~~..~~
Tony: How could I, I've only been down
the hall? You'd think it was 10 days camel
ride.
Norma: There's no need to be sarcastic,
sonny!
Tony: Just because you're patronising every
~~refuse~~ that crawls into the county, it
doesn't mean that you.....
Norma: ~~...~~ ~~...~~ you little ~~...~~ What
the Hell!
~~...~~ Knock Knock
Oh, lor' if he heard that —9!!, "Come in
Abraham.
Abraham: Is anybody home?

Tony: No, we've gone out for the night.. ~~...~~
Abie: ~~...~~ Ho, Ho, Enter left
unwanted Abraham, Ho.
Norma: [gushing] He's only joking, aren't
you Tony
~~Tony~~ ~~—~~ yes, and a bunch of toast.
Abie: Well Norma, are you ready?
Norma: Coming. (Exit)
Tony: ~~...~~ Did you see that, ~~mother~~?
(Enter Mother)
Mother: No dear, what happened?
Tony: Oh nothing startling, it's just the way
she tags that poor ~~cnit~~ along. He's ~~a fool~~
a mug not to see through her. It doesn't
take much to see what she's after. I should
have thought it was as plain as the nose
on his face.
Mother: I thought she rather liked him.
Tony: Liked him? She likes him like Abie
likes bacon.
[Knock, Knock] [Enter Mrs. Penn]
What is it this time, Penn?
Penn: I wondered if your ma had such
a thing as a cup of sugar, I ~~can~~ seem to
have left it off me list.
Mother: Tony, See if you can find some.
Here, take Mrs. Penn's cup. [Tony exit]
Penn: Thanks, luv; [slight pause] ...and how's

HERE TODAY...   (20)

(1) And if I ~~sorry~~ SAID
I really knew you well
(What would your answer be) ~~what would you have to say?~~
(~~If you were here with me~~)
If you were here today......

(2) Well knowing you....
You'd probably laugh and say
That we were world's apart
If you were here today
    here today)

But
~~Well~~ as for me
I still remember how it was before
And I ~~am~~ holding back the tears no more
~~See no point I~~ I love you

What about the ~~time~~ we met
Well I suppose that you could say that we
    were playing hard to get
Didn't understand a thing
    but we could always sing —

(3) LAST VERSE
And if I ~~said day~~
I really loved you
and I was glad you came along
~~THEN~~ you were here today
For you were in my song
ooh.... here today...

What about
the ~~night~~ we cried
because there wasn't any reason left
To keep it all inside
Never ~~understood~~ a word
but ~~you were~~ always there with
● smile

280

Left top: Story written with John Lennon, late 1950s

Above: With George Harrison, John Lennon and Stuart Sutcliffe. Hamburg, 1960

Right: With John Lennon. Trident Studios, London, 1968

Hey Jude

WRITERS Paul McCartney and John Lennon
ARTIST The Beatles
RECORDED Trident Studios, London
RELEASED Single, 1968
Hey Jude, 1970

Hey Jude, don't make it bad
Take a sad song and make it better
Remember to let her into your heart
Then you can start to make it better

Hey Jude, don't be afraid
You were made to go out and get her
The minute you let her under your skin
Then you begin to make it better

And anytime you feel the pain
Hey Jude, refrain
Don't carry the world upon your shoulder
For well you know that it's a fool
Who plays it cool
By making his world a little colder

Hey Jude, don't let me down
You have found her, now go and get her
Remember to let her into your heart
Then you can start to make it better

So let it out and let it in
Hey Jude, begin
You're waiting for someone to perform with
And don't you know that it's just you
Hey Jude, you'll do
The movement you need is on your shoulder

Hey Jude, don't make it bad
Take a sad song and make it better
Remember to let her under your skin
Then you begin to make it better
Better, better, better, better, better

Hey Jude

THE FIRST TIME I PLAYED THIS SONG FOR JOHN AND YOKO WAS on what we called the 'Magic Piano' in my music room. I was facing one way, and they were standing behind me almost on my shoulder. So when I sang, 'The movement you need is on your shoulder', I immediately turned around to John and said, 'Don't worry, I'll change that,' and he looked at me and said, 'You won't, you know. It's the best line in it.' So, this line that I was going to junk got to stay in. It's a great example of how we collaborated. He was so firm about keeping it in that when I sing 'Hey Jude' now, I often think of John, and it's become this emotional point in the song for me.

It was a delicate moment, of course, because I'm not even sure he knew at the time that the song was for his son Julian. The song had started when I was travelling out one day to see Julian and his mother Cynthia. At this point John had left Cynthia, and I was going out to Kenwood as a friend to say hi and see how they were doing. People have suggested I fancied Cynthia, as people will, but that's not at all the case. I was thinking about how tough it would be for Jules, as I called him, to have his dad leave him, to have his parents go through a divorce. It started out as a song of encouragement.

What often happens with a song is that it starts off in one vein - in this case my being worried about something in life, a specific thing like a divorce - but then it begins to morph into its own creature. The title early on was 'Hey Jules', but it quickly changed to 'Hey Jude' because I thought that was a bit less specific. I realised no one would know exactly what this was about, so I might just as well open it up a bit. Ironically, for a time John thought it was about him and my giving permission for him to be with Yoko: 'You have found her, now go and get her'. I didn't ever know a person called Jude. It was a name I liked - partly, I believe, because of 'Pore Jud Is Daid', that plaintive song from *Oklahoma!*

What happens next is that I start adding elements. When I write, 'You were made to go out and get her', there's now another character, a woman, in the scene. So it might now be a song about a breakup or some romantic mishap. By this stage the song has moved on from being about Julian. It could now be about this new woman's relationship. I like my songs to have an everyman or everywoman element.

Another element that was added to the song is the refrain. 'Hey Jude' wasn't meant to be that length, but we were having such fun ad-libbing at the end that it turned into an anthem, and the orchestra gets built up and built up partly because it has the time to do that.

A funny thing happened in the studio during the recording. Thinking everyone was ready, I started the song, but Ringo had run off to the toilet. Then, as we were recording, I felt him tiptoe back in behind me, and he got to his kit just in time to hit his intro without missing a beat. So even as we're recording it, I'm thinking, 'This is the take, and you put a little more into it.' We were having so much fun that we even left in the swearing around halfway through, when I made a mistake on the piano part. You have to listen carefully to hear it, but it's there.

After we'd mixed it, Mick Jagger heard an early acetate of the recording at the Vesuvio Club on Tottenham Court Road. I handed a copy to the DJ when I got there and asked him to sneak it on at some point in the night to see how it went down. After it played, Mick came over and said, 'That's something else! It's like two songs!'

'Hey Jude' was also the first single on our new Apple record label, and I believe it became our biggest single. The song was too long for a standard seven-inch single, so the engineers had to do some studio trickery with the volume to get it to fit on one side, and it ended up going to number one pretty much everywhere. It was fun starting up the label. The Apple logo was inspired by a René Magritte painting I'd bought, and on the record disc's labels we put a green Granny Smith apple on side A and a cross section of it on side B. Some people thought the B-side was a little suggestive, perhaps even pornographic, but it was just a visual pun on 'Apple Corps'.

The song has since become a highlight of our live show, and the refrain has taken on a life of its own. When people ask me why I still tour, I tell them it's because of communal moments like this. There can be crowds of tens, if not hundreds, of thousands all singing, and it's joyous. The lyrics are so simple that anyone can sing along!

So, 'Hey Jude' started off as my being worried for Julian, and it morphed into this moment of celebration. I also welcome the fact that people put their own interpretations on my songs. I'm always glad when the lyrics get a bit screwed up. When people mishear them, it shows that they've 'taken ownership of them', as they say. I've let the song go. It's yours now. Now you may make of it what you will. It's as if you get to carry the song on your own shoulder.

Above: Cynthia Lennon photographed by Paul. London, February 1964

Right: With Julian Lennon. Weybridge, 1968

Hey Jude don't make it bad,
take a sad song and make it better,
Remember to let her into your heart,
then you can start to make it better.

Hey Jude don't be afraid
You were made to go out and get her,
the minute you let her under your skin
Then you'll begin to make it better.

And any time you feel the pain
hey Jude refrain don't carry the world upon
                                        your shoulders

For well you know that's it, a fool who plays it cool
by making his (life world) a little colder.

Hey Jude, don't let me down.
She had found you now make it better
Remember to let her into your heart,
then you can start to make it better.

So let it out and let it in, hey Jude begin
you waiting for someone to perform with
+ don't you know that it's just you

Above left: With Martha standing beside the Magritte painting that inspired the Apple logo. London, 1968

Above right: Apple Corps catalogue, 1968

Right: Acetate of 'Hey Jude' single, 1968

SO YOU THINK YOU'VE GOT TALENT?

Whatever it is – songs, singers, ...
Send it to APPLE
Our address is 94 Baker St. W.1

So you think you're TALENTED?

Most people are.
Singers, songwriters, musicians.
Send it to Apple 94 Baker St

Left: Ringo Starr during recording sessions for *The Beatles*. Abbey Road Studios, London, 1968

Above and right: Sketches and final poster for Apple Corps advertisement, 1969

At home with the Magic Piano, photographed by daughter Mary. London, 2018

Hi, Hi, Hi

WRITERS	Paul McCartney and Linda McCartney
ARTIST	Paul McCartney and Wings
RECORDED	Abbey Road Studios, London
RELEASED	'Hi, Hi, Hi'/'C Moon' double A-side single, 1972

Well when I met you at the station
You were standing with a bootleg in your hand
I took you back to my little place for a taste
Of a multicoloured band

We're gonna get hi, hi, hi
The night is young
I'll put you in my pocket, little mama
Gonna rock it and we've only just begun

We're gonna get hi, hi, hi
With the music on
Won't say bye-bye, bye-bye, bye-bye, bye-bye
Til the night is gone
I'm gonna do it to you, gonna do ya, sweet banana
You've never been done
We're going to get hi, hi, hi
In the midday sun

Well well take off your face
Recover from the trip you've been on
I want you to lie on the bed
Getting ready for my polygon
I'm gonna do it to you, gonna do ya, sweet banana
You've never been done
Yes so like a rabbit, gonna grab it
Gonna do it til the night is done

We're gonna get hi, hi, hi
With the music on
Won't say bye-bye, bye-bye, bye-bye, bye-bye
Til the night has gone
I'm gonna do it to you, gonna do ya, sweet banana
You've never been done

We're gonna get hi, hi, hi
We're going to get hi, hi, hi
We're going to get hi, hi, hi
In the midday sun

Hi, hi, hi
Hi, hi, hi
Hi, hi, hi
In the midday sun

THE ABSURDIST DRAMATIST ALFRED JARRY FIGURES IN A COU-
ple of my songs, including 'Maxwell's Silver Hammer'. He was a real
character, and his writing was very playful. I first came across him in
a radio production of his play *Ubu Cocu*, the sequel to the much better
known *Ubu Roi*, around the time of writing *Sgt. Pepper*. One of the main
characters in *Ubu Cocu* is a character called Achras, who is a breeder of
'polyhedra'. That's why I use the term 'polygon' in this song. 'Hi, Hi, Hi' was
banned by our friends at the BBC for being sexually suggestive. I believe
they thought I was singing 'body gun' rather than 'polygon'. I'm not sure if
that's more, or less, suggestive.

Before that, the idea of 'I met you at the station' is familiar enough from
the blues tradition:

> *Yeah, when the train left the station*
> *It had two lights on behind*
> *Whoa, the blue light was my baby*
> *And the red light was my mind*

That's from 'Love in Vain', the Robert Johnson song that was covered by
The Rolling Stones in 1969, three years before 'Hi, Hi, Hi' was released.

The 'bootleg' reference goes back to a visit we had on our farm in Scotland by a guy from Norman, Oklahoma. This guy showed up one day with a
vinyl record in a sacking bag - a burlap sack - which was, he announced, a
bootleg. So that was probably what I was thinking of at the start of the song.

Then there's 'going to get hi, hi, hi'. I have to confess that might be a little
cheeky. The BBC certainly thought so. As it happens, this was a moment
when everyone was getting high in the h-i-g-h sense. Everyone was smoking pot. We even got arrested for growing it on our farm in Scotland. Of
course, it might also refer to a legalised drug like alcohol.

The bottom line here is that sex and drugs are two of the staples of rock
and roll. More than that, this is a genre that openly recognises sex and drugs
as being fun.

People say to me, 'Wow, my God, how do you do it?' and I say, 'Sex and
drugs' - which isn't, strictly speaking, true but is loosely true. One of the
features of rock and roll that keeps it vital is that it entertains possibilities
of transgression - or what is usually thought of as transgression.

People say to me, 'Wow, my God, how do you do it?' and I say, 'Sex and drugs' - which isn't, strictly speaking, true but is loosely true. One of the features of rock and roll that keeps it vital is that it entertains possibilities of transgression.

Left and below: Cover for
the 'Hi, Hi, Hi'/ 'C Moon'
double A-side single, 1972

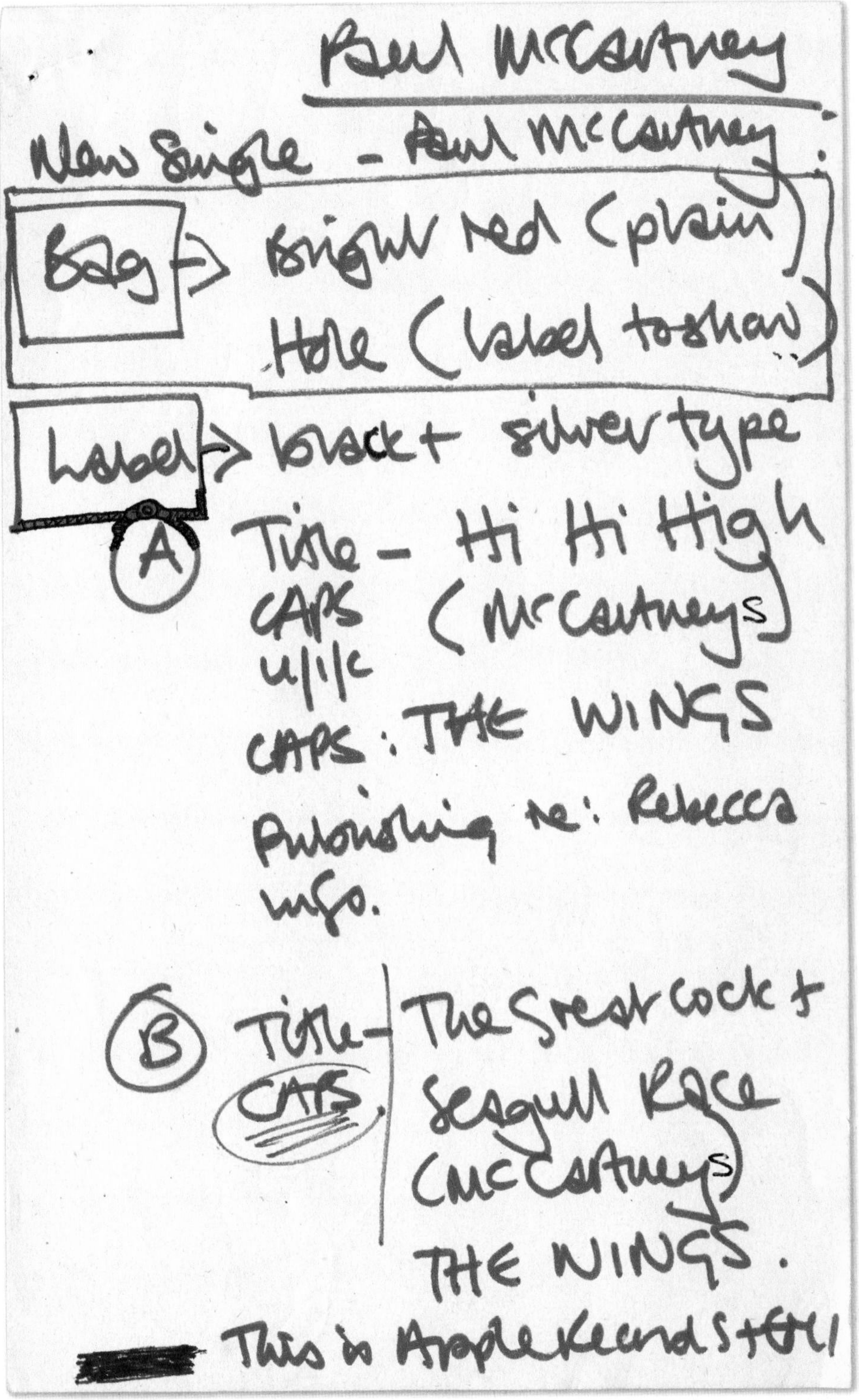

Paul McCartney

New Single — Paul McCartney

Bag → Bright red (plain)
Hole (label to show)

Label → black + silver type

(A) Title — Hi Hi High
CAPS (McCartneys)
u/l/c
CAPS: THE WINGS
Publishing re: Rebecca
info.

(B) Title — The Great cock +
CAPS Seagull Race
(McCartneys)
THE WINGS.

— This is Apple record still

Artwork notes for 'Hi, Hi, Hi'
single with originally planned
B-side 'The Great Cock and
Seagull Race', 1972

Well —
    when I met you at the station
You were standing with a bootleg in your
                                        hand

    Drove you back to my little place
    For a taste of a multicolour band
    were gonna get high high high
        The night is young
Put you in my pocket little mama
gonna rock it and we're only just begun

We're gonna get high high high
    with the music on
we won't say bye bye bye bump —
    till the night has gone
I'm gonna do it to you, gonna do you
    sweet banana
like you've never been done
    Gonna get high, high, high,
    in the midday sun.

Well - Take off your face, recover from the trip
                                    you've been on
    I want you to lie on the bed, getting ready
for my polygon,
I'm gonna do it to you, gonna do you sweet banana
like you've never been done
    + like a rabbit gonna grab it gonna do it
                                    till the night is done

Honey Pie

WRITERS Paul McCartney and John Lennon
ARTIST The Beatles
RECORDED Trident Studios, London
RELEASED *The Beatles*, 1968

She was a working girl
North of England way
Now she's hit the big time in the USA
And if she could only hear me
This is what I'd say

Honey Pie, you are making me crazy
I'm in love but I'm lazy
So won't you please come home?

Oh Honey Pie, my position is tragic
Come and show me the magic
Of your Hollywood song

You became a legend of the silver screen
And now the thought of meeting you
Makes me weak in the knee

Oh Honey Pie, you are driving me frantic
Sail across the Atlantic
To be where you belong
Honey Pie, come back to me

Will the wind that blew
Her boat across the sea
Kindly send her sailing back to me?

Now Honey Pie, you are making me crazy
I'm in love but I'm lazy
So won't you please come home?
Come, come back to me, Honey Pie

Honey Pie
Honey Pie

'CAN'T SING. CAN'T ACT. BALDING. CAN DANCE A LITTLE.' I always liked that quote from the screen test for Fred Astaire. Fred is a bit of an inspiration to me, and sometimes, when I'm singing, I'll pretend to be him to get that 'little' voice. It helps me reach a very particular place. Sometimes I'll be Fats Waller, and that helps me reach a place too.

I was definitely thinking of Fred and the whole world of the silver screen when I was writing 'Honey Pie'. I fell in love not only with Fred but with all those other beautiful singers I'd heard throughout my childhood. For example, I can still remember standing in the kitchen at Forthlin Road and hearing 'When I Fall in Love' by Nat King Cole. I was reaching for an HP sauce bottle at the time and thinking, 'My God, this is good.'

If I'd have to choose anyone, I'd be very happy to be thought of as a channeller of Nat King Cole or Fats or Fred. I don't think there's any denying the idea of being a medium. I definitely dreamt 'Yesterday', so I'm sure I've channelled many other songs.

'Honey Pie', then, is a throwback to the 1930s or even the 1920s, the flapper era and Hollywood ('You became a legend of the silver screen'). The use of sound effects was, as always, a lot of fun. The engineers used a lot of EQ technology to adjust the frequencies, which gives it that little trebly megaphone feel.

Sometimes people get the idea that by the late 1960s, the focus on studio work had begun to take its toll, keeping The Beatles from playing concerts. It's exactly the opposite. The live playing was taking us away from recording. When we were in the studio, we were four artists plus George Martin and an engineer. Six artists, in fact, who were making something, diligently and carefully, having a lot of fun and a lot of artistic freedom. Out on the road it was pretty much the opposite. We were bundled into a car or a hotel room or suffocated in a lift or stuck in a crowd with everyone screaming.

The catalyst for the shift from playing live to focusing on the studio was our experience at Candlestick Park in San Francisco, when we all got totally fed up. I had usually been the one with the optimistic view who said, 'Don't worry, guys. It'll blow over. We'll figure it out.' Finally, I agreed with the other three and was as pissed as they were. We'd been stuck in a steel-lined meat wagon, sliding around just like cattle in a boxcar, as we were being taken away from Candlestick Park. That was the last straw. We'd had it.

Honey Pie.

① Honey Pie, you are driving me frantic
Sail across the Atlantic
To be where you belong.

② Honey Pie my position is tragic
Come + show me the magic
Of your Hollywood song.

You became a legend of the silverscreen

① Obla die Obla da.
③ Mother Natures Son.
⑤ Back in the USSR
⑦ Rocky Racoon
⑨ Junk

Left: With George Martin, Ringo Starr, John Lennon and George Harrison during *The Beatles* recording sessions. Trident Studios, London, 1968

Right: With George Martin during *The Beatles* recording sessions. Abbey Road Studios, London, 1968

Hope of Deliverance

WRITER   Paul McCartney
ARTIST   Paul McCartney
RECORDED   Hog Hill Mill, Sussex
RELEASED   UK single, 1992
              US single, 1993
              Off the Ground, 1993

I will always be hoping, hoping
You will always be holding, holding
My heart in your hand
I will understand

I will understand someday, one day
You will understand always, always
From now until then

When it will be right, I don't know
What it will be like, I don't know
We live in hope of deliverance
From the darkness that surrounds us

Hope of deliverance
Hope of deliverance
Hope of deliverance
From the darkness that surrounds us

And I wouldn't mind knowing, knowing
That you wouldn't mind going, going
Along with my plan

When it will be right, I don't know
What it will be like, I don't know
We live in hope of deliverance
From the darkness that surrounds us

Hope of deliverance
Hope of deliverance
Hope of deliverance
From the darkness that surrounds us

Hope of deliverance
Hope of deliverance
I will understand

Above: With Robbie McIntosh on the set of the video for 'Hope of Deliverance', 1992

CERTAIN COSMIC THEMES GO WAY, WAY BACK THROUGH THE ages. In the Bible or the Quran or the Torah, you get these very profound ideas that are also quite primal. One of them is about how to get out of the dark.

It's true not just for us but for animals, who live their lives looking back over their shoulders. I think it's a cosmic feeling, that we all want to be delivered from something, from the dark, and it's a very rewarding theme for a song. You're bound to be feeling all the problems of the world, so let me help you out, and here's how I'd like to do it. That's the essential story line.

'Deliverance', to me, is a religious word, a biblical word that you hear in church, and I'm glad to be using it in a secular context - in the context of a love song, that's to say. We want deliverance from all the darkness that surrounds us.

I wrote this song up in the attic of my house to get some peace and quiet to myself. It has a little ladder leading up to a trap door so that once you close it, no one else can reach you. I brought a Martin twelve-string guitar up with me, with a capo on it about halfway up the guitar neck to change the sound. It sounds much more jingly that way, which reminds me of Christmas and churches. Maybe that's what led me to the idea of hope and deliverance.

There's a lot of imagery of the clouds, darkness, light, torches, candles, and fires. It's all very primeval. 'We live in hope of deliverance / From the darkness that surrounds us' - that can be anything. For a sailor at sea, it literally is darkness of the night and the hope of seeing a lighthouse, but especially for people in the US, it could be political turmoil, because polarisation exists these days, and we're looking for a way out of that darkness. Romantically, it can mean that you're not getting on well with your partner, and you need deliverance. You're thinking one way, and then you've suddenly got to change. That change may involve just flicking a little switch in your brain.

When I am touring with my band, we actually sing this song in our rehearsals quite often. Normally, we do it without drums, as an acoustic thing, with all of us except Wix Wickens, our keyboard player, and Abe Laboriel, our drummer, who plays an acoustic guitar for this and sings harmony with me. We really enjoy performing it, but it hasn't made it onto the main set list. Not yet, at any rate.

Above: With Linda. 'Hope of Deliverance' music video, 1992

Right: Album notes for Off the Ground, 1992

ALBUM IMAGES -

Ground. (Vid. (We can all fly!)
Still. feet.

Looking. Still. 9 illustrations cat, rabbit, monkey.
(Chrissie?)

Vid. holding animals (approaching cam.)

Hope. vid. religions (Sally army / cosmic)
(Spiritual)

Mistress. Vid. hologram game operated by humans....

hologram
illustrates
words of
song

Still. 50's/60's
flat with couple.

(_0 it al. vid. French caves /
locations mentioned in words)

Bikers. Icon pic. vid. wild ones movie.

Get Out. Vid. illustrates words.

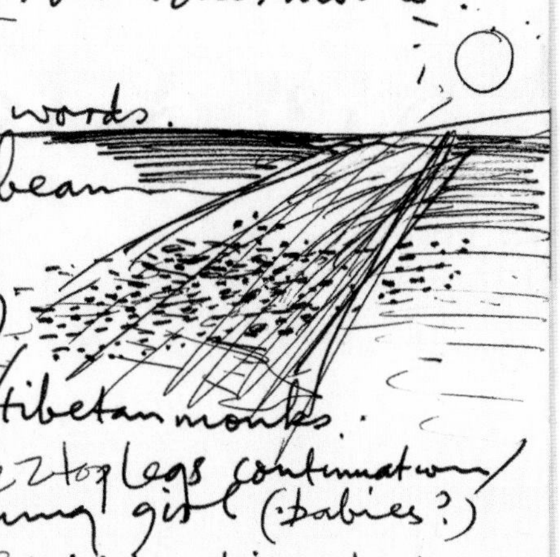

Golden Still. fish in a sunbeam
(or vid.)

Peace. neighbourhood barbacue -
(veggie of course)

Cmon People ancient minstrels / tibetan monks.

Winedark. Style. Vid. 22 toy legs continuation /
spinning girl (babies?)

Long Leather illustration of story? Lichtenstein style.

305

House of Wax

WRITER — Paul McCartney

ARTIST — Paul McCartney

RECORDED — Abbey Road Studios, London

RELEASED — *Memory Almost Full*, 2007
B-side of 'Ever Present Past' single, 2007

Lightning hits the house of wax
Poets spill out on the street
To set alight the incomplete
Remainders of the future

Hidden in the yard
Hidden in the yard

Thunder drowns the trumpets' blast
Poets scatter through the night
But they can only dream of flight
Away from their confusion

Hidden in the yard
Underneath the wall
Buried deep below a thousand layers
Lay the answer to it all

Lightning hits the house of wax
Women scream and run around
To dance upon the battleground
Like wild demented horses

Hidden in the yard
Underneath the wall
Buried deep below a thousand layers
Lay the answer to it all

WHEN I WROTE *BLACKBIRD SINGING* WITH ADRIAN MITCHELL, I was doing a little tour with him, and I'd said, 'Why don't we resurrect that sixties thing where we'll play a backing track and you recite a poem?' He liked that idea, so we did it.

Adrian was my go-to poet, just because I knew him so well, so I asked him various things about poetry. Around that time I think I was trying to write something that was moving more towards poetry. I'm always trying to stretch myself, trying to push my boundaries a little bit, and to educate myself and not get stuck in a rut. If I've just written something very straightforward, like 'It's so sweet, oh baby', then it's kind of nice not to do another one of those immediately. I was in a poetical frame of mind.

'Lightning hits the house of wax' - I remember saying these words to Adrian and being quite proud of the phrase. The phrase 'house of wax' has various references. It could be either a Madame Tussauds or a place where they make records - wax being records, as in 'waxing a disc'. I suppose the best-known 'house of wax' is the one in the 1953 horror movie by that name, which stars Vincent Price and is as hair-raising as a film can be. I didn't have a specific house of wax in mind, and I can't imagine that I was inspired by the gruesome Price murderer - that's just not my thing - but I did like the idea of a house of wax.

As I read it now from a distance, I can see that it's a very fiery first verse. I'm not sure I was consciously trying to go, 'Wow, fire!' You get on a train of thought, and things just come in without you noticing. The poets are about 'To set alight the incomplete / Remainders of the future'. I think that's just a way of saying 'to clarify things'.

'Hidden in the yard / Underneath the wall / Buried deep below a thousand layers / Lay the answer to it all'. I just enlarged upon the image of women, screaming, running around, 'Like wild demented horses'. The song itself gets quite dramatic. I had this little idea that the 'remainders of the future' were sort of buried somewhere in the yard, just like a hidden treasure. Meaning that we don't know the answer to these incomplete remainders, we don't know what's going to happen. I mean, here we are in the midst of the COVID crisis and we really don't know what's going to happen, but I've seen children completely at ease with masks, so this generation of kids is just going to think, 'Oh yeah, everyone wears masks, don't they?'

We had lightning, so we're going to have thunder, and the thunder drowns the trumpets' blast. It's kind of like a film; there's a sort of heraldic score going on and the thunder's blasting it out, so it's like a soundtrack to a film. I wrote this on a piano, so I didn't build it so much while I was writing it, but more when I was recording it. I would think, 'Okay, it should get a bit more dramatic here; the accompaniments should be a bit more dramatic and we should start to build it that way.' We've played it live, but we had to have a large whisky and slap ourselves round the back of our heads to remember it. It's moody. I like to play it, the band likes to play it, and some people in the audience like to hear it played.

In general, though, songs like this one don't hang about in your repertoire, because you realise they're the ones where people are going for a beer, and you think, 'Well, let me just pull 'em back with "Lady Madonna".' I saw Prince and was quite unhappy that he didn't do 'Purple Rain', but he was probably pissed to the eyeballs with 'Purple Rain'. It's a big decision you have to make as a performing artist - whether to just go with your own whims: 'Okay, lads, tonight we're just going acoustic, and we're gonna do all these songs no one's ever heard of.' When you're in front of fifty thousand Brazilians, you don't get the feeling that that'd be the best thing to do. You think, 'Well, I tell you what; let's just do a couple of hits.' So that's what I tend to do, but if we're in a little club situation we can pull out the lesser-known things and watch songs like 'House of Wax' come to life again.

These days we still do little venues, on purpose, if we're getting ready for a tour or we're between things. A couple of years ago we did Coachella; it's a two-weekend festival in the California desert. You play on the Saturday, and then there's a week off and you play the following Saturday. We wanted to keep up to speed, so we booked a little place called Pappy & Harriet's, which is in the Joshua Tree area, near where Coachella is held, so our equipment was nearby. It was just a little, kind of honky-tonk club, held three hundred people, and it was good fun. It wasn't a billed show. We just told people on the day.

We brought David Hockney along. I told him, 'Oh, I'm gonna go to this place; you might enjoy this, David.' And he brought his iPad and sketched a bit. He's only eighty-three.

I Don't Know

WRITER	Paul McCartney
ARTIST	Paul McCartney
RECORDED	Henson Studios, Los Angeles;
	Hog Hill Mill, Sussex; and Abbey Road Studios, London
RELEASED	'Come On to Me'/'I Don't Know' double A-side single, 2018
	Egypt Station, 2018

I got crows at my window
Dogs at my door
I don't think I can take any more
What am I doing wrong?
I don't know

My brother told me
Life's not a pain
That was right when it started to rain
Where am I going wrong?
I don't know

But it's alright, sleep tight
I will take the strain
You're fine, love of mine
You will feel no pain

Well I see trouble
At every turn
I've got so many lessons to learn
What am I doing wrong?
I don't know

Now what's the matter with me?
Am I right, am I wrong?
Now I've started to see
I must try to be strong

I tried to love you
Best as I can
But you know that I'm only a man
Why am I going wrong?
I don't know

But it's alright, sleep tight
I will take the strain
You're fine, little love of mine
You will feel no pain

I got crows at my window
Dogs at my door
But I don't think I can take any more
What am I doing wrong?
I don't know

Now what's the matter with me?
I don't know, I don't know
What's the matter with me?
I don't know, I don't know
What's the matter with me?
I don't know, I don't know

PARENTHOOD IS AN INTERESTING BUSINESS. WE HAVE BABIES FOR the pure joy of bringing a little creature into the world, and everything that goes with that. But sometimes you forget that they'll grow up one day. I've known people who say, 'Oh, I don't like them when they're babies. I like them when they get a bit older.' I don't agree. I like them when they're babies, but let's say it gets more interesting as they get older because things other than 'goo-goo' and 'mama' come into the conversation. The vocabulary is extended a bit. It's sometimes 'challenging', as they say, and this was one of those times.

I was going through a couple of days where I was a bit frantic with what was happening on the home front – things that happen to us all. So the song starts off 'I got crows at my window / Dogs at my door' because that's how I was feeling, and it just kind of spilled out, like, 'Jesus Christ, I'm feeling so bad; I'm just going to tell all.' Once I'd finished it, I felt as if I'd had a session on a psychiatrist's couch.

It's not often that I feel quite so down, but on this occasion I was shouldering a real burden. I've had a couple of verses of moaning to myself, with the rain as a symbol of sadness, and then I think, 'What's the flip side of this? Is it going to work out badly or can I still find some consolation?' I suppose that, as a parent, I wanted to say, 'It's alright, it's okay, don't worry.' Then comes this bridge section: 'But it's alright, sleep tight / I will take the strain / You're fine, love of mine / You will feel no pain'.

So that sets out the basic idea. I'm talking about my troubles as I would in a blues song. 'Well I see trouble / At every turn / I've got so many lessons to learn.' When you've got the blues, you've got the blues. If I'm going to sing a song about sadness, given my musical tastes through the years, it tends to lean towards the blues, the form that's the bedrock of rock and roll. It feels good to sing in those terms. It feels good to embody a sadness rather than just saying, 'I'm very sad today.'

In many ways, that's what poetry or music is all about – the ability to project or show something through the art itself, to raise all these kinds of emotions to a higher level, just the way a good writing teacher will sometimes ask you to 'show' rather than just 'tell'.

This is one song we haven't done yet in concert, because it's a little complicated, and I walk a fine line between doing music that's very simple – rock and roll with three chords, four at most, very minimal – or the music of my dad's era, because of the melodies and the harmonies and the wit of those songs. I think of the great writers of standards of Dad's era, like Harold Arlen, Cole Porter, the Gershwins, who all came out of that tradition. It was a time when Broadway was exploding and Hollywood was exploding, so these people who'd become rather adept at devising clever little rhymes made this a huge American tradition.

I've always been very interested in that period, maybe a time that lasted just until after I was born, when there was a piano in every house, when there was a widespread tradition in many homes of making up little ditties for someone's birthday. Everyone then was a songwriter of sorts. So, sometimes I move away from the three or four chords and explore other formations.

'I Don't Know' is one of those songs where I went out of my comfort zone. It's not just C, F, G. There are A-flats and E-flats in there. There's a little more colour. I like to try different things and experiment.

I often say that writing a song is like talking to a psychiatrist, and this song is just like that. It's me getting my troubles and thoughts out and wondering what I'm doing wrong. But the answer is, 'I don't know'.

Egypt Station II painting by Paul

Above: *Egypt Station* recording sessions. Henson Studios, Los Angeles, 22 February 2016

Right: Limited edition 'I Don't Know' 7" white label promo single

I Lost My Little Girl

WRITER	Paul McCartney
ARTIST	Paul McCartney
RECORDED	Limehouse Studios, London
RELEASED	*Unplugged (The Official Bootleg)*, 1991

Written in 1956 but unreleased until 1991

Well I woke up late this morning
My head was in a whirl
And only then I realised
I lost my little girl
Uh huh huh huh

Well her clothes were not expensive
Her hair didn't always curl
I don't know why I loved her
But I loved my little girl
Uh huh huh huh huh huh

YOU WOULDN'T HAVE TO BE SIGMUND FREUD TO RECOGNISE that the song is a very direct response to the death of my mother. She died in October 1956 at the terribly young age of forty-seven. I wrote this song later that same year. I was fourteen at the time.

Because my dad played trumpet, I'd learnt it a little bit. I gave that up because I couldn't sing with the mouthpiece in my mouth. The point being that I liked the idea of singing, and I was watching loads of people who were coming onto the scene. When you look back and think about it, rock and roll was only just being born.

Since the trumpet was indeed a bit of a non-starter in rock and roll, I ended up with a guitar, of sorts. A Zenith acoustic. It was right-handed, because they didn't sell left-handed guitars, so I had to do a botch job, turn it over so that now the fat, low strings were going into the thin holes and the thin, high strings were going into the fat holes. I had to carve out the thin holes to allow the fat strings to go in, and then put a little match in each fat hole so that the thin string could lie on top of it. I now had pretty much a left-handed guitar, and I had a couple of chords that I'd learnt - very basic chords, as we all do.

The chords in 'I Lost My Little Girl' were going from G to G7 to C, which was descending, so we had a ding-ding-ding effect. I wanted the melody to go upwards as the chord progression was going down. So I was already try-ing to sort of think these things out at fourteen, maybe because music had always been played in our home by my dad or his friends or our aunties, and I'd probably seen them improvising a little. So I decided that while the gui-tar was going down, I would go up with the singing.

The opening line 'Well I woke up late this morning', or some version of it, is a staple of American blues. I'm not at all sure whether I had a particular blues song in my head. It was a very familiar setup. Blues 101. The line 'Her

Above: Early photograph of The Quarry Men with Arthur Kelly, George Harrison and John Lennon

hair didn't always curl' made me cringe a few times over the years but, come on, I was fourteen. And that, as they say, was the start of it.

Things really started, needless to say, when I met John Lennon. We'd been introduced by a mutual friend named Ivan Vaughan, who took me to see John play at the Woolton Village Fête at St Peter's Church. The stage was a flatbed truck, and I thought he was pretty good. He was singing a song called 'Come Go With Me', by The Del-Vikings, and I vaguely knew it. It became clear to me that he only vaguely knew it too and was making it up as he went along. He was singing something like 'Come, come, come, come, go with me, down to the penitentiary'. Those are definitely not the words, but he must have pulled that from Lead Belly or somebody else. I thought that was pretty ingenious of him.

John and I then met up in the break between his daytime show and the evening show, which was in the village hall – the church hall – and there was a little backstage area there. I recall there was a piano, and I had my guitar with me. So I played the song 'Twenty Flight Rock', which was my party piece, and apparently he was very impressed that I knew all the words.

I've a feeling he didn't really want to associate with me, because I was a bit younger than him, but he had to sort of admit there was, well, a little bit of talent there.

I went to his evening show and sort of hung out with Ivan and him. They weren't a great band, but John was good. About a week later, one of John's friends, Pete Shotton, caught up with me when I was out on my bicycle and said, 'They want you in the band.' I paused and said, 'I'll give it some consideration.'

I wasn't exactly playing hard to get. But I was a careful young fellow. I wondered whether I really wanted to be in a band. Was this a good thing, or should I be trying to study for school?

Anyway, I did get back to them and said, 'Yeah.'

Things really started, needless to say, when I met John Lennon. We'd been introduced by a mutual friend named Ivan Vaughan, who took me to see John play at the Woolton Village Fête at St Peter's Church. The stage was a flatbed truck, and I thought he was pretty good.

Woolton Parish Church
Garden Fete
and
Crowning of Rose Queen
Saturday, July 6th, 1957

To be opened at 3p.m. by Dr. Thelwall Jones

PROCESSION AT 2p.m.

LIVERPOOL POLICE DOGS DISPLAY
FANCY DRESS PARADE
SIDESHOWS   REFRESHMENTS
BAND OF THE CHESHIRE YEOMANRY
THE QUARRY MEN SKIFFLE GROUP

ADULTS 6d., CHILDREN 3d.   OR BY PROGRAMME

GRAND DANCE

at 8p.m. in the Church Hall

GEORGE EDWARDS' BAND
THE QUARRY MEN SKIFFLE GROUP

Tickets 2/-

Above: Zenith guitar drawing
found in a schoolbook copy
of Hamlet, late 1950s

Right: With Ivan Vaughan.
London, 1968

Playing the Zenith guitar on the set of the 'Early Days' music video. Los Angeles, 5 March 2014

I Saw Her Standing There

WRITERS	Paul McCartney and John Lennon
ARTIST	The Beatles
RECORDED	Abbey Road Studios, London
RELEASED	*Please Please Me*, 1963
	B-side of 'I Want to Hold Your Hand' US single, 1963
	Introducing… The Beatles, 1964

Well she was just seventeen
You know what I mean
And the way she looked was way beyond compare
So how could I dance with another
Ooh when I saw her standing there

Well she looked at me
And I, I could see
That before too long I'd fall in love with her
She wouldn't dance with another
Ooh when I saw her standing there

Well my heart went boom
When I crossed that room
And I held her hand in mine

Oh we danced through the night
And we held each other tight
And before too long I fell in love with her
Now I'll never dance with another
Ooh when I saw her standing there

Well my heart went boom
When I crossed that room
And I held her hand in mine

Oh we danced through the night
And we held each other tight
And before too long I fell in love with her
Now I'll never dance with another
Ooh since I saw her standing there
Since I saw her standing there
Since I saw her standing there

I'VE WRITTEN A LOT OF SONGS, BUT CERTAIN ONES STAND out, and if I had to choose what I thought was my best work over the years, I would probably include 'I Saw Her Standing There'. No, I would *definitely* include this one.

I first played this song to John when he and I got together to smoke tea in my dad's pipe. (And when I say tea, I mean tea.) I said, 'She was just seventeen. She'd never been a beauty queen.' And John said, 'I'm not sure about that.' So our main task was to get rid of the beauty queen. We struggled with it, but then it came.

Singing it now - and this happens with all the Beatles songs I sing, particularly from the earlier period - I realise I'm reviewing the work of an eighteen-to-twenty-year-old boy. And I think this is very interesting because it's got a naïveté - a kind of innocence - that you can't invent.

Mind you, Jerry Seinfeld did a great sort of satirical thing with it. We went to the White House, and Jerry says, 'Paul, you know, I've been looking at "She was just seventeen / You know what I mean"; I'm not sure we *do* know what you mean, Paul!'

In any case, we'd heard all this stuff - I was around twenty, and we wrote this at my dad's at Forthlin Road - and now we're going, 'She was just seventeen / You know what I mean / And the way she looked was way beyond compare'. That rhythm echoes Stanley Holloway's version of 'The Lion and Albert'. It's a comic poem written by Marriott Edgar, and it has a similar metre.

I was loaded with all the tunes I'd heard. Hoagy Carmichael's writing, Harold Arlen's writing, George Gershwin's writing, Johnny Mercer. I'd heard all this stuff growing up. I hadn't written anything much myself, but it had all gone in. And then at school I'd heard my English teacher, Alan Durband, talking about the rhyming couplet at the end of a Shakespeare sonnet. I don't know where 'beyond compare' came from, but it might have come out of Sonnet 18: 'Shall I compare thee to a summer's day?' I may even have been conscious, as a child, of the Irish song tradition - of a woman being described as 'beyond compare'.

In any case, it's not what you would expect in rock and roll. And like I say, I don't know where I dredged it from, but in the great trawling net of my youth, it just got caught up like a dolphin.

Above: Alan Durband, Head of English at Liverpool Institute High School for Boys

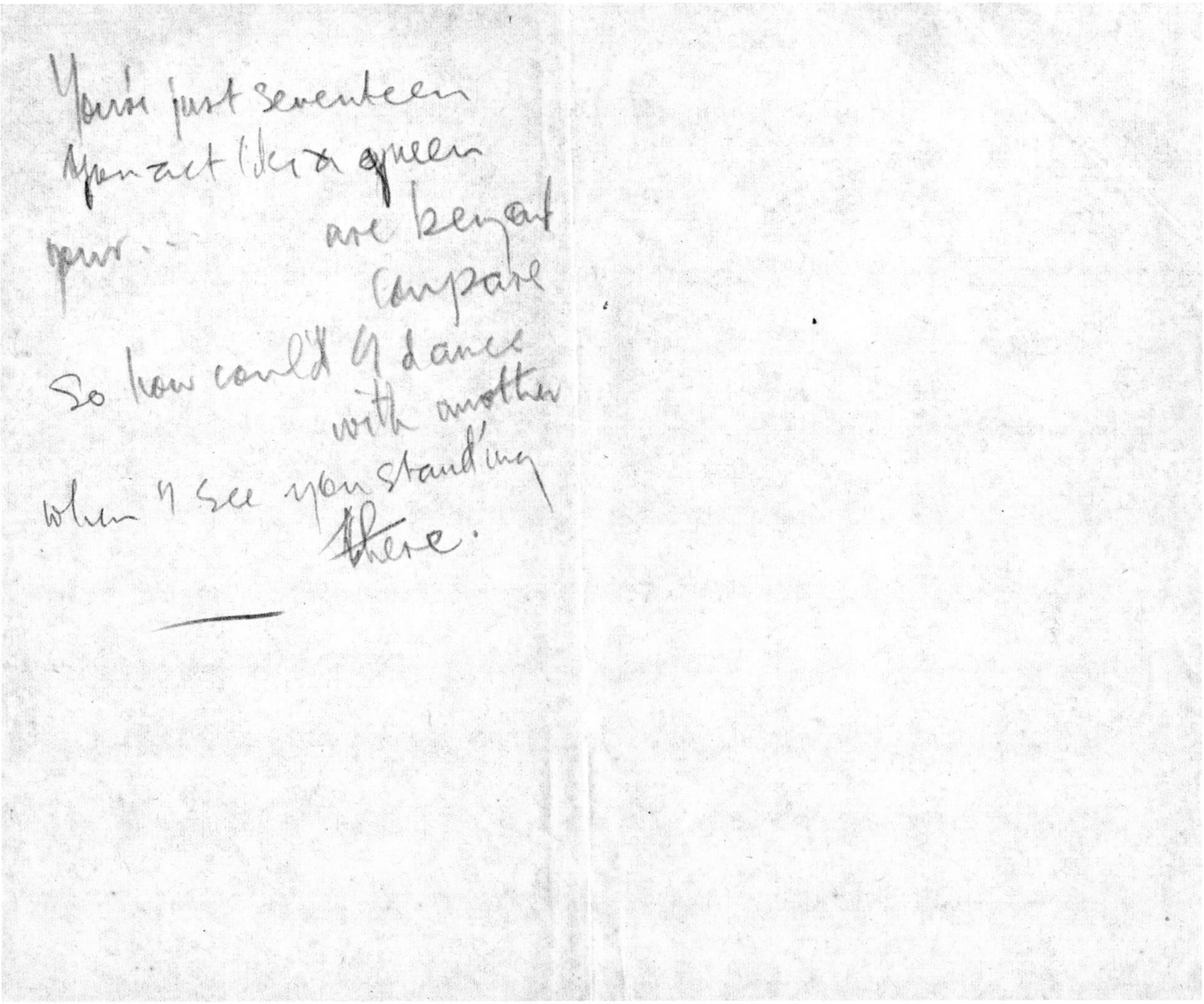
You're just seventeen
You act like a queen
your... are beyond
compare
So how could I dance
with another
when I see you standing
there.

Left: With John Lennon.
Liverpool, late 1950s

With John Lennon
writing 'I Saw Her
Standing There'.
Forthlin Road,
Liverpool, 1962

Writing with John
Lennon, photographed
by brother Mike.
Forthlin Road,
Liverpool, early 1960s

I Wanna Be Your Man

WRITERS   Paul McCartney and John Lennon
ARTIST   The Beatles
RECORDED   Abbey Road Studios, London
RELEASED   *With The Beatles*, 1963

I wanna be your lover, baby
I wanna be your man
I wanna be your lover, baby
I wanna be your man

Love you like no other, baby
Like no other can
Love you like no other, baby
Like no other can

I wanna be your man
I wanna be your man
I wanna be your man
I wanna be your man

Tell me that you love me, baby
Let me understand
Tell me that you love me, baby
I wanna be your man

I wanna be your lover, baby
I wanna be your man
I wanna be your lover, baby
I wanna be your man

I wanna be your man
I wanna be your man
I wanna be your man
I wanna be your man

I wanna be your lover, baby
I wanna be your man
I wanna be your lover, baby
I wanna be your man

Love you like no other, baby
Like no other can
Love you like no other, baby
Like no other can

I wanna be your man
I wanna be your man
I wanna be your man
I wanna be your man

WE ALWAYS WROTE A SONG FOR RINGO ON EACH ALBUM, because he was very popular with the fans, and as Keith Richards once said to me, 'You had four singers in your group. We only had one.' And it's true. Ringo wasn't the best vocalist in the group, but there's no doubt he could hold a song. He'd always done a song called 'Boys', which was originally sung by The Shirelles.

The gay audience must have been very happy to hear The Beatles' drummer singing about boys, but we never really thought about that. And to people who fussed over lyrics we used to say, 'Nobody listens to the words. It's just the sound of the song.'

Now I'm not so sure about that. I think times have changed. But in the early days we didn't always worry too much about the words or their nuances. 'I wanna be your lover, baby / I wanna be your man / I wanna be your lover, baby / I wanna be your man'. Pretty basic, but it was a cool enough little song, and Ringo did it really well.

One day, around the time we moved down to London from Liverpool in the summer of 1963, John and I were in Charing Cross Road, which was guitar central. We would get a taxi and go down there, just to look at the guitars. The whole place in the early sixties was guitar shops, and we'd just go there and gaze longingly all afternoon at guitars we could not afford.

Besides, Dick James's office was there. He was our publisher then. That was probably the real reason for going. Anyhow, we were looking at the guitars one day when a black London cab went by and we noticed Mick Jagger and Keith Richards in it. So we yelled, 'Hey!' They saw us waving, so they pulled over. We ran up and said, 'Hey, give us a lift.' 'Yeah, alright. Where are you going?' 'We're going to north London.'

So, we were just chatting in the car about what we were doing. 'Oh, we've got a recording contract,' Mick told us. We knew that already, because George Harrison had got it for them. Dick Rowe was the guy who turned down The Beatles and didn't want us for Decca, and I have to say, if you listen to our audition tape, it wasn't brilliant, but there was something there. So George was at a cocktail party, and Dick Rowe said, 'Do you know any good groups? I made one mistake, and I'm looking to sign someone good.' George said, 'Yeah, they're called The Rolling Stones. You should try and sign them.' He told Rowe the Stones were at the Station Hotel in Richmond, where they often played, and Rowe went along to see them and signed them pretty much on the spot.

So there we were in the taxi, talking, and Mick said, 'The only trouble is, we haven't got a new single.' They asked us if we had any songs, and I said, 'Well, there's a song that we've done on our latest record, *With The Beatles*, but it's an album track. It hasn't been a single, and it won't be, because it's Ringo doing it. But I think it would work great for you guys.' So we sent 'I Wanna Be Your Man' over to them, and they recorded it. Our version was a bit more of a Bo Diddley shuffle; theirs is quite raw and distorted, almost punk-like, and it was their first big hit.

After that we would hang out with each other; we would talk about what music they were making. I would go hang at Keith's flat, so we were quite friendly. John and I sang on one of their songs – 'We Love You' - in 1967, so we had a lot of interaction. But the idea that we were rivals was just something started by the media, and then people started to ask, 'Who do you like, The Beatles or the Stones?' And it became an either/or thing. It wasn't framed like that for the first couple of years, but it got built up by the press as we became more successful. And it just wasn't true. Mick used to come over to my house in London so that I could play him all the new American records while all this was being written.

So, that was the kind of relationship we had. But with the press, you need them and they need you, as we would discover throughout our careers, but things are said that can stick. For instance, they called what we did 'Mersey Beat' - which took its name from a local entertainment paper - and we thought, 'Well, bloody hell. That's so corny.' We never thought of ourselves as Mersey, we thought of ourselves as Liverpool, and it's an important difference if you come from there. But 'Mersey Beat' and 'Mop Tops' - all these catchphrases stuck and were quite annoying. You'd do something you wouldn't even think about, but then it would be a huge story.

Stones, Beatles - we were big buddies, forever and ever, but the fans started to believe there was some truth in the manufactured rivalry. There never was.

I Want to Hold Your Hand

WRITERS   John Lennon and Paul McCartney
ARTIST   The Beatles
RECORDED   Abbey Road Studios, London
RELEASED   Single, 1963
                 Meet The Beatles! 1964

Oh yeah I'll tell you something
I think you'll understand
When I say that something
I want to hold your hand

I want to hold your hand
I want to hold your hand

Oh please say to me
You'll let me be your man
And please say to me
You'll let me hold your hand

Now let me hold your hand
I want to hold your hand

And when I touch you I feel happy inside
It's such a feeling that my love
I can't hide
I can't hide
I can't hide

Yeah you got that something
I think you'll understand
When I say that something
I want to hold your hand

I want to hold your hand
I want to hold your hand

And when I touch you I feel happy inside
It's such a feeling that my love
I can't hide
I can't hide
I can't hide

Yeah you got that something
I think you'll understand
When I feel that something
I want to hold your hand

I want to hold your hand
I want to hold your hand
I want to hold your hand

THERE WAS AN EROTICISM BEHIND IT ALL. IF I'D HEARD myself use that word when I was seventeen, there would have been a guffaw. But eroticism was very much a driving force behind everything I did. It's a very strong thing. And, you know, that was what lay behind a lot of these love songs. 'I want to hold your hand', open brackets, [and probably do a lot more!]

By the time this song was written, when I was about twenty-one, we had come to London. Our manager had gotten The Beatles a flat: Apartment L, 57 Green Street, Mayfair. It was all very exciting; Mayfair is a posh part of London. For some reason I was the last one to go down there and see it, and they'd left me a small room. The others had bagged all the great rooms. They'd left me this crappy little room.

But by then I had a girlfriend, Jane Asher, who was a very classy girl whose father was a Wimpole Street doctor and whose mother was a wonderful lady, a music teacher, called Margaret Asher. So I would go round to their house to visit. I loved it there because it was such a *family*. Margaret and I got on very well. She sort of mothered me. It was what I'd been used to before my mum died, when I was fourteen, though I'd never seen a family quite like this. The only people I'd seen were working-class Liverpool. This was classy London; all of them had diaries that stretched from eight in the morning to six or seven at night – jam-packed. There was not a second that wasn't accounted for. Jane would go off to her agent, then read for a play, then meet someone for lunch, then have a vocal coach teaching her a Norfolk accent for her next thing. So I was quite infatuated with all this. It was like a story, like a novel I was living in.

Eventually I ended up living with the Ashers. I'd already stayed over quite a bit, but Margaret must have said, 'Well, you know, we'll let you have the attic room.' So I ended up there, and they got a piano up in that room.

When John came to visit, there was a piano in the basement as well – a little music room where I think Margaret took students. So, we would write there in the basement, both on the piano at the same time, or eyeball to eyeball on our guitars.

'I Want to Hold Your Hand' is not about Jane, but it was certainly written when I was with her. To tell you the truth, I think we were writing more to a general audience. I may have been drawing on my experience with a person I was in love with at the time – and sometimes it was very specific – but mostly we were writing to the world.

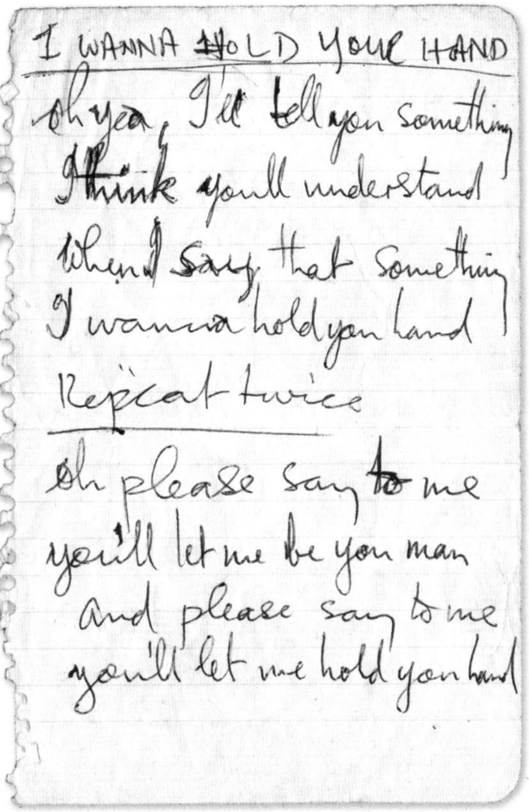

I WANNA HOLD YOUR HAND

Oh yea, I'll tell you something
I think you'll understand
When I say that something
I wanna hold your hand

Repeat twice

Oh please say to me
you'll let me be your man
And please say to me
you'll let me hold your hand

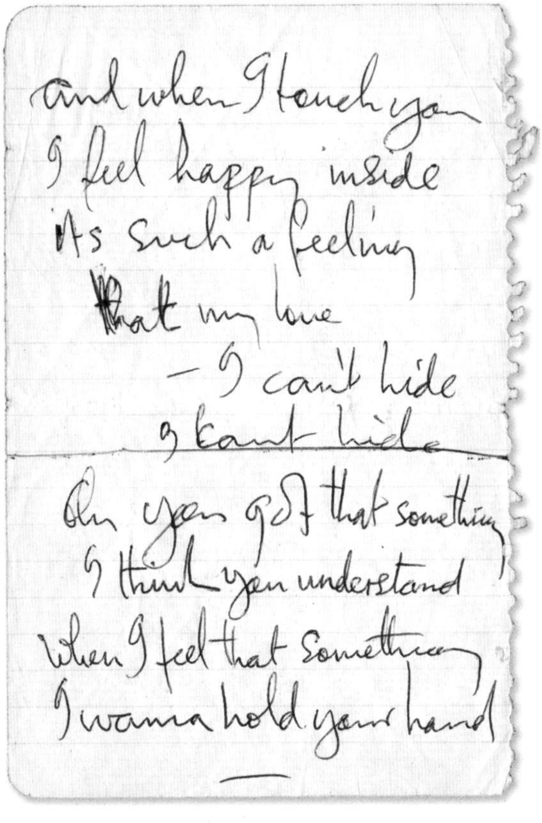

And when I touch you
I feel happy inside
Its such a feeling
that my love
— I can't hide
I can't hide

Oh yea you got that something
I think you understand
When I feel that something
I wanna hold your hand

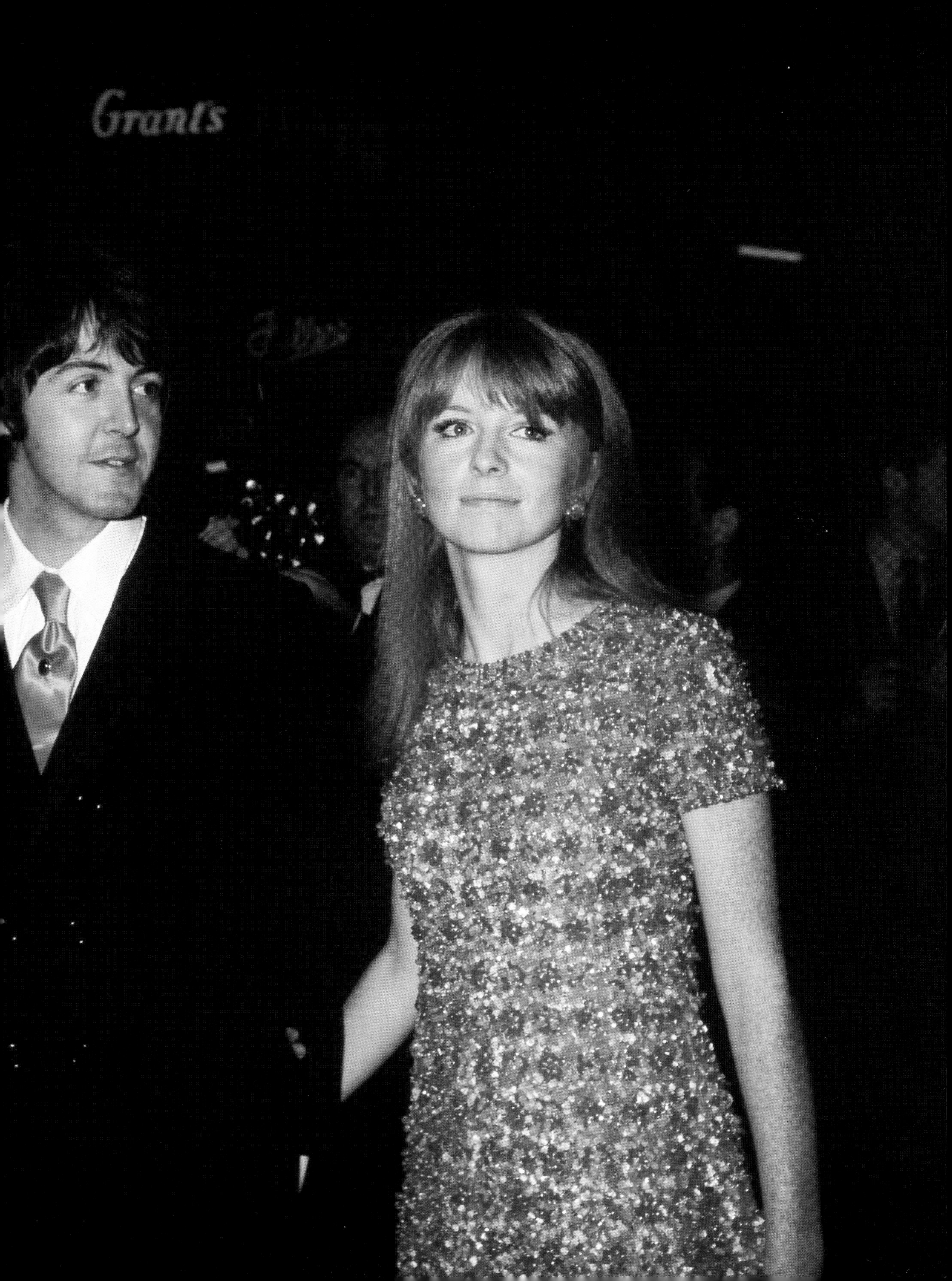
Grant's

I Will

WRITERS   Paul McCartney and John Lennon
ARTIST   The Beatles
RECORDED   Abbey Road Studios, London
RELEASED   *The Beatles*, 1968

Who knows how long I've loved you
You know I love you still
Will I wait a lonely lifetime
If you want me to I will

For if I ever saw you
I didn't catch your name
But it never really mattered
I will always feel the same

Love you forever and forever
Love you with all my heart
Love you whenever we're together
Love you when we're apart

And when at last I find you
Your song will fill the air
Sing it loud so I can hear you
Make it easy to be near you
For the things you do endear you to me
You know I will
I will

Above: With Jane Asher
and the Maharishi.
Rishikesh, India, April 1968

ALAN-A-DALE. THE MINSTREL WANDERING AROUND SHERWOOD Forest in the Robin Hood legend. That's me. This song finds me in my troubadour mode.

There's a theory that the most interesting love songs are ones about love gone wrong. I don't subscribe to it. This is a song about the joy of love. Those are sometimes thought of as being soppy or sweet or saccharine. Yes, I understand that. But love can be the mightiest, strongest force on the planet. Right now in Vietnam, or in Brazil, there are people falling in love. They often want to have children. It's a strong, universal force. It's not soppy at all.

When I sit down to try and write a song, I'm often thinking, 'Oh, I wish I could capture that feeling of first being in love.' This song was started in February 1968, when I was in India with Jane Asher. As I recall, the melody had been around for a while, and the music came together quite quickly. It's still one of my favourites of the melodies I've written. The words took a bit longer. That seems strange, I know, because it's a pretty basic set of ideas. The folk singer Donovan, who spent some time with us on our trip to visit Maharishi Mahesh Yogi, helped with an early version of the lyric, but it didn't quite pass muster. It was even more basic, all moon/June stuff.

Yet again, just because I was involved with Jane at the time doesn't mean this song is addressed to, or about, Jane. When I'm writing, it's as if I'm setting words and music to the film I'm watching in my head. It's a declaration of love, yes, but not always to someone specific. Unless it's to a person out there who's listening to the song. And they have to be ready for it. It's almost definitely not going to be a person who's said, 'There he goes again, writing another of those silly love songs.' So, this is me in my troubadour mode.

This is a song about the joy of love. Those are sometimes thought of as being soppy or sweet or saccharine. Yes, I understand that. But love can be the mightiest, strongest force on the planet. Right now in Vietnam, or in Brazil, there are people falling in love. They often want to have children. It's a strong, universal force. It's not soppy at all.

I'll Follow the Sun

WRITERS   Paul McCartney and John Lennon
ARTIST   The Beatles
RECORDED   Abbey Road Studios, London
RELEASED   *Beatles for Sale*, 1964; *Beatles '65*, 1964

One day you'll look
To see I've gone
For tomorrow may rain, so
I'll follow the sun

Some day you'll know
I was the one
But tomorrow may rain, so
I'll follow the sun

And now the time has come
And so, my love, I must go
And though I lose a friend
In the end you will know, oh

One day you'll find
That I have gone
But tomorrow may rain, so
I'll follow the sun

Yes tomorrow may rain, so
I'll follow the sun

And now the time has come
And so, my love, I must go
And though I lose a friend
In the end you will know, oh

One day you'll find
That I have gone
But tomorrow may rain, so
I'll follow the sun

THE LAST HOUSE I LIVED IN IN LIVERPOOL WAS 20 FORTHLIN Road. By then we'd moved up in the world. My mum had great aspirations for us, and she'd found this house in a comparatively nice area. There were lace curtains, which is probably why I've still got lace curtains everywhere. An Irish thing, maybe. So people can't look in. I remember standing in the living room with my guitar, singing this song. When you think about it, it's a 'Leaving of Liverpool' song. I'm leaving this rainy northern town for someplace where more is happening.

It's an interesting melody too. I'd been searching for striking new combinations of notes. There's something quite original about it. One of my favourite songs of my dad's era was 'Cheek to Cheek', the Fred Astaire song, and what I liked was that it starts with 'Heaven, I'm in heaven', and it goes through two verses and comes back at the end of the middle eight to 'heaven'. It's a single sentence. It was like our house in Forthlin Road. You went in the front door, went around through the living room, dining room, kitchen, hall, and ended up back where you started. 'I'll Follow the Sun' does that too.

Even if we were open to influencers, one of the great things about The Beatles was our aversion to repeating ourselves. We were intelligent young lads; we didn't like being bored. When we played Hamburg, we sometimes had an eight-hour stretch to fill. We tried to learn enough songs so we didn't have to repeat them. Some bands just had an hour's set, took an hour off, and then played a whole hour's set all over again. We tried to vary it, because we'd decided we simply weren't going to survive otherwise. By the time we came back to England, we had a large repertoire, and I think when we started making records, that idea persisted. Why repeat ourselves? Why make the same record twice?

It's true that, as I've said, there was a certain formula to some of the early songs - the recurrence of the pronouns 'I', 'you', 'me', 'him', 'her', 'my', 'she' – but that was because we wanted to be in contact with the fans. To engage with them. But they weren't formulaic. What made The Beatles such a great band was that no two tracks are the same. It's pretty amazing when you think of that output. The other thing is that John and I wrote close to three hundred songs in sessions lasting just a few hours or a single day, and we never, ever came away from one of those sessions without finishing a song. Whenever we sat down to write a song, we didn't leave that room until we had one.

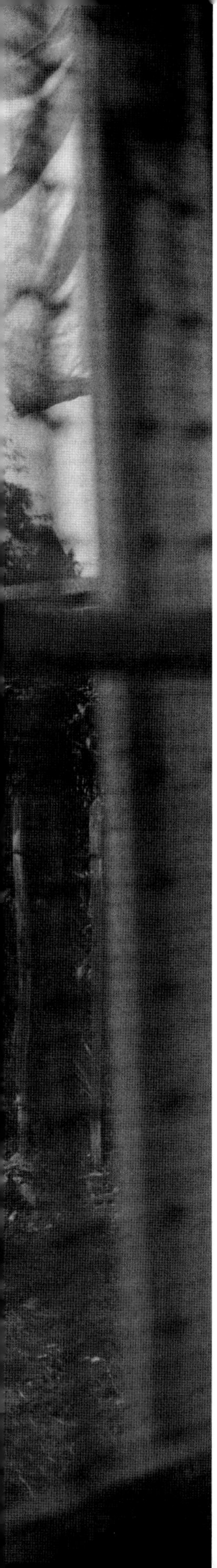

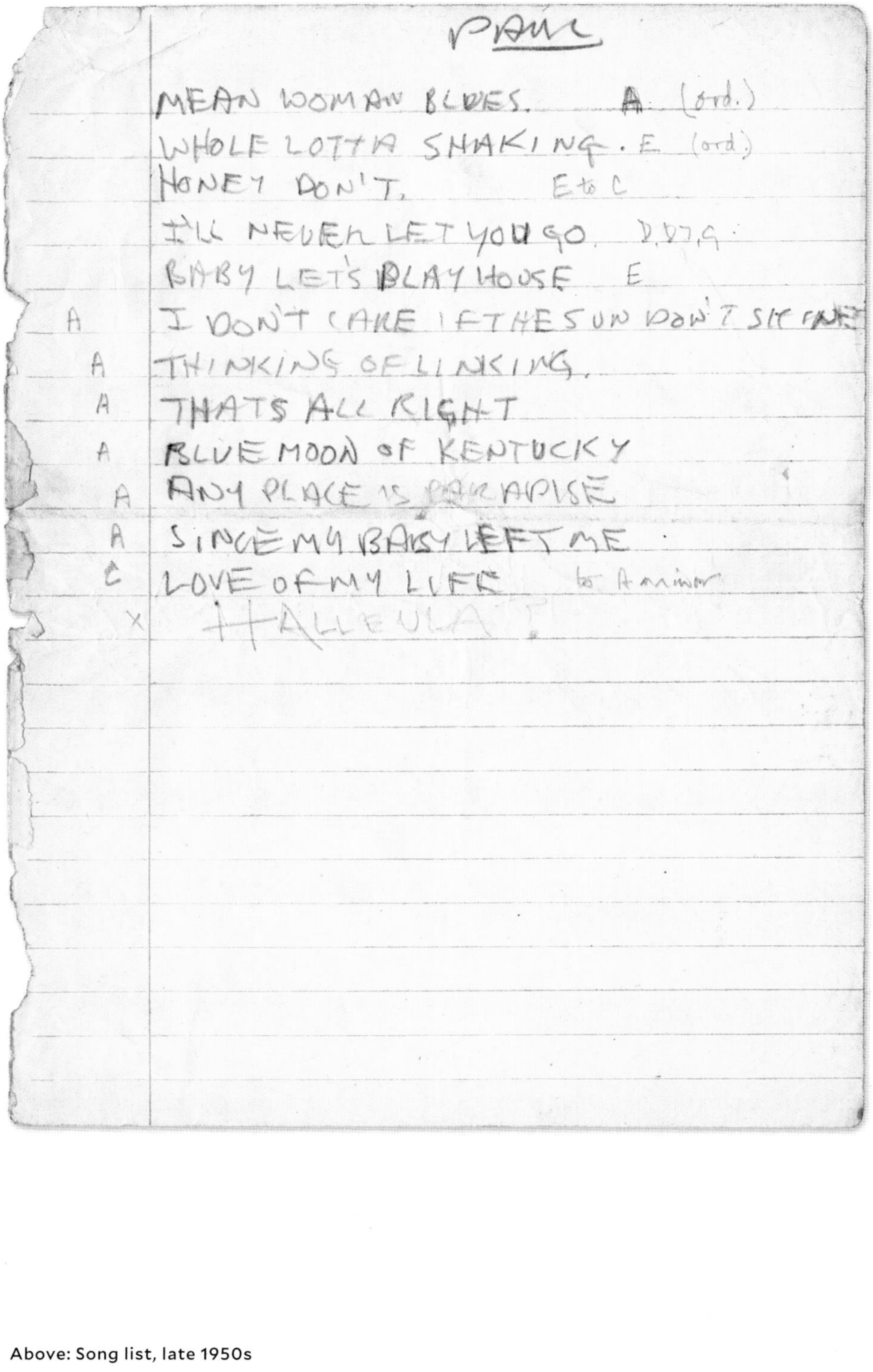

PAUL

	MEAN WOMAN BLUES.	A (ord.)
	WHOLE LOTTA SHAKING.	E (ord.)
	HONEY DON'T.	E to C
	I'LL NEVER LET YOU GO.	D. D7. G.
	BABY LET'S PLAY HOUSE	E
A	I DON'T CARE IF THE SUN DON'T SHINE	
A	THINKING OF LINKING.	
A	THAT'S ALL RIGHT	
A	BLUE MOON OF KENTUCKY	
A	ANY PLACE IS PARADISE	
A	SINCE MY BABY LEFT ME	
C	LOVE OF MY LIFE	to A minor
X	HALLELULA	

Above: Song list, late 1950s

Left: In the garden of 20 Forthlin Road, photographed by brother Mike, Liverpool, early 1960s. This image was later used for the cover of the 2005 album *Chaos and Creation in the Backyard*

I'll Get You

WRITERS   Paul McCartney and John Lennon
ARTIST   The Beatles
RECORDED   Abbey Road Studios, London
RELEASED   B-side of 'She Loves You' single, 1963
               The Beatles' Second Album, 1964

Oh yeah, oh yeah
Oh yeah, oh yeah

Imagine I'm in love with you
It's easy 'cause I know
I've imagined I'm in love with you
Many, many, many times before
It's not like me to pretend
But I'll get you, I'll get you in the end
Yes I will, I'll get you in the end
Oh yeah, oh yeah

I think about you night and day
I need you and it's true
When I think about you, I can say
I'm never, never, never, never blue
So I'm telling you, my friend
That I'll get you, I'll get you in the end
Yes I will, I'll get you in the end
Oh yeah, oh yeah

Well there's gonna be a time
When I'm gonna change your mind
So you might as well resign yourself to me
Oh yeah

Imagine I'm in love with you
It's easy 'cause I know
I've imagined I'm in love with you
Many, many, many times before
It's not like me to pretend
But I'll get you, I'll get you in the end
Yes I will, I'll get you in the end

Oh yeah, oh yeah
Oh yeah, oh yeah, oh yeah

THIS SONG WAS WRITTEN ON MENLOVE AVENUE, IN LIVERPOOL, where John still lived with his Aunt Mimi. She was a good and very strong-willed woman; she definitely knew her own mind. What's odd about that is that Mimi didn't care so much for our music and would just as soon not have had us around, because she thought we were encouraging John to devote more time to his guitar instead of his studies. Mimi always said, 'The guitar's all right for a hobby, John, but you'll never make a living at it!'

The word and idea of 'imagine' is something John would repurpose in his own song 'Imagine'. It's also a bit like the opening of 'Lucy in the Sky With Diamonds', with its exhortation to 'Picture yourself . . .' So it's a filmic thing, as well as a literary thing. When I say 'literary', I think of the imagined world of Lewis Carroll that John and I both loved so much. Carroll was a big influence on both of us; that can really be seen in John's books *In His Own Write* and *A Spaniard in the Works*.

With regard to the musical structure, that's a really effective opening – a D major chord as we sing 'oh yeah' in an octave. We'd learnt the sort of C, A minor, F, G, and D sequences – the straight, 'triady' things. But then you start to juxtapose them a bit, and the opening of 'I'll Get You' is an example of what happens. Otherwise, these are fairly standard chords, until you get to 'It's not like me to pretend'. That's a weird chord under 'pretend'. It doesn't quite belong, and that's the secret of this song.

It may be a bit much to say that the chord is commenting on the word 'pretend' – suggesting that the character in the song may not be taken at face value, that he's actually pretending to feel, to present a feeling he's not really committed to. That he might just be playing around. In general, though, the sentiment in these early songs is pretty straight up. Not a lot of irony. And that's why people liked, and like, these songs. They say what they mean. 'It's not like me to pretend / But I'll get you, I'll get you in the end'. Mind you, I think it's fair to say there might be a little bit of schoolboy humour hovering around the idea too.

Dear

John.
I have to
go for Mimi about
1-30pm so I have left
her clothes here I will
be back in an hour 12-30pm
Mimi.

Above: The Beatles rehearsing. The Cavern Club, Liverpool, early 1960s

Right: With John Lennon and brother Mike, photographed by George Harrison. The Cavern Club, Liverpool, early 1960s

I'm Carrying

WRITER   Paul McCartney

ARTIST   Wings

RECORDED   *Fair Carol*, Virgin Islands; and Abbey Road Studios, London

RELEASED   *London Town*, 1978

                B-side of 'London Town' single, 1978

By dawn's first light I'll come back to your room again
With my carnation hidden by the packages
I'm carrying
Something
I'm carrying something for you

Ah long time no see, baby, sure has been a while
And if my reappearance lacks a sense of style
I'm carrying
Something
I'm carrying something for you

I'm carrying
Can't help it
I'm carrying something for you

I'm carrying
Something
I'm carrying something for you

FOLLOWING THE BEATLES WAS ALWAYS GOING TO BE DIFFICULT. I was carrying baggage in many people's minds. But after a few solo releases, I wanted to get back to the camaraderie of being in a band, and I could have approached Wings in one of two ways: either I could come in at the top as a Beatle alongside a former member of Small Faces or Cream and make what they used to call a 'supergroup', or I could just start something that felt good and try to build it up like The Beatles had. I chose the latter. The only trouble was that we'd have to make our mistakes in public this time around. With The Beatles it had all been in private, because there was no one much in the clubs of Hamburg to hear us mess up.

It was a slog at first, because we didn't have any Wings songs and I didn't want to play anything by The Beatles. I wanted to have a clean break. All the big-name promoters at the time said, 'Are you going to do "Yesterday"?' and you could tell by the looks on their faces that was what they wanted, and that was what we had to fight against. It's just who I am; I am loath to duplicate anything or anyone, so I wanted Wings to be successful in its own right. From the beginning, then, it was obvious that we had to be resigned to the fact it would take time. We started off with little things, got a little bit bigger, went abroad. We weren't a very good band at the beginning, a bit rough around the edges. It was a little gig here and a little gig there, turning up at universities and asking to play the student union that night with nothing to play that people knew. But then we started to get better, and we started to get more used to each other. Then, by the mid-seventies, we suddenly had hits, like 'Band on the Run', 'Silly Love Songs' and enough of our own stuff to actually be known for that rather than The Beatles.

People say, 'What does this song mean?' and I say, 'Well, it's up to you.' It can mean a million things. What am I carrying here? I kind of make it clear that it's packages. So I'm like Dapper Dan, with my carnation hidden by the packages. I'm bringing presents for you, I'm carrying something for you, but also, when a woman is having a baby, she's carrying. There are a couple of other meanings that rule themselves out. One is carrying a gun. Another is carrying drugs. One meaning that might have a little traction is the idea of one person 'carrying' a band, with the others riding on the coattails. I'm not even sure about that. I'm just playing with the word 'carrying'. It's a very ambiguous little song, but that was the sort of freedom of Wings, to do something a little bit ambiguous.

It's been suggested that this song sounds Lennon-esque. I'd admit to it if it were, but to me it sounds more McCartney-esque: just the little voice. I couldn't imagine John doing quite such a little voice. But you know, if it's seen as Lennon-esque, that's no great problem. We did learn how to write songs together, after all.

People say, 'What does this song mean?' and I say, 'Well, it's up to you.' It can mean a million things.

Left: *London Town*
recording sessions.
Virgin Islands, 1977

Top: Wings departing for
their *University Tour*, 1972

Above: Gatefold artwork
for *London Town*, 1979

I'm Down

WRITERS   Paul McCartney and John Lennon
ARTIST   The Beatles
RECORDED   Abbey Road Studios, London
RELEASED   B-side of 'Help!' single, 1965

You tell lies thinkin' I can't see
You can't cry 'cause you're laughing at me

I'm down (I'm really down)
I'm down (down on the ground)
I'm down (I'm really down)
How can you laugh when you know I'm down?
(How can you laugh?) When you know I'm down?

Man buys ring
Woman throws it away
Same old thing
Happen every day

I'm down (I'm really down)
I'm down (down on the ground)
I'm down (I'm really down)
How can you laugh when you know I'm down?
(How can you laugh?) When you know I'm down?

We're all alone
And there's nobody else
You still moan
Keep your hands to yourself

I'm down (I'm really down)
Oh babe, I'm down (down on the ground)
I'm down (I'm really down)
How can you laugh when you know I'm down?
(How can you laugh?) When you know I'm down?

Oh babe, you know I'm down (I'm really down)
Oh yes I'm down (I'm really down)
I'm down on the ground (I'm really down)
I'm down (I'm really down)
Ah baby, I'm upside down
Oh yeah, yeah, yeah, yeah, yeah

IT'S A ROCK AND ROLL SCREAMER, AND THE VOICE BELONGS to Little Richard. Early on, I'd sung 'Long Tall Sally' at an end-of-term party. You could bring your guitar into school on the last day. We had a history teacher named Walter Edge, though we called him 'Cliff' Edge because we thought that was really funny. He was one of our favourite teachers. I got to stand up on the desk in front of all my mates in the class and sing 'Long Tall Sally' with my guitar because he let us.

I've never really thought much about my voice. I've been lucky enough not to have to. People say to me, 'Do you use your head voice or your chest voice?' I say, 'I'm afraid I don't know the difference.' I haven't analysed it.

With the Little Richard thing, you just have to give yourself over to it. You can't really think about it. On one occasion I was thinking about it when we were recording 'Kansas City' with The Beatles. John had asked me, weeks before, how I did that Little Richard thing. I said, 'It just comes out the top of my head.' So I was recording 'Kansas City' and having trouble with it, because now I'm thinking, 'This has got to be my best performance ever,' and I wasn't doing too well. And John was up in the control room with all the other guys while I was down in the body of the studio doing the vocal, and he walks down for a minute, comes in and whispers in my ear, 'Comes out the top of your head. Remember?'

In the course of writing that first verse, you've pretty much established everything that's going on. You just elaborate on that. Also, when you're shouting a rock and roll song, you want to be immediate; you don't want to get too fancy. Your natural rhyming pattern is trying to find the two rhymes. 'Man buys ring / Woman throws it away / Same old thing / Happen every day.' It's like a telegram.

One of the great things about rock and roll and blues is that it's very economical. In the first verse you find your little rhyming pattern, and then normally you stick to that in successive verses. It's going to be a three-minute song; there's no time to be too fancy. We have to bang this out and get it said, powerfully and quickly, in two and a half or three minutes. Of course, the songs started getting a wee bit longer after that. They were up to three minutes, or maybe three minutes ten or three minutes thirty seconds.

Pages 356–357: The Beatles with Little Richard. The Tower Ballroom, New Brighton, Merseyside, 12 October 1962

In Spite of All the Danger

WRITERS	Paul McCartney and George Harrison
ARTIST	The Quarry Men
RECORDED	Phillips Sound Recording Service, Liverpool
RELEASED	*Anthology 1*, 1995
	Originally recorded in summer 1958

In spite of all the danger
In spite of all that may be
I'll do anything for you
Anything you want me to
If you'll be true to me

In spite of all the heartache
That you may cause me
I'll do anything for you
Anything you want me to
If you'll be true to me

I'll look after you
Like I've never done before
I'll keep all the others
From knocking at your door

In spite of all the danger
In spite of all that may be
I'll do anything for you
Anything you want me to
If you'll be true to me

In spite of all the heartache
That you may cause me
I'll do anything for you
Anything you want me to
If you'll be true to me
I'll do anything for you
Anything you want me to
If you'll be true to me

WE ALWAYS HAD TROUBLE WITH DRUMMERS. IN THE VERY early days, when we were just innocent boys starting to form our group, John and George were quite set that we three were going to be in it, but we were never quite sure who'd be drumming for us. For a while we even started telling people the rhythm came from the guitars.

We were often throwing pebbles at a drummer's window saying, 'We've got a gig on Tuesday.' He'd be trying to sleep, or his wife or girlfriend would shout at us. It was also difficult in those years to find someone who had actually bought and owned a drum kit. We could get away with a guitar; that was easier to acquire. But there was a guy called Colin Hanton who was a little older than us and had come over from John's group, The Quarry Men; he was with us for a while. So this was the beginning of The Beatles: me, John, George, Colin Hanton on drums, and a school friend of mine, John 'Duff' Lowe, who could play piano.

There's an arpeggio, as I later learnt it's called, at the beginning of 'Mean Woman Blues' by Jerry Lee Lewis. It's a spread arpeggio - which basically means you play the notes of a chord individually rather than at the same time, and really quickly across several octaves - and none of us could do that, but Duff could, so we were quite impressed with that, and for that reason alone we got him in the group.

The name 'The Quarry Men' came from John's grammar school, Quarry Bank High School. George and I went to what I liked to think was a better grammar school, the Liverpool Institute High School for Boys, which is now the Liverpool Institute for the Performing Arts. But while he was at Quarry Bank, John had formed a group and called them The Quarry Men, so we kind of inherited that title, which we didn't mind. It was just a name.

At some point in 1958 we wanted to make a record to say, 'Look, this is us,' just to show our wares. We found an advert for a little studio, Percy Phillips in Kensington - Liverpool's Kensington, not quite as posh as London's Kensington. It was about half an hour away by bus. It cost you five pounds to make a demo record on shellac; that's the old-fashioned way of doing it. Each of us had managed to scrape a pound together, which wasn't too hard once we set our minds to it. If it had been five each, that might have been a bit more challenging.

So we showed up at Percy Phillips's recording studio, which was basically a small room with one mic. We were young kids with our own equipment, and you'd have to wait your turn, like at a doctor's office. When it was us, he just said, 'Okay, you go in there and we'll run through the song, and then you can record it. Let me know what you want to record as the A-side, the B-side and all that.' And we said okay.

There was the Buddy Holly song, now a real classic, called 'That'll Be the Day', which we liked a lot, and we decided we wanted to record it. And then for the B-side we had a self-penned epic, which was called 'In Spite of All the Danger'. John and I had already started our writing careers, and we had a few songs at that time. He had a couple and I had a couple, and when we got together we fixed each other's songs up, and they still, in fact, remain unrecorded, which is probably a good thing because they weren't very good songs. But we did have these two that we took in - 'That'll Be the Day' and 'In Spite of All the Danger' - and we recorded them in this little, dark recording studio, and we paid the five pounds.

The only problem was that there was only one copy of the record, so we happily shared it, the deal being that we would each keep it for a week. We'd play it for all our relatives and say, 'Look at this. This is what we did.' We were quite thrilled just to hear ourselves on a record because we'd never really done that before. As it turned out, John had it for a week, then gave it to me. I had it for a week, George had it for a week, Colin had it for a week, and then Duff Lowe had it for twenty-three years.

We more or less forgot about it, once each of us had heard it for a week. There wasn't an awful lot more to do with it. We didn't have any promoters or managers to play it to. It was really just for ourselves and our families. I got it back in 1981 and made a few copies for friends and family. You can't play the original acetate really, because the shellac would wear out. It's said to be one of the most valuable records in the world, but really, for me it's about the memories in those grooves.

'In Spite of All the Danger' has often been thought by some to be a cry for help, that it somehow reflects John's angst about everything, which really got bad when his mum Julia died very shortly after we recorded the song; it might even have been only days afterwards. But in this case, John was not involved in the start of the song. I realise that many of our songs, especially the very old ones, are thought to come from me, as in 'I Saw Her Standing There', which did start with me, with John helping me fix a couple of lines.

It's true that while some of these songs did start from me, and others began with John or us collaborating, the most important thing to know about 'In Spite of All the Danger' is that this is the only McCartney-Harrison writing credit on record. This was really before we understood writing credits. George made up the solo but some of it did come from John. It was the first song we ever recorded, the first thing on which our names appeared, the first official recording of what later became The Beatles.

Country · Western · Rock 'n' Roll · Skiffle

The Quarry Men

LEOSDENE,
VALE ROAD, WOOLTON.   OPEN FOR ENGAGEMENTS
LIVERPOOL.

Right: Early song list
written by John Lennon

SUSAN

UP A LAZY RIVER.
AIN'T SHE SWEET
MAILMAN.
VACATION TIME
BEAUTIFUL DELILAH.
I'LL NEVER LET YOU GO.
KEEP A KNOCKIN
KEEP LOOKING THAT WAY,
TRUE LOVE
BLUE SUEDE SHOES.
GONNA BACK UP BABY
DANCE IN THE STREETS
MEMPHIS TENNASSEE

Above: 'In Spite of All the
Danger' original 1958
acetate

I've Got a Feeling

WRITERS   Paul McCartney and John Lennon
ARTIST   The Beatles
RECORDED   Apple Corps rooftop, London
RELEASED   *Let It Be*, 1970

I've got a feeling
A feeling deep inside, oh yeah
I've got a feeling
A feeling I can't hide, oh no
I've got a feeling

Oh please believe me
I'd hate to miss the train, oh yeah
And if you leave me
I won't be late again, oh no
I've got a feeling

All these years I've been wandering around
Wondering how come nobody told me
All that I've been looking for was
Somebody who looked like you

I've got a feeling
That keeps me on my toes, oh yeah
I've got a feeling
I think that everybody knows, oh yeah
I've got a feeling

Everybody had a hard year
Everybody had a good time
Everybody had a wet dream
Everybody saw the sunshine
Oh yeah

Everybody had a good year
Everybody let their hair down
Everybody pulled their socks up
Everybody put their foot down
Oh yeah

Everybody had a good year
   (I've got a feeling)
Everybody had a hard time
   (A feeling deep inside, oh yeah)
Everybody had a wet dream
   (Oh yeah)
Everybody saw the sunshine

Everybody had a good year
   (I've got a feeling)
Everybody let their hair down
   (A feeling deep inside, oh no)
Everybody pulled their socks up
   (Oh no)
Everybody put their foot down
Oh yeah
I've got a feeling

THIS SONG IS A SHOTGUN WEDDING BETWEEN MY OWN 'I'VE GOT a Feeling' and a piece John had written, called 'Everyone Had a Bad Year'. One of the most exciting things about writing with John was that he would very often come in from another angle. If I were saying, 'It's getting better all the time,' John might easily say, 'It can't get no worse,' which immediately opens the song right up.

It had been a rough year or two for John. The breakup of his marriage. His estrangement from Julian. A problem with heroin. And there was the generally poor state of affairs in the band by this time. That's encapsulated in the combination of the phrases 'Everybody pulled their socks up' and 'Everybody put their foot down'. Those lines refer in some way to the state of the nation, or the state of The Beatles.

As I continue to write my own songs, I'm still very conscious that I don't have him around, but I still have him whispering in my ear after all these years. I'm often second-guessing what John would have thought – 'This is too soppy' – or what he would have said differently, so I sometimes change it. But that's what being a songwriter is about; you have to be able to look over your own shoulder.

I have to do this by myself these days. And if anyone asks me what was it like to work with John, the truth is it was easier – much easier, because there were two minds at work. Mine would be doing this, his would be doing that, and the interplay was just miraculous. And that's why people are still listening to the songs we wrote. They didn't just go away like your average pop song. The climate that the two of us created in writing wasn't a soppy pop song climate. We created an environment in which we might grow, try new things, maybe even learn a thing or two.

Now that John is gone, I can't sit around sighing for the old days. I can't sit around wishing he was still here. Not only can I not replace him, but I don't need to, in some profound sense. When Bob Dylan was asked once why he didn't write another 'Mr. Tambourine Man', he said, 'I'm not that guy anymore.' The same is true of me.

Above: Filming the *Let It Be* documentary, 1969

I've got a ~~feeling~~ .

I've got a feeling
a feeling deep inside   Oh yea .

I've got a feeling
a feeling I can't hide .

_____

Oh please believe me
I'd hate to miss the train
And if you leave me
I wont be ~~here~~ late again ,

All these years I've been wandering around
wondering how come nobody told me)
All that I was looking for was somebody)
who looked like you .

(I've got a feeling
(that everybody knows) oh yea
(I've got a feeling
(that keeps me on my toes) ~~Oh~~
)know
knows

Right: Writing with
John Lennon during *The
Beatles* sessions. Abbey
Road Studios, London, 1968

Jenny Wren

WRITER	Paul McCartney
ARTIST	Paul McCartney
RECORDED	AIR Studios, London; and Ocean Way Recording Studios, LA
RELEASED	*Chaos and Creation in the Backyard*, 2005
	Single, 2005

Like so many girls
Jenny Wren could sing
But a broken heart
Took her song away

Like the other girls
Jenny Wren took wing
She could see the world
And its foolish ways

How we spend our days
Casting love aside
Losing sight of life
Day by day

She saw poverty
Breaking up a home
Wounded warriors
Took her song away

But the day will come
Jenny Wren will sing
When this broken world
Mends its foolish ways

Then we'll spend our days
Catching up on life
All because of you
Jenny Wren
You saw who we are
Jenny Wren

T HERE'S A CANYON IN LOS ANGELES WHERE I PARTICULARLY LIKE to go walking. You have to drive there, so I often go on my own, and the day I wrote this song I found a quiet parking space along the side of the road in a very rural area and, instead of going on a walk, I thought, 'I'm going to write a song.'

People often think of Liverpool as an industrial city, but I had no trouble pursuing bird-watching when I was a kid. I liked to be able to get out of the workaday world, and this was allowed by the simple fact that we were living in Speke in south Liverpool, only about a mile away from quite deep country-side. I had a little pocket book, *The Observer's Book of Birds*, and I used to go on my own for a walk, for a little bit of solitude. I enjoyed being away from the normal stuff - school, family life, radio, television, errands, whatever it was - and just being off on my own, able to meander and meditate. Pretty soon I started being able to recognise the birds, and the wren became probably my favourite bird - very little, very private, a very sweet little thing. You wouldn't see it that often, but suddenly you'd see it flit from one little bush to another. So whenever we're talking about birds - blackbirds, also amongst my favourites, or larks or Jenny Wrens - it's something I've long had an affection for.

It's always good, when you're writing something, to write about a world you enjoy. So, the minute I'm talking about Jenny Wren, I'm first recalling fiction, that brave girl from Dickens' *Our Mutual Friend* whose positive attitude allowed her to overcome her painful deformities, then I'm seeing the bird, but then I'm seeing a person again, and in this story she's a great singer. The kids may no longer have heard of her, but my parents' and grand-parents' generations knew of the great Swedish opera singer Jenny Lind, whom they used to refer to as 'Jenny Wren'.

In my telling, it turns out that Jenny Wren, her soul having been taken from her, has stopped singing as a form of protest. Then the song becomes a bit reflective about our society - how we screw things up and how we sym-pathise with the person who protests. She has seen our foolish ways, and the way we cast love aside, the way we lose sight of life - poverty breaking up homes, creating wounded warriors. She has seen who we are, and like everyone else, she's just looking for that better way. And if it's, say, an elec-tion year, and it could be anywhere around the world, you're hoping that the mess - 'this broken world' we're in at the moment - will go away, as will the people who created it, and someone better will come in so that we can get back to the better side of ourselves, mend our 'foolish ways'. You know that better side is there, but it's not always so easy to access.

Still, I have to remain the optimist - what with my being a war baby and Britain having come out of the darkest days of the Second World War - so I'm still convinced it's a good old world, really, but I do think we have screwed it up. It's highly obvious with the ocean filling with plastic; it didn't get there by itself. Thinking that climate change is a hoax is another screw-up, one that I hope we can still fix for our children and our children's children.

I'm aware that I'm singing to people who may be having a hard time, because the people I came from, lots of them, had a hard time through lack of money, and I've never forgotten that there's a load of things you don't get if you haven't got money. So, I'm always very much aware of the power that a beautiful song can have, for I know that when I heard one - even a song from a little bird - back growing up in Liverpool, it gave me hope and made me happy. I understood how valuable that feeling was to me. But I'm now the guy saying, 'Look, things aren't always bad.' It gives me somewhere to go in a song, and it also gives me somewhere that I'd like to be. This is really like the Charlie Chaplin song 'Smile'. It's OSS - Optimistic Song Syndrome.

Songs are so often in conversation with other songs, and this one is obviously in conversation with 'Blackbird'. I think that when you're sitting down with an acoustic guitar, there are a few ways you can go. With 'Blackbird', it's a guitar part that you sing against, rather than strumming chords, and I think 'Jenny Wren' has the same idea. I think I was probably writing another 'Blackbird', and intentionally so. I wouldn't admit that to anyone if I weren't working on this book - 'Catching up on life' - and all because of Jenny Wren.

Below: Jamaica, 1979

Right: Driving. Sussex, England, 1978

Songs are so often in conversation with other songs, and this one is obviously in conversation with 'Blackbird'. I think that when you're sitting down with an acoustic guitar, there are a few ways you can go. With 'Blackbird', it's a guitar part that you sing against, rather than strumming chords, and I think 'Jenny Wren' has the same idea.

Like so many birds
(Jenny wren) could sing
morning Dove)
but a broken heart
took
kept her song away

Like the other birds
(a wren?) ~~took going~~
(high above)
she could see the world
& its foolish ways

She saw poverty
Breaking up a home
So much violence
Took her song away
CH. How we spend our days

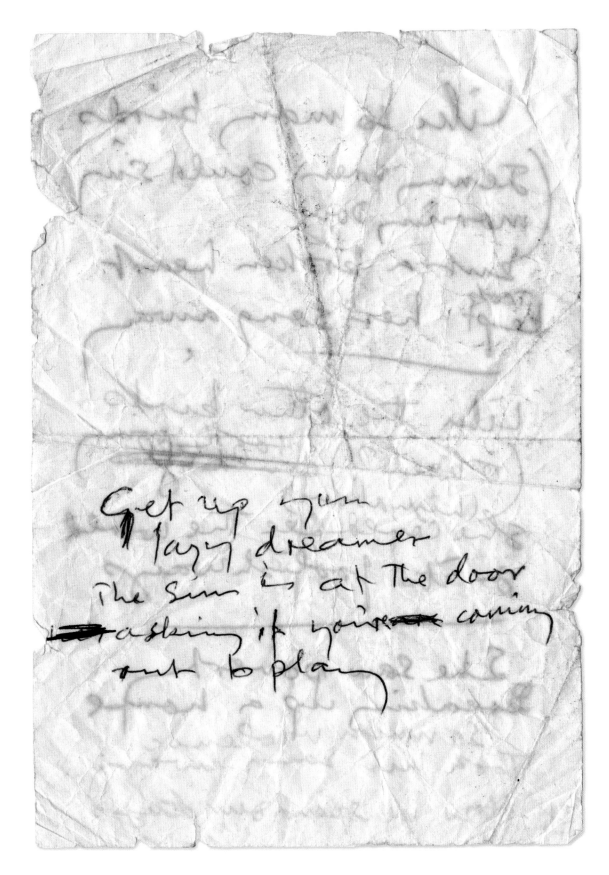

Get up you
lazy dreamer
The sun is at the door
asking if you're coming
out to play

Jet

WRITERS   Paul McCartney and Linda McCartney
ARTIST   Paul McCartney and Wings
RECORDED   EMI Studios, Lagos; and AIR Studios, London
RELEASED   *Band on the Run*, 1973
           Single, 1974

Jet
Jet
Jet, I can almost remember their funny faces
That time you told them that you were going to be
    marrying soon
And Jet, I thought the only lonely place was on the
    moon
Jet
Jet

Jet, was your father as bold as the sergeant major
How come he told you that you were hardly old
    enough yet
And Jet, I thought the major was a lady suffragette
Jet
Jet

Ah Mater
Want Jet to always love me
Ah Mater
Want Jet to always love me
Ah Mater
Much later
Jet

And Jet, I thought the major was a lady suffragette
Jet
Jet

Ah Mater
Want Jet to always love me
Ah Mater
Want Jet to always love me
Ah Mater
Much later

Jet, with the wind in your hair of a thousand laces
Climb on the back and we'll go for a ride in the sky
And Jet, I thought that the major was a little lady
    suffragette

Jet
Jet
And Jet, you know I thought you was a little lady
    suffragette
Jet

A little lady
My little lady, yes

WHEN WE WERE IN THE BEATLES, WE'D LEARNT TO WRITE HIT songs. We were The Beatles, after all, so we had to. We couldn't write flops. That wouldn't have been right for The Beatles.

So, I had developed a knack for writing a popular song or a hit. At this time I was deliberately trying to make Wings sound different to The Beatles, but the tricks of the trade still applied, so when it came to 'Jet', I had loads of tricks that I could use. One of them is shouting; that works. A shout is always a good song opener.

'Jet' was actually the name of a pony, a little Shetland pony that we had for the kids on the farm. My daughter Mary was born in 1969, so in 1973, when the song was written, she was four. Stella would have been two, so they were little. But to know that Jet is a pony is about as important, or unimportant, as knowing that Martha in 'Martha My Dear' is a sheepdog.

I remember exactly how the song started. We were in Scotland. I had my guitar, surprise, surprise. There was a big hill which had the site of a fortress on top of it, an old Celtic fort. It's now primarily an ordnance survey marker. It was an extraordinarily good vantage point. The kind of place where you could imagine the Vikings coming up the hill while we poured oil on them or, if that didn't work, threw some spears at them. There were some lovely little spots on the hillside where we all liked to hang out.

I had told Linda I'd be gone for a while, and as I lay there on this beautiful summer's day, I let my mind wander. Some of the imagery is drawn from the relationship between Linda and her father. He was a cool guy - very accomplished - but he was a little bit too patriarchal for my liking. I got on well with him, but he was a bit strict. That's partly where the 'sergeant major' comes from. He also comes partly from Gilbert and Sullivan and 'the very model of a modern Major-General'. Partly, too, from *Bootsie and Snudge*,

Left: Linda's dad, Lee
Eastman. Sussex, 1983

Right: Mary and Jet, late
1970s

the UK television sitcom, which had a character called Sergeant-Major
Claude Snudge.

'Mater', or 'mother', goes back to my Latin class in school. This is an
imaginary mother figure, though I think it's fair to say that the ghost of my
real mother always loomed somewhere in the background.

Anyhow, I made it all up, played it on the guitar, came back to the farm-
house and played it for Linda. I asked her what she thought. She liked it! And
that was what came out of my afternoon up on the hill. This wasn't Mount
Sinai and I didn't come back with the Tablets of the Law, but I did come back
with 'Jet'.

ready for take off...

JET

PAUL McCARTNEY
and
WINGS

Apple Single 1871

Junior's Farm

WRITERS   Paul McCartney and Linda McCartney
ARTIST   Paul McCartney and Wings
RECORDED   Soundshop Recording Studios, Nashville
RELEASED   Single, 1974

You should have seen me with the poker man
I had a honey and I bet a grand
Just in the nick of time I looked at his hand
I was talking to an Eskimo
Said he was hoping for a fall of snow
When up popped a sea lion ready to go

Let's go, let's go, let's go, let's go
Down to Junior's Farm where I want to lay low
Low life, high life, oh let's go
Take me down to Junior's Farm

At the Houses of Parliament
Everybody's talking 'bout the President
We all chip in for a bag of cement
Ollie Hardy should have had more sense
He bought a gee-gee and he jumped the fence
All for the sake of a couple of pence

Let's go, let's go, let's go, let's go
Down to Junior's Farm where I want to lay low
Low life, high life, oh let's go
Take me down to Junior's Farm
Let's go, let's go
Down to Junior's Farm where I want to lay low
Low life, high life, oh let's go
Take me down to Junior's Farm
Everybody tag along

I took my bag into a grocer's store
The price is higher than the time before
Old man asked me, why is it more?
I said, you should have seen me with
    the poker man
I had a honey and I bet a grand
Just in the nick of time I looked at his hand

Let's go, let's go, let's go, let's go
Down to Junior's Farm where I want to lay low
Low life, high life, oh let's go
Take me down to Junior's Farm
Let's go, let's go
Down to Junior's Farm where I want to lay low
Low life, high life, oh let's go
Take me down to Junior's Farm
Everybody tag along
Take me down to Junior's Farm

Take me back
Take me back
I want to go back
Yeah, yeah, yeah

Above: With Stella and James. Scotland, 1982

LINDA AND I ELOPED – ACROSS THE SCOTTISH BORDER, BYPASSING Gretna Green, which is actually on the way – and went up to the farm I'd acquired a few years before. I hadn't been massively keen on it, frankly, but Linda was. She opened my eyes to how beautiful it was.

We spent quite a bit of time on the farm, just raising the kids and farming. It became a refuge of sorts, and it was nice to get away from London and everything – both the good and bad – that comes with the city. I would drive a Massey Ferguson 315 tractor and mow the hay, and I loved that because I'd been a nature fiend as a kid, and this freedom just gave me time to think – 'Down to Junior's Farm where I want to lay low'. It was such a relief to get out of those business meetings with people in suits, who were so serious all the time, and to go off to Scotland and be able just to sit around in a T-shirt and corduroys. I was very much in that mindset when I wrote this song. The basic message is, let's get out of here. You might say it's my post-Beatles getting-out-of-town song.

Wings went to Nashville to bond as a band. We'd lost a guitarist and drummer before we recorded *Band on the Run*, and now we had two new members. So the idea was to rehearse and record a couple of songs, this being one of them. We stayed at the home of a songwriter called Curly Putman, who wrote 'The Green, Green Grass of Home'. I think he and his wife had gone on holiday, so we had the place to ourselves.

My own farm was in the background, but here we were staying on a kind of ranch, very American and very different to Scotland. Flat plains instead of rolling hills. And rocking chairs on the porch. So I decided to get into a fantasy for the verses. Bob Dylan's 'Maggie's Farm' had come out nearly a decade before, in 1965, and that definitely was an influence on this song. And the 'Eskimo' is probably Mighty Quinn from Dylan's song 'Quinn the Eskimo'. The verse 'I took my bag into a grocer's store / The price is higher than the time before' – well, that's always very relevant because many people were feeling the pinch, since the early seventies was a tough financial time for so many people, and money was tight. Why is everything much more expensive than it used to be?

Now, that second verse. I don't always sing that bit when we play this song live, so it's sometimes not included in the lyric: 'At the Houses of Parliament / Everybody's talking 'bout the President / We all chip in for a bag of cement'. This song was recorded in the summer of 1974 and released in October of the same year. Around the same time of Richard Nixon and his impeachment hearing; in fact, I think he'd had to resign in disgrace that summer. The idea in the song was to give him the so-called Mafia send-off. I don't think there's any reason we don't perform that verse now. It may just be that it makes the song too long and we get through around forty songs in our sets.

There are fashions in music and in songs, and at the time of the album *Band on the Run*, which this song followed, there was a fashion for the idea of the desperado, partly because of the Eagles song by that name – not to mention how popular *Butch Cassidy and the Sundance Kid* was. We just took this to a larger and more personal level. The idea was that we were *all* on the run from the law. When you were smoking pot, policemen became something you had to worry about, in case they sort of went, 'What's that smell?' You know you're not guilty, but you feel guilty because you think you're going to be accused of some misdemeanour, and they're going to be able to bust you for it. It was different when I was growing up; a policeman to me then was just a friendly old bobby walking his beat, and there wasn't an awful lot of negative association with the police. Once, though – once or twice – I got stopped in a new car, my first car, a Ford Consul Classic. I was a little too young to have such a shiny car, and this policeman stopped me, 'Where'd you get this car?' You know, I was a Liverpool guy, and I looked like I might've just stolen it. I said, 'It's mine. I bought it.'

'Junior's Farm' remains a good live song, and we usually put it in at the start of the set. It's got a lot of elements that work well – a recognisable introduction and a good steady rock and roll beat, and then these interesting, slightly surreal lyrics and a rousing chorus of 'Let's go, let's go'. That gets people in the mood to set out, 'just in the nick of time', for their *own* version of 'Junior's Farm', whatever that might be – wherever they want to disappear and hide out and just lie low.

Above left: Scotland, 1974

Above right: Nashville, 1974

But just in the nick of time I looked at his hand.

lets go, lets go –

② I was talking to an Eskimo —
said he was hoping for a fall of snow –
And up popped a sea lion ready to go

CHORUS lets go ·· ·· ·· ·· down to juniors farm
where I wanna lay low
when
low life ~~lets~~ high life oh lets go (go life, go!)
Take me
heading down to Juniors Farm

·· ··· _students union_ – – – ···

③ At the houses of Parliament,
Everybody's talkin bout the President
All chip in for a bag of cement.
(Everybody Tags along.)

④ Ollie Hardy should have had
more sense
He bought a geegee and he
jumped a
fence
All for the sake of a couple
3 — of pence.

③ Took my bag into a grocery store (Gross restore)
The prices too higher than the time before
Old man asking John is it more? (Everybody tags along)

Junk

WRITER   Paul McCartney
ARTIST   Paul McCartney
RECORDED   At home, London; and Morgan Studios, London
RELEASED   *McCartney*, 1970

Motor cars, handlebars, bicycles for two
Broken-hearted jubilee
Parachutes, army boots, sleeping bags for two
Sentimental jamboree

Buy, buy, says the sign in the shop window
Why? Why? says the junk in the yard

Candlesticks, building bricks, something old and new
Memories for you and me

Buy, buy, says the sign in the shop window
Why? Why? says the junk in the yard

WILFRID BRAMBELL WAS AN IRISH ACTOR WHO PLAYED THE character of my 'very clean' grandfather in the Beatles film *A Hard Day's Night*. He was also one of the stars of *Steptoe and Son*, a well-known sitcom on the BBC. The series focused on the constant conflict between Albert Steptoe, often referred to as a 'dirty old man', and his son Harold, a character doomed to having social aspirations which never seem to materialise. I think we're all familiar with that scenario!

If I may use a fancy word, the *milieu* of 'Junk' was influenced by the rag-and-bone shop, or junkyard, that was the main setting of *Steptoe and Son*. That junkyard was as familiar to British audiences in the 1960s and '70s as the ranch in *Bonanza* or the mansion in *The Beverly Hillbillies*.

The song started, as so many do, with a chord sequence that I liked, and then the melody. I know it may sound strange, but the chord at the start of this song actually put me in mind of a scrapyard or the back of a shop. The kind of atmospheric place in which, if I were writing a novel, I'd like to set a scene. Dickens often does that. The back of a shop or a basement, or even the Rouncewell ironworks in *Bleak House*. Here we have 'Motor cars, handlebars, bicycles for two'. Many people will recognise that last phrase as being recycled from the song 'Daisy Bell (Bicycle Built for Two)', which has the lines 'Daisy, Daisy, / Give me your answer do!' That's Harry Dacre's song of 1892, with which Nat King Cole had such a big hit in 1963.

Not that recycling was much of a feature back in the 1960s. That's partly because the idea of built-in obsolescence hadn't quite taken off. In those days, if you bought a car, it was meant to last you a long time. It might even be handed down within a family. When I was a kid, you held on to things. I have an instinct now to hold on to things and, more than that, I expect things to last. So, this is a comment on consumer society. It's one thing you do as a writer: you comment on society, and you put across an opinion. I put opin-

Above: With Wilfred Bramble. *A Hard Day's Night*, 1964

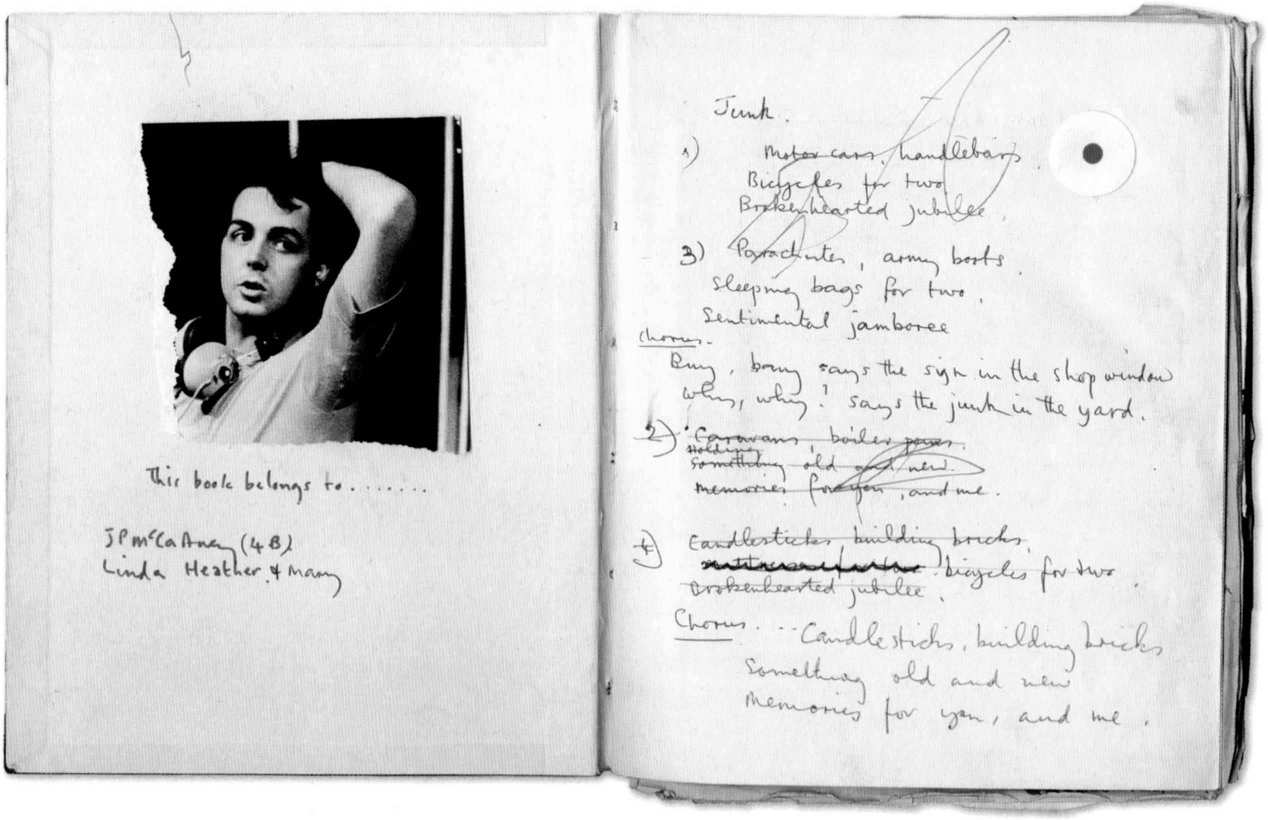

Junk.

1)   Motor cars, handlebars,
     Bicycles for two,
     Brokenhearted jubilee.

3) Parachutes, army boots
     Sleeping bags for two,
     Sentimental jamboree

Chorus.
     Buy, buy, says the sign in the shop window
     Why, why? says the junk in the yard.

2) Caravans, boiler ~~pipes~~
~~Holding~~ Something old ~~and~~ new
     memories for ~~you~~, and me.

4) Candlesticks, building bricks,
~~intrase of pipes~~ bicycles for two
~~Brokenhearted jubilee~~.

Chorus. ...Candlesticks, building bricks
     Something old and new
     Memories for you, and me.

This book belongs to.........

J P McCartney (4B)
Linda Heather & Mary

ions in my songs – not always an opinion I hold, but just an opinion I've heard or I like or that interests me. So, the idea that stuff is going to be useless after you buy it is a comment on consumer society. Apparently, it was only in the 1960s that we crossed the line from having needs to having wants and then acting upon those wants. So, this song is of a piece with that.

But it's mostly a love song. The 'bicycles for two' merge into the 'sleeping bags for two'. Then there's the line 'Buy, buy, says the sign in the shop window', which sounds like one lover saying, 'Bye-bye,' and then the other plaintively asking, 'Why, why?' even as 'the junk in the yard' demands an explanation for the urge to acquire something, or somebody, new.

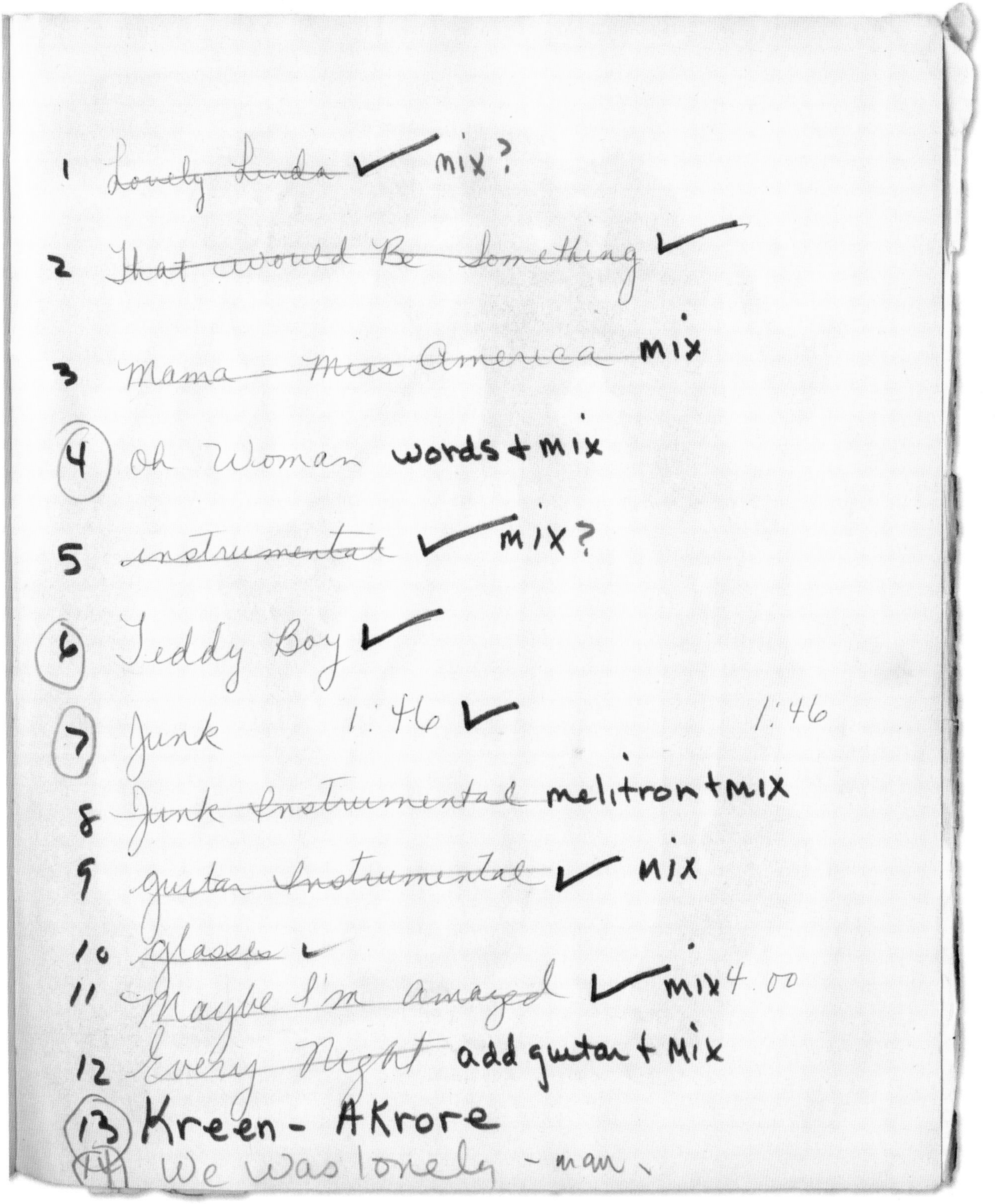

1 ~~Lovely Linda~~ ✓ mix?

2 ~~That would Be Something~~ ✓

3 ~~Mama – Miss America~~ mix

(4) Oh Woman words + mix

5 ~~instrumental~~ ✓ mix?

(6) Teddy Boy ✓

(7) Junk 1:46 ✓ 1:46

8 ~~Junk Instrumental~~ melitron + mix

9 ~~guitar Instrumental~~ ✓ mix

10 ~~glasses~~ ✓

11 ~~Maybe I'm amazed~~ ✓ mix 4.00

12 ~~Every Night~~ add guitar + mix

(13) Kreen-Akrore

(14) We was lonely – man.

Notes for *McCartney*, 1970

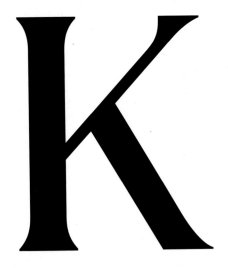

The Kiss of Venus

WRITER   Paul McCartney
ARTIST   Paul McCartney
RECORDED   Hog Hill Mill, Sussex
RELEASED   *McCartney III* , 2020

The kiss of Venus
Has got me on the go
She scored a bullseye
In the early morning glow
Early morning glow

Packed with illusions
Our world is turned around
This golden circle has a
Most harmonic sound
Harmonic sound

And in the sunshine
When we stand alone
We came together with
Our secrets blown
Our secrets blown

Now moving slowly
We circle through the square
Two passing planets in the
Sweet, sweet summer air
Sweet summer air

And in the sunshine
When we stand alone
We came together with
Our secrets blown
Our secrets blown

Reflected mountains in a lake
Is this too much to take?
Asleep or wide awake?
And if the world begins to shake
Will something have to break?
We have to stay awake

Packed with illusions
Our world is turned around
This golden circle has a
Most harmonic sound
Harmonic sound

And in the sunshine
When we stand alone
We came together with
Our secrets blown
Our secrets blown

The kiss of Venus
Has got me on the go
She scored a bullseye
In the early morning glow
Early morning glow

The kiss of Venus
Has got me on the go

A LITTLE BOOK OF COINCIDENCE IN THE SOLAR SYSTEM, BY JOHN Martineau, is a mini-treatise on the planets and their orbits, and the revolutions of the sun and the moon. I read it recently, and it's an absolutely fascinating read because whoever designed this book visualised those orbits and revolutions. For example, geocentrically, Venus draws a pentagram around the Earth every eight years.

When I first read the book, I was amazed to see these complex designs in the universe, and it made me think, 'Yes, it *is* magical – this life, the interdependence of everything, trees giving oxygen; there's so much magical stuff going on.'

Speaking of magical, when I played the Glastonbury Festival in 2004, I loved the idea that we were probably on the confluence of ley lines, the lines that crisscross the globe and along which our ancestors are thought to have set up significant sites. I like that kind of history. Glastonbury is also said to be the place where King Arthur is buried. So, one way or another, it's a very special place and it has a very definite vibe. There's simply no denying that it has a distinct aura.

Ever since the sixties I've been interested in constellations and cosmology and cosmic sounds. Martineau's book also goes into sound – the music of the spheres – where each of the planets sounds a different note. This, to me, is very 'hippie' – this whole idea of just enjoying the simple things in life and being in tune with nature. 'We came together with / Our secrets blown' – we're not trying to hide anything, we're naked out in the rain, and the cosmos is going on about its business.

When you think of these larger things, it's all so humbling. Here we are, these little specks on this planet, which itself is a speck in the universe, and yet at the heart of it all, you have this pattern of the lotus flower which at least a couple of religions – Buddhism and Hinduism – have divined as an important symbol.

Another thing I learnt from Martineau's book is that every so often Venus passes very close to the Earth; the phenomenon is known as 'the kiss of Venus'. That was enough to fire my imagination. That's really what got me going.

'Two passing planets in the / Sweet, sweet summer air'. It's as if, as people, we're passing planets – a bit like ships that pass in the night. The phrase 'Now moving slowly / We circle through the square' reminds me of 'through the fair', a phrase used in a lot of ballads, including the traditional Irish ballad, 'She Moved Through the Fair'. The idea of 'squaring the circle' – of doing something impossible – is also lurking somewhere in the undergrowth of that phrase. There's a sense in which every song is overcoming tremendous odds to get written at all.

HARMONIC SOUND

1. Packed with illusion
   my world is ~~turning~~ turned around
   ~~The~~ This ~~kiss of Venus~~ golden circle
   Has a most harmonic sound
   (harmonic sound)

   ~~Any golden circles~~

2. The kiss of Venus
   Has got me on the go
   ~~She~~ scored a bulls eye
   In the early morning glow
   (~~early morning~~ glow)

CH And in the sunshine
    where we stand alone
    we came together
    with our secrets blown
    (secrets blown)

3. Now moving slowly
   we circled in the square
   ~~Two passing planets~~
   ~~and came together~~ in the
   sweet sweet summer air
   (sweet summer air)

CH. And in the sunshine ... etc.

[MID] Reflected mountains
      in a lake
      Is this too much to take.
      Asleep or wide awake

1. Packed with illusion
   my world is turned around
   This golden circle
   Has a most harmonic sound.

THE KISS OF VENUS

① The kiss of Venus
   Has got me on the go
   She scored a bullseye
   In the early morning (glow) (show)
      (" ")

② Packed with illusion
   Our world is turned around
   This golden circle has a
   Most harmonic sound
      (" / " ")

(Bridge) And in the sunshine
   When we stand alone
   We came together with
   Our secrets blown
      (" ")

③ Now moving slowly
   We circle through (in) the square
   Two passing planets in the
   Sweet sweet summer air
      (" " ")

(Bridge) And in the sunshine when we stand alone
   We came together with our secrets blown (our)

[MID] Reflected mountains in a lake / is this too much to take?
   Asleep or wide awake / REPEAT
   And if the world begins to shake / will something have to
   We have to stay awake   break?

④ The kiss of Venus
   Has got me on the go
   She scored a bullseye
   In the early morning (show)(glow)
      (" " ")

V1
V2
① B
V3
② B
m
V2 / B ③
m
V1
end

Headlining Glastonbury
Festival, 26 June 2004